THE LANGUAGE OF
DICKENS

THE LANGUAGE LIBRARY

EDITED BY ERIC PARTRIDGE AND SIMEON POTTER

ALREADY PUBLISHED

G. L. BROOK

THE LANGUAGE OF DICKENS

ANDRE DEUTSCH

FIRST PUBLISHED 1970 BY
ANDRE DEUTSCH LIMITED
105 GREAT RUSSELL STREET
LONDON WC1
COPYRIGHT © 1970 BY G. L. BROOK
ALL RIGHTS RESERVED
PRINTED IN GREAT BRITAIN BY
TONBRIDGE PRINTERS LTD
TONBRIDGE KENT
233 96131 3

145905

To my Wife

CONTENTS

PREFACE

Two motives have combined to make me write a book on the language of Dickens. The first is that I believe that such a study can help in the understanding of both the history of the English language and the novels of Dickens. The second is that I enjoy reading Dickens, and the collection of material for this book has provided me with an excuse for re-reading the novels and calling it work and not mere self-indulgence. My aim has been to suggest possible ways of approaching the language of Dickens, not to treat the subject exhaustively. Such an exhaustive treatment must await, among other things, the establishment of a satisfactory text of the novels, a task which has been begun by the publication of Professor Kathleen Tillotson's edition of *Oliver Twist*. I have had in mind the reader whose interest in Dickens is mainly literary, but the substandard language used by many of the characters in the novels seemed to call for a more linguistic treatment, and this I have tried to provide in the Appendix.

It is often important to notice which Dickensian characters indulge in particular linguistic eccentricities. Sam Weller, the Artful Dodger, the Game Chicken and Squeers all use substandard English, but each of them has his own special variety. For this reason, in quoting examples I have given the name of the speaker whenever it seemed to me to have any significance. When no name is given, the speaker is usually a minor or unidentified character.

I am deeply indebted to my wife, Professor John Jump and Professor Brian Cox, who read the book in typescript and allowed me to profit from their comments. I am grateful to the Governors of the John Rylands Library, Manchester, and the Librarian, Mr Ronald Hall, for permission to make use of material in two articles which I contributed to *The Bulletin of the John Rylands Library*. For help on specific points I am indebted to Professor Marcus Cunliffe, of the University of Sussex, and to my colleagues at Manchester, Professor P. M. Bromley, Professor Denis Welland and Mr Noel Lees.

January 1969

G. L. Brook.

ABBREVIATIONS

The following abbreviations refer to the titles of books by Dickens.

AN	*American Notes*
BH	*Bleak House*
BR	*Barnaby Rudge*
CB	*Christmas Books*
CS	*Christmas Stories*
DS	*Dombey and Son*
ED	*Edwin Drood*
GE	*Great Expectations*
HT	*Hard Times*
LD	*Little Dorrit*
MC	*Martin Chuzzlewit*
MHC	*Master Humphrey's Clock*
NN	*Nicholas Nickleby*
OCS	*The Old Curiosity Shop*
OMF	*Our Mutual Friend*
OT	*Oliver Twist*
PP	*Pickwick Papers*
SB	*Sketches by Boz*
TTC	*A Tale of Two Cities*

Other abbreviations are:

Fr	French
ME	Middle English
MnE	Modern English
OE	Old English
OF	Old French
RP	Received Pronunciation

PHONETIC SYMBOLS

The following letters are used as phonetic symbols with their usual English values: p, b, t, d, k, g, f, v, s, z, h, w, l, r, m, n. Other symbols are used with the values indicated by the italicised letters in the key-words which follow:

CONSONANTS

ʃ	*sh*ip	θ	*th*in
ʒ	plea*s*ure	ð	*th*en
tʃ	*ch*in	j	*y*es
dʒ	*judg*e	ç	German i*ch*
ŋ	si*ng*		

VOWELS

i	s*i*t	ɑ:	f*a*ther
i:	s*ee*	ɔ	h*o*t
e	g*e*t	ɔ:	s*aw*
a	f*a*t	u	p*u*t
ə	fath*er*	u:	s*oo*n
ə:	b*ir*d	ʌ	b*u*t

DIPHTHONGS

ei	d*ay*	ɔi	b*oy*
ou	g*o*	iə	h*ere*
ai	fl*y*	ɛə	th*ere*
au	n*ow*	uə	g*ou*rd

Square brackets are used to enclose phonetic symbols. A colon after a phonetic symbol indicates length.

I

STYLE

The study of the language used by an author serves two purposes. It can lead the way to a better understanding of the author's meaning and a fuller appreciation of his literary skill, and it can provide material for the study of the history of the language. The two approaches to a literary work are closely intertwined and one helps the other. The use which any author makes of a language is a part of the history of that language, and, if the author's works are widely read, his linguistic habits are likely to exert an important influence on others who use the language. On the other hand, a knowledge of the state of the language at the time when the author wrote is of the utmost importance in understanding what the author meant. Without that knowledge we are in danger of attributing to his words modern senses which he did not intend them to bear and of seeking special significance in turns of phrase, unusual to us, which were the normal way of expressing ideas at the time when the author wrote.

In studying novels or plays it is always necessary to distinguish between the language of the author himself and that which he puts into the mouths of his characters. In this chapter I am concerned primarily with the language used by Dickens in the descriptive and narrative parts of his novels; in the subsequent chapters I shall be concerned chiefly with the language which he puts into the mouths of his characters.

Dickens makes use of many different styles. He was not afraid of writing highly mannered passages that would today be condemned as 'fine writing'. Such passages, aiming at a strong appeal to the emotions, were highly regarded in the nineteenth century. An example is the opening of chapter 46 of *Bleak House*:

> Darkness rests upon Tom-all-Alone's. Dilating and dilating since the sun went down last night, it has gradually swelled until it fills every void in the place. For a time there were some dungeon

lights burning, as the lamp of Life burns in Tom-all-Alone's, heavily, heavily, in the nauseous air, and winking – as that lamp, too, winks in Tom-all-Alone's – at many horrible things. But they are blotted out. The moon has eyed Tom with a dull cold stare, as admitting some puny emulation of herself in his desert region unfit for life and blasted by volcanic fires; but she has passed on, and is gone. The blackest nightmare in the infernal stables grazes on Tom-all-Alone's, and Tom is fast asleep.

There are other passages, like the description of the Gordon Riots in *Barnaby Rudge*, where a high emotional pitch is maintained for several chapters of detailed description and narrative. Nicholas Nickleby's return to London by stage-coach provides the occasion for a graphic description of London consisting of a series of contrasting pictures showing how splendour and misery are to be found side by side:

As they dashed by the quickly-changing and ever-varying objects, it was curious to observe in what a strange procession they passed before the eye. Emporiums of splendid dresses, the materials brought from every quarter of the world; tempting stories of everything to stimulate and pamper the sated appetite and give new relish to the oft-repeated feast; vessels of burnished gold and silver wrought into every exquisite form of vase, and dish, and goblet; guns, swords, pistols, and patent engines of destruction; screws and irons for the crooked, clothes for the newly-born, drugs for the sick, coffins for the dead, churchyards for the buried – all these jumbled each with the other and flocking side by side, seemed to flit by in motley dance like the fantastic groups of the old Dutch painter, and with the same stern moral for the unheeding restless crowd.

Nor were there wanting objects in the crowd itself to give new point and purpose to the shifting scene. The rags of the squalid ballad-singer fluttered in the rich light that showed the goldsmith's treasures; pale and pinched-up faces hovered about the windows where was tempting food; hungry eyes wandered over the profusion guarded by one thin sheet of brittle glass – an iron wall to them; half-naked shivering figures stopped to gaze at Chinese shawls and golden stuffs of India. There was a christening party at the largest coffinmaker's, and a funeral hatchment had stopped some great improvements in the bravest mansion. Life and death went hand in hand; wealth and poverty stood side by side; repletion and starvation laid them down together. (*NN*, ch. 32)

At the other extreme Dickens often uses a more colloquial style. The description of Todgers's boarding house in *Martin Chuzzlewit* includes a phrase of the kind that one of its residents might have used: 'It had not been papered or painted, hadn't Todgers's, within the memory of man' (ch. 8).

Sometimes Dickens uses a style of sustained banter. In the description of the dinner parties given by Mr Merdle in *Little Dorrit* the prevailing tone is light, but the author makes his satirical purpose plain by allowing the banter to give way from time to time to a sentence or two of bitter denunciation. Thus, in the conversation between Mr Merdle and Bar about Mr Merdle's three pocket boroughs, a long passage of ornate eloquence is followed by the brief comment:

> The three places in question were three little rotten holes in this Island, containing three little ignorant, drunken, guzzling, dirty, out-of-the-way constituencies that had reeled into Mr Merdle's pocket. (Bk II, ch. 12)

There is a similar piece of anticlimax near the end of the novel, when the speculation aroused by the suicide of Mr Merdle is described. A long sentence describing the honours that had been showered upon him ends with the words:

> he, the shining wonder, the new constellation to be followed by the wise men bringing gifts, until it stopped over certain carrion at the bottom of a bath and disappeared – was simply the greatest Forger and the greatest Thief that ever cheated the gallows. (Bk II, ch. 25)

Another style which Dickens adopts from time to time is the mock-heroic. Long passages in praise of the beauty of the heroine were a common feature of the novels with which Dickens would be familiar in his youth. When he introduces such passages, he seems to be laughing at both the literary convention and himself. A point of linguistic interest in the following mock-heroic passage is that it shows that, when he wanted, Dickens could construct a gigantic sentence.

> To have seen Miss Squeers now, divested of the brown beaver, the green veil, and the blue curl-papers, and arrayed in all the virgin splendour of a white frock and spencer, with a white muslin bonnet, and an imitative damask rose in full bloom on the inside thereof – her luxuriant crop of hair arranged in curls so tight that it was impossible they could come out by any accident, and her bonnet-cap trimmed with little damask roses, which might be supposed to be so many promising scions of the big rose – to have seen all this, and to have seen the broad damask belt, matching both the family rose and the little roses, which encircled her slender

waist, and by a happy ingenuity took off from the shortness of the spencer behind, – to have beheld all this, and to have taken further into account the coral bracelets (rather short of beads, and with a very visible black string) which clasped her wrists, and the coral necklace which rested on her neck, supporting, outside her frock, a lonely cornelian heart, typical of her own disengaged affections – to have contemplated all these mute but expressive appeals to the purest feelings of our nature, might have thawed the frost of age, and added new and inextinguishable fuel to the fire of youth. (*NN*, ch. 39)

References to Sally Brass are usually of the ironical kind that is normal in mock-heroic writing. Her unattractive appearance is described in some detail (*OCS*, ch. 33), but she is afterwards 'the charming Sarah', 'the beautiful virgin', 'the fair enslaver', 'the absent charmer', 'the beauty', 'the gentle Sarah', 'the lovely damsel' and 'the lovely Sarah' (chs. 59, 60, 62, 66). In one reference to her the use of the archaic third person singular ending -*eth* gives the reader a warning of the author's playful intention:

. . . the beautiful Sally was already at her post, bearing in her looks a radiance, mild as that which beameth from the virgin moon. (ch. 58)

Much has been written about the polysyllabic humour of the Victorians. The form that it usually takes is the use of grandi- loquent language to describe trivial events, thus emphasizing their triviality and causing the reader to smile at the incongruity between the language and the occasion. Dickens imparts a legal flavour to his account of an inn servant taking the poker away:

The brandy and water luke and the inkstand having been carried into the little parlour, and the young lady having carefully flattened down the coals to prevent their blazing, and carried away the poker to preclude the possibility of the fire being stirred, without the full privity and concurrence of the Blue Boar being first had and obtained, Sam Weller sat himself down . . . (*PP*, ch. 33)

Elsewhere a blow is described as 'a manual compliment' (*MC*, ch. 9), and a pawnbroker's assistant is somewhat coyly described as 'the David of the – how shall it be phrased? – the triumvirate of golden balls' (*MC*, ch. 27).

In some passages Dickens's style seems to show the influence of Carlyle. The following description of Jo in *Bleak House* has the declamatory and repetitive quality of many passages in Carlyle, and it concludes with an apostrophe very much in Carlyle's manner:

Dirty, ugly, disagreeable to all the senses, in body a common creature of the common streets, only in soul a heathen. Homely filth begrimes him, homely parasites devour him, homely sores are in him, homely rags are on him: native ignorance, the growth of English soil and climate, sinks his immortal nature lower than the beasts that perish. Stand forth, Jo, in uncompromising colours! From the sole of thy foot to the crown of thy head, there is nothing interesting about thee. (*BH*, ch. 47)

A passage in much the same style is the description of the death of Krook:

Plenty will come in, but none can help. The Lord Chancellor of that Court, true to his title in his last act, has died the death of all Lord Chancellors in all Courts, and of all authorities in all places under all names soever, where false pretences are made, and where injustice is done. Call the death by any name Your Highness will, attribute it to whom you will, or say it might have been prevented how you will, it is the same death eternally – inborn, inbred, engendered in the corrupted humours of the vicious body itself, and that only – Spontaneous Combustion, and none other of all the deaths that can be died. (*BH*, ch. 32)

In descriptive passages Dickens felt no urge to follow the old precept of grammarians that every sentence must contain a verb. The opening chapter of *Bleak House* contains a vivid description of a November day; the following passage from that chapter is only a part of a long description in which finite verbs play little part:

Fog everywhere. Fog up the river, where it flows among green aits and meadows; fog down the river, where it rolls defiled among the tiers of shipping, and the waterside pollutions of a great (and dirty) city. Fog on the Essex marshes, fog on the Kentish heights. Fog creeping into the cabooses of collier-brigs; fog lying out on the yards, and hovering in the rigging of great ships; fog drooping on the gunwales of barges and small boats. Fog in the eyes and throats of ancient Greenwich pensioners, wheezing by the firesides of their wards; fog in the stem and bowl of the afternoon pipe of the wrathful skipper, down in his close cabin; fog cruelly pinching the toes and fingers of his shivering little 'prentice boy on deck. Chance people on the bridges peeping over the parapets into a nether sky of fog, with fog all round them, as if they were up in a balloon, and hanging in the misty clouds.

Some writers are chiefly interested in the ideas that they want to express and regard preoccupation with details of expression as unhealthy; others regard the manner of expression as all-important, but no author whose work is of lasting value is likely to be completely indifferent to the language that he uses to express his ideas. Dickens had a lifelong interest in language, but his knowledge was obtained by the careful observation of life and by the study of the work of English authors, not by reading books on rhetoric and composition. When he uses technical terms, they are quite likely to be wrongly used, as in his comment on Mrs MacStinger's reference to Captain Cuttle's 'guzzlings and his muzzlings'. Dickens's comment is: 'Mrs MacStinger used the last word for the joint sake of alliteration and aggravation, rather than for the expression of any idea' (*DS*, ch. 39). She may have aimed at aggravation, but she did not on this occasion achieve alliteration.

Dickens's interest in language began to show itself in his childhood in a way not uncommon among schoolboys. Two of his schoolfellows later described his invention of a private language, formed by adding a group of sounds to every word used. It was the ambition of Dickens and his friends, when using this gibberish in the streets, to be mistaken for foreigners (Forster, I, 3). This private language seems to have been similar to that used in a very different social environment by the children of the Mitford family and described by Jessica Mitford in *Hons and Rebels*.

Although Dickens wrote very little literary criticism, he remained all his life a critic of language and introduced into his novels critical comments on the use of words, either in his own capacity of author or through the mouths of his characters. An example of Dickens's comments in his capacity of author is that occasioned by Peter Magnus's use of the words 'Never mind':

There must be something very comprehensive in this phrase 'Never mind', for we do not recollect to have ever witnessed a quarrel in the street, at a theatre, public room, or elsewhere, in which it has not been the standard reply to all belligerent inquiries. 'Do you call yourself a gentleman, sir?' – 'Never mind, sir.' 'Did I offer to say anything to the young woman, sir?' – 'Never mind, sir.' 'Do you want your head knocked up against that wall, sir?' – 'Never mind, sir.' It is observable, too, that there would appear to be some hidden taunt in this universal 'Never mind', which rouses more indignation in the bosom of the individual addressed, than the most lavish abuse could possibly awaken. (*PP*, ch. 24)

Dickens had enormous zest and he shared the tendency of the Crummles family to overact. He is very fond of superlatives. When Tom Pinch buys a piece of steak, the butcher wraps it up in a cabbage-leaf and the author describes the leaf as 'perhaps the greenest cabbage-leaf ever grown in a garden', (*MC*, ch. 39). Barbara's kitchen in *The Old Curiosity Shop* is 'such a kitchen as was never before seen or heard of out of a toy-shop window' (ch. 22), and when Kit takes Barbara out to supper, the waiter brings 'the newest loaves, and the freshest butter, and the largest oysters, ever seen' (ch. 39). Of Mrs Varden's house we are told that 'there was not a neater, more scrupulously tidy or more punctiliously ordered house in Clerkenwell, in London, in all England' (*BR*, ch. 4), and when the Vardens paid a series of visits, 'never were people so glad to see other people' (*BR*, ch. 19). One of the reasons for the wide appeal of Dickens is the pleasure that he takes in simple things, joined with the power of conveying this pleasure to the reader. Very often the effect is achieved simply by enumeration, but for this method to be effective it is necessary for the author to choose his list with care. When Maggy in *Little Dorrit* is describing the delights of being in hospital, she enumerates the attractions:

'Such beds there is there! Such lemonades! Such oranges! Such d'licious broth and wine! Such Chicking! Oh, AIN'T it a delightful place to go and stop at!' (Bk I, ch. 9)

Such unselfconscious pleasure in simple things is no doubt intended to reveal one aspect of Maggy's character, but it is a characteristic which the author himself shares. The last chapter of *Pickwick Papers* describes the house in which Mr Pickwick is to spend his declining years, and the author carries the practice of rhapsodical enumeration even further than Maggy does:

Everything was so beautiful! The lawn in front, the garden behind, the miniature conservatory, the dining-room, the drawing-room, the bed-rooms, the smoking-room, and above all the study with its pictures and easy chairs, and odd cabinets, and queer tables, and books out of number, with a large cheerful window opening upon a pleasant lawn and commanding a pretty landscape, dotted here and there with little houses almost hidden by the trees; and then the curtains, and the carpets, and the chairs, and the sofas! Everything was so beautiful, so compact, so neat, and in such exquisite taste, said everybody, that there really was no deciding what to admire most. (ch. 57)

There is a similar example of infectious enthusiasm in the description of the Cheerybles' dinner-party at the close of *Nicholas Nickleby*. The description begins characteristically 'Never was such a dinner as that, since the world began', and the effect is achieved simply by enumerating the names of the guests, each with its appropriate adjective or pair of adjectives:

> . . . Then there was Mrs Nickleby, so grand and complacent; Madeline and Kate, so blushing and beautiful; Nicholas and Frank, so devoted and proud; and all four so silently and tremblingly happy; there was Newman, so subdued yet so overjoyed, and there were the twin Brothers so delighted and interchanging such looks, that the old servant stood transfixed behind his master's chair, and felt his eyes grow dim as they wandered round the table. (ch. 63)

The mere listing of a large number of incongruous objects becomes very effective in the description of a scene of disorder. In the following description of Mrs Jellyby's house the long parenthesis plays havoc with the sentence-structure but it gives a very convincing picture of muddle and neglect:

> Poor Mr Jellyby, who very seldom spoke, and almost always sat when he was at home with his head against the wall, became interested when he saw that Caddy and I were attempting to establish some order among all this waste and ruin, and took off his coat to help. But such wonderful things came tumbling out of the closets when they were opened – bits of mouldy pie, sour bottles, Mrs Jellyby's caps, lettuces, tea, forks, odd boots and shoes of children, firewood, wafers, saucepan-lids, damp sugar in odds and ends of paper bags, footstools, blacklead brushes, bread, Mrs Jellyby's bonnets, books with butter sticking to the binding, guttered candle-ends put out by being turned upside down in broken candlesticks, nutshells, heads and tails of shrimps, dinner-mats, gloves, coffee-grounds, umbrellas – that he looked frightened, and left off again. (*BH*, ch. 30)

There is a similar, but more attractive, catalogue in the description of the contents of the hamper sent round to the convalescent Dick Swiveller (*OCS*, ch. 66).

This method of enumeration can be used very effectively in descriptive passages where a vivid picture can be presented by the careful building up of detail. A good example is provided by this description of the scenes visited by the Dorrit family:

> Among the day's unrealities would be, roads where the bright red vines were looped and garlanded together on trees for many miles; woods of olives; white villages and towns on hill-sides, lovely without, but frightful in their dirt and poverty within; crosses by the way; deep blue lakes with fairy islands, and clustering boats with awnings of bright colours and sails of beautiful forms; vast piles of building mouldering to dust; hanging-gardens where the weeds had grown so strong that their stems, like wedges driven home, had split the arch and rent the wall; stone-terraced lanes, with the lizards running into and out of every chink; beggars of all sorts everywhere: pitiful, picturesque, hungry, merry: children beggars and aged beggars. (*LD*, Bk II, ch. 3)

This careful observation of detail is one of Dickens's most valuable qualities, and he is always ready, by a fanciful touch, to prevent it from becoming dull. Thus, Fanny Dorrit, over-whelmed by boredom and self-pity, steps on to the balcony after taking leave of Mr Merdle:

> Waters of vexation filled her eyes; and they had the effect of making the famous Mr Merdle, in going down the street, appear to leap, and waltz, and gyrate, as if he were possessed by several Devils. (*LD*, Bk II, ch. 24)

Dickens was very sensitive to smells, especially unpleasant ones, and he describes them in some detail. In *Great Expectations* convicts travelling by coach are described as 'bringing with them that curious flavour of bread-poultice, baize, rope-yarn, and hearthstone, which attends the convict presence' (ch. 28). When Flora Finching visited Mr Dorrit, 'a singular combination of perfumes was diffused through the room, as if some brandy had been put by mistake in a lavender-water bottle, or as if some lavender-water had been put by mistake in a brandy-bottle' (*LD*, Bk II, ch. 17).

One feature of Dickens's style that is to be noticed in some of the passages already quoted is his readiness to use adjectives freely. As we have seen, the adjectives are often conventional, adding little to a description that a reader could not have imagined for himself, but they are sometimes very effective, giving a life-like picture in a very concise way. There is, for example, the guest at Mr Perker's dinner party, who is described as 'a small-eyed peremptory young gentleman' (*PP*, ch. 47). Sometimes the adjective is more fanciful but nevertheless effective, as in the description of the tract read by Arthur Clennam when a child, which 'had a parenthesis in every other line with some such hiccupping reference as 2. Ep. Thess. c. iii. v. 6 & 7' (*LD*, Bk I, ch. 3). Sometimes an adjective used by one of the characters in a novel is unexpected but amusing, as when Flora Finching describes her late husband's will, which had left her comfortably off, as 'a beautiful will' (*LD*, Bk I, ch. 13). It is not only adjectives which are well chosen to express much in little. There is, for example, a good deal of concise satire in the word *jewel-stands* for society women (*LD*, Bk I, ch. 21). The verb is well chosen in the description of 'a mysterious old lady who lurks behind a pair of spectacles' (*SB*, 'The Couple who coddle themselves'), and so is the adverb when Thomas Gradgrind, the victim of a careful education, 'stood sniffing revengefully at the fire' (*HT*, Bk I, ch. 4).

Some of the words used by Dickens are unusual, though the meaning is generally clear from the context. A cabman eyes Mr Pickwick 'askant' (*PP*, ch. 2), and the recipient of a dirty look from Mrs Wilfer is described as 'the beglared one' (*OMF*, Bk III, ch. 16). Sometimes an unexpected word is an elegant variation of a cliché, as when Mr Pickwick, in his indignation with Peter Magnus, 'looked encyclopaedias' at him (*PP*, ch. 19), which we may understand as meaning looking volumes, only more so.

Critics sometimes speak of the elaborate circumlocutions which are common in Dickens, and they say with truth that this is a form of humour that has not worn well. But circumlocution represents only one form of Dickensian humour and that not the best. Dickens was a master of the concise phrase. Here are four examples from a single novel: Georgiana Podsnap is accompanied by 'six feet one of discontented footman' (*OMF*, Bk II, ch. 4); Twemlow is first introduced as 'an innocent piece of dinner-furniture' (Bk I, ch. 2); his cousin, Lord Snigsworth, is described as having 'gout in the temper' (Bk II, ch. 3); and Mr and Mrs Boffin, unhappy with their newly-inherited wealth, are described as sitting after breakfast 'a prey to prosperity' (Bk I, ch. 15). Examples abound in all the novels. The description of Mrs Clennam's house in *Little*

Dorrit contains a number of expressive phrases: the deserted rooms have 'settled down into a gloomy lethargy' and the furniture 'hid in the rooms rather than furnished them' (Bk I, ch. 5). The payment of debts was regarded by the prisoners in the Marshalsea as 'a disease that occasionally broke out' (*LD*, Bk I, ch. 8). A chapel in Coketown is 'a pious warehouse of red brick' (*HT*, Bk I, ch. 5). Miss Miggs welcomes Dolly Varden 'with a sort of hysterical gasp, intended for a smile' (*BR*, ch. 41). The cheers of the pupils at Dotheboys Hall are 'sighs of extra strength with the chill on' (*NN*, ch. 8). The 'weak-eyed young man' who opens the door for Mr Dombey when he visits Doctor Blimber's Academy is concisely described as 'all meekness and incapacity' (*DS*, ch. 11). When Mrs Chick is about to pick a quarrel with her friend Miss Tox, she is described as 'labouring under a peculiar little monosyllabic cough; a sort of primer, or easy introduction to the art of coughing' (*DS*, ch. 29). Joe Gargery in his Sunday clothes looks 'like a scarecrow in good circumstances' (*GE*, ch. 3). The children of the Smallweed family are 'complete little men and women' who 'bear a likeness to old monkeys with something depressing on their minds' (*BH*, ch. 21).

Sometimes the phrases used to describe everyday matters show an ability to see the funny side of things not usually regarded as funny. Pip, as narrator, in *Great Expectations* speaks of Mr Wopsle's great-aunt as having 'conquered a confirmed habit of living into which she had fallen' (ch. 16), and says that when he was a child he was regaled with 'those obscure corners of pork of which the pig, when living, had had the least reason to be vain' (*GE*, ch. 4). Such phrases seem amusing or facetious according to the temperament of the reader or the mood of the moment.

Both in the narrative of the novels and in the conversations Dickens sometimes obtains a comic effect by the deliberate use of a slightly inappropriate word. When the Micawbers' servant, the Orfling, is about to leave, the phrase used is that she 'was about to be disbanded' (*DC*, ch. 12). A word that would be appropriate if applied to a whole army emphasizes the forlorn solitariness of the Orfling and the poverty of her employers. Some of Dickens's attractive simple-minded characters have a great capacity for misplaced admiration, and so we find Toots praising the Game Chicken for his 'great intelligence' (*DS*, ch. 50) and Captain Cuttle treating Bunsby with a veneration that he does little to justify.

Although the novels of Dickens belong only to the last century, there have been such linguistic changes that their language often stands in need of annotation. We no longer use *mother-in-law* in the sense 'stepmother', yet Tony Weller's second wife is repeatedly described as Sam Weller's mother-in-law (*PP*, ch. 22) and Edmund Sparkler is said to be Mr Merdle's son-in-law (*LD*, Bk I, ch. 21). These meanings were common in the early nineteenth century: Jane Austen describes Mrs Weston as Frank Churchill's mother-in-law (*Emma*, ch. 5). Some words need annotation because the objects described are no longer familiar. No doubt many readers of *Pickwick Papers* have been puzzled by the allusion in the account of the meeting of the Brick Lane Temperance Association to 'a little emphatic man, with a bald head, and drab shorts' who began the proceedings (ch. 33). In *Great Expectations* the returned convict, Magwitch, tries to decide what clothes he will wear:

> He cherished an extraordinary belief in the virtues of 'shorts' as a disguise, and had in his own mind sketched a dress for himself that would have made him something between a dean and dentist. (ch. 40)

The use of *shorts* to describe trousers which leave the knees bare is comparatively modern; in Victorian English the word generally means 'knee-breeches'. Another word which had a similar meaning in Victorian times was *smalls* (for *small clothes*). One of Sir Leicester Dedlock's footmen is described as wearing 'peach-blossomed smalls' (*BH*, ch. 54). Again, there is the word *housewife*; Miss Peecher is described as 'a little pin-cushion, a little housewife, a little book, a little workbox, a little set of tables and weights and measures, and a little woman, all in one' (*OMF*, Bk I, ch. 16). The meaning of the word becomes clear when it is used in a compound: Little Dorrit 'took out her little pocket-housewife, threaded her needle, and began to hem' (*LD*, Bk I, ch. 24). Mrs Gamp's apartment contains a number of 'pippins', which are described as falling on Mrs Gamp like a 'wooden shower-bath' (*MC*, ch. 49). Another word that occurs in Dickens in a sense no longer generally current is *promiscuous(ly)* in the sense 'by chance'. It is so used in *Sketches by Boz* (*Tales*, ch. 1). Captain Cuttle uses it in the same sense. He tells Rob the Grinder:

> go you to Brig Place and whistle that 'ere tune near my old moorings – not as if you was a meaning of it, you understand, but as if you'd drifted there, promiscuous. (*DS*, ch. 32)

The evidence to be found in the novels of Dickens about the senses in which words were used in Victorian England is all the more valuable because Dickens was interested in linguistic details. In *Great Expectations* Pip, as narrator, interrupts a description to say that a bow-window is not the same thing as a bay-window (ch. 46), though he does not go on to say what the difference is. Moreover, Dickens made a serious attempt to achieve verisimilitude in making the language of his characters appropriate to their personality. This is harder to achieve in long passages of narrative than in conversation. When Esther Summerson in *Bleak House* seems to be speaking out of character, she hastens to add that she is quoting somebody else, though her anxiety is not always justified, as when she says that Mr Boythorn was 'incapable (as Richard said) of anything on a limited scale' (ch. 9).

Apart from words describing objects no longer familiar Dickens occasionally uses learned words, as when Bunsby in *Dombey and Son* is described as having a waistband so very broad and high that it became a succedaneum for a waistcoat (ch. 23).

Much may be learnt from the novels of Dickens about the drinking habits of the Victorians. Punch enters largely into the arrangements for any party, but there are other names of various kinds of strong drink that are less well-known today. When Mr Pickwick joined the one-eyed bagman at the Bush, 'he and the landlord were drinking a bowl of bishop together' (*PP*, ch. 48), and this seems to be the same as negus, for the bagman ladles out a glass of negus from the bowl. Mrs Gamp's requirements after the death of Anthony Chuzzlewit, are described in some detail:

> In her drinking too, she was very punctual and particular, requiring a pint of mild porter at lunch, a pint at dinner, half-a-pint as a species of stay or hold fast between dinner and tea, and a pint of the

celebrated staggering ale, or Real Old Brighton Tipper, at supper; besides the bottle on the chimney-piece, and such casual invitations to refresh herself with wine as the good breeding of her employers might prompt them to offer. (*MC*, ch. 19)

Flip was a heated and sweetened mixture of small beer and brandy, drunk at the end of a meal. At the Six Jolly Fellowship-Porters the company are described as 'not having yet arrived at the flip-stage of their supper, but being as yet skirmishing with strong ale' (*OMF*, Bk IV, ch. 12).

In describing the proceedings of the Brick Lane Temperance Association, the author is so considerate as to give the recipe for dog's nose. The secretary of the Association reports on one convert to the cause:

H. Walker, tailor, wife, and two children. When in better circumstances, owns to having been in the constant habit of drinking ale and beer; says he is not certain whether he did not twice a week, for twenty years, taste 'dog's nose', which your committee find upon inquiry, to be compounded of warm porter, moist sugar, gin, and nutmeg (a groan, and 'So it is!' from an elderly female). (*PP*, ch. 33)

Many of the strong drinks were served hot. At the Six Jolly Fellowship-Porters one could not only have mulled ale, but they also 'heated for you those delectable drinks Purl, Flip, and Dog's Nose' (*OMF*, Bk I, ch. 6). The first of these was a speciality of the house, and was common enough for Dickens to have noticed that it was usually described by the adjective 'early'; the Fellowship-Porters bore the inscription 'The Early Purl House'.

In no sphere, perhaps, have there been so many changes as in the various types of road vehicle. The carriage in which Mr Pickwick is taken to the Fleet prison is described as 'a queer sort of fresh painted vehicle', but the attempt to describe it further tells us less about the vehicle itself than about the wide variety of carriages that were available to the Victorians:

The vehicle was not exactly a gig, neither was it a stanhope. It was not what is currently denominated a dog-cart, neither was it a taxed-cart, nor a chaise-cart, nor a guillotined cabriolet, and yet it had something of the character of each and every of these machines. (*PP*, ch. 40)

'Mr Dombey's chariot' is described as a *rumble* (*DS*, ch. 20).
Mrs Skewton in a barouche, fifty years before the events of
Dombey and Son, was thought to resemble Cleopatra in her
barge (*DS*, ch. 21).

Dickens took a delight in collecting the technical vocabulary
of various occupations, and he uses it to give local colour. When
Sam Weller is cleaning the boots at the White Hart, it is
natural that he should have a rather specialized way of identifying
the guests:

> There's a wooden leg in number six; there's a pair of Hessians in
> thirteen; there's two pair of halves in the commercial; there's
> these here painted tops in the snuggery inside the bar; and five
> more tops in the coffee-room. (*PP*, ch. 10)

Sergeant Buzfuz shows an unexpected familiarity with the
vocabulary of children's games, when he says of Master Bardell:

> his infant sports are disregarded when his mother weeps; his 'alley
> tors' and his 'commoneys' are alike neglected; he forgets the long
> familiar cry of 'knuckle down', and at tip-cheese, or odd and even,
> his hand is out. (*PP*, ch. 34)

When Pecksniff and his daughter visit Todgers's, they find
a table laid for breakfast and on it 'an instance of that particular
style of loaf which is known to housekeepers as a slack-baked,
crummy quartern' (*MC*, ch. 28). Later, in describing the
dessert at a dinner at the same establishment, Dickens uses a
word unfamiliar to readers of today: 'stacks of biffins' (ch. 9).
Other examples of his fondness for technical language are
Chuffey's use of the commercial terms *Tare and Tret* (*MC*,
ch. 19), and the reference to change-ringing in *Triple-bob-major*
(*MC*, ch. 30). The introduction of the Game Chicken into
Dombey and Son provides an opportunity for the use of the slang
of prize-fighting, including the name of the Game Chicken
himself and that of his adversary the Larkey Boy.

The difficulty of identifying words, with which all readers of
early texts are familiar, is one that the reader of Dickens does
not entirely escape. Slight differences in spelling can change
the appearance of a word, as in *Caffre* (*BH*, ch. 11) for the
word now usually spelt *Kaffir*. A word now obsolete may be
confused with another word with which it happens to be
identical in form. At the game of cards at the Christmas party

at Dingley Dell 'Mr Tupman and the spinster aunt established a joint-stock company of fish and flattery' (*PP*, ch. 6). A reader who takes the word *fish* at its face value is likely to think that this is rather a strange game of cards, but it is from French *fiche* and means a gambling token. The word re-appears, together with another technical term, in the account of the party given by Bob Sawyer at his lodgings. Supper was served 'when the last "natural" had been declared, and the profit and loss account of fish and sixpences adjusted' (*PP*, ch. 32). The language of games has a way of seeming to the uninitiated to be more difficult than one would expect it to be. Mr Pickwick is clearly an expert at the special language of whist:

> 'Two by honours makes us eight,' said Mr Pickwick. Another hand. 'Can you one?' inquired the old lady. 'I can,' replied Mr Pickwick. 'Double, single, and the rub.' (*PP*, ch. 6)

Dickens was fond of the apparent *non sequitur* which, on closer examination, turns out to have a logic of its own. Sometimes the apparent *non sequitur* seems not to be deliberate but to be the result of clumsy sentence-construction. In the following sentence in *Great Expectations* the significance of the word *but* is not immediately apparent:

> Mr Jaggers never laughed; but he wore great, bright, creaking boots;

Everything becomes clear by the time that the reader reaches the end of the sentence, but he should not have to wait so long. The sentence goes on:

> and, in poising himself on those boots, with his large head bent down and his eyebrows joined together, awaiting an answer, he sometimes caused the boots to creak, as if they laughed in a dry and suspicious way. (ch. 24)

More often, however, the *non sequitur* is clearly deliberate and is a source of humour that has affinities with dramatic irony. The author, the speaker and the reader have enough knowledge to understand the connexion of ideas, but they realize that the person addressed probably has not, and the reader enjoys the mystification that he realizes the remark may cause. Sometimes the explanation is given; sometimes it is left for the reader to work out for himself. In *Bleak House* Alan Woodcourt calls on

Mr Snagsby to make enquiries about Jo. Mr Snagsby's reply is likely to puzzle Alan Woodcourt until the explanation is added:

'Are you a married man, sir?'
'No, I am not.'
'Would you make the attempt, though single,' says Mr Snagsby, in a melancholy whisper, 'to speak as low as you can? For my little woman is a-listening somewheres, or I'll forfeit the business and five hundred pound!' (ch. 47)

An example of an apparent *non sequitur* being left for the reader to work out for himself is provided by Vholes, the shady lawyer in *Bleak House*. He assures Richard Carstone with apparent irrelevance: 'I never impute motives; I both have, and am, a father, and I never impute motives' (ch. 39). The relevance becomes clear when we remember that Vholes has made frequent references to his three daughters and his father in the Vale of Taunton, mentioning his care for them as evidence of the disinterested rectitude of which his refusal to impute motives is but another example. An easier example is provided by Mr Boffin. Rokesmith is understandably puzzled on hearing of Silas Wegg that 'professionally he declines and he falls' (*OMF*, Bk I, ch. 9), but the reader, who knows from what book he is to read, finds no difficulty in the statement.

Professor Ian Gordon[1] describes one of the features of romantic prose:

The task set by the originators of romantic prose was to find ways of writing which would communicate excited feeling. Pathos, terror, and warm sentiment, they discovered, could be induced by syntax, through variations in the sentence-structure. A favourite device was the series of short sentences, either in parataxes or in simple co-ordination.

Professor Gordon goes on to say that this manner became almost standardized for the pathos of a death scene with the romantic novelists, and he quotes as an example the description of the death of Little Nell:

For she was dead. There, upon her little bed, she lay at rest. The solemn stillness was no marvel now. (*OCS*, ch. 71)

It is not only in death scenes that Dickens makes use of this device; it is also used in descriptive passages:

[1] *The Movement of English Prose* (Longmans, 1966), p 150.

> . . . The iron was rusty, the stone was slimy, the wood was rotten, the air was faint, the light was dim. (*LD*, Bk I, ch. 1)

The device is used, reinforced by inversion, to give an impression of haste and hustle:

> Up go the steps, bang goes the door, 'Golden-cross, Charing-cross, Tom,' says the waterman; 'Good-bye grandma,' cry the children, off jingles the coach at the rate of three miles an hour. (*SB*, *Scenes*, ch. 7)
>
> Up went the steps, bang went the door, round whirled the wheels, and off they rattled. (*OCS*, ch. 41)
>
> Out came the chaise – in went the horses – on sprung the boys – in got the travellers. (*PP*, ch. 9)

From time to time Dickens made use of the figure of speech known to medieval rhetoricians as epanaphora, a series of parallel phrases each beginning with the same word or group of words:

> Like a well, like a vault, like a tomb, the prison had no knowledge of the brightness outside. (*LD*, Bk I, ch. 1)

Dickens made use of the same device in his letters. In one of his letters to Forster three sentences begin with the words 'I wish you could have seen' (Forster, III, 2).

Dickens made frequent and effective use of similes. Those in *Sketches by Boz* are usually homely and ludicrous:

> The boarders were seated, a lady and a gentleman alternately, like the layers of bread and meat in a plate of sandwiches. (*Tales*, ch. 1)
>
> And Mr Octavius Budden departed, leaving his cousin looking forward to his visit on the following Sunday, with the feelings of a penniless poet to the weekly visit of his Scotch landlady. (*Tales*, ch. 2)
>
> as happy as a tomtit on birdlime. (*Tales*, ch. 2)
>
> They dressed in the most interesting manner – like twins! and looked as happy and comfortable as a couple of marigolds run to seed. (*Tales*, ch. 3)
>
> Tom looked as happy as a cock on a drizzly morning. (*Tales*, ch. 5)
>
> One of those young women who almost invariably, though one hardly knows why, recall to one's mind the idea of a cold fillet of veal. (*Tales*, ch. 11)

Other similes are more elaborate and sustained. An example is the description of Mr Pickwick falling asleep after dinner:

Like a gas lamp in the street, with the wind in the pipe, he had exhibited for a moment an unnatural brilliancy; then sunk so low as to be scarcely discernible: after a short interval he had burst out again, to enlighten for a moment, then flickered with an uncertain staggering sort of light, and then gone out altogether. His head was sunk upon his bosom; and perpetual snoring, with a partial choke occasionally, were the only audible indications of the great man's presence. (*PP*, ch. 2)

Another, less elaborate, example from the same novel is the description of the end of the quarrel between Pickwick and Tupman:

The unwonted lines which momentary passion had ruled in Mr Pickwick's clear and open brow, gradually melted away, as his young friend spoke, like the marks of a black-lead pencil beneath the softening influence of India rubber. (ch. 15)

The effect of the long vacation on the region of Chancery Lane is thus described:

The Temple, Chancery Lane, Serjeants' Inn, and Lincoln's Inn even unto the Fields, are like tidal harbours at low water; where stranded proceedings, offices at anchor, idle clerks lounging on lop-sided stools that will not recover their perpendicular until the current of Term sets in, lie high and dry upon the ooze of the long vacation. (*BH*, ch. 19)

There is sometimes a special appropriateness in Dickensian similes and metaphors. The similes used in the description of the schoolmistress Miss Peecher's official residence are clearly suggested by her occupation, when the house is described as having 'little windows like the eyes in needles, and little doors like the covers of school-books' (*OMF*, Bk II, ch. 1).

When, in *Bleak House*, Mr George visits his old friend Matthew Bagnet, the whole atmosphere of the party is very military, and this is reflected in the choice of metaphors:

At first Mrs Bagnet trusts to the combined endearments of Quebec and Malta to restore him; but finding those young ladies sensible that their existing Bluffy is not the Bluffy of their usual frolicsome acquaintance, she winks off the light infantry, and leaves him to deploy at leisure on the open ground of the domestic hearth. (ch. 34)

Comparison does not always take the form of a simile. Silas Wegg's loss of sleep when the mounds of dust are being cleared away is graphically described:

So continually broken was his rest through these means, that he led the life of having wagered to keep ten thousand dog-watches in ten thousand hours, and looked piteously upon himself as always getting up and yet never going to bed. So gaunt and haggard had he grown at last, that his wooden leg showed disproportionate, and presented a thriving appearance, in contrast with the rest of his plagued body, which might almost have been termed chubby. (*OMF*, Bk IV, ch. 14)

The head waiter at Bella Wilfer's marriage dinner is described as 'a solemn gentleman in black clothes and a white cravat, who looked much more like a clergyman than *the* clergyman, and seemed to have mounted a great deal higher in the church'. The comparison is sustained by the comment that when the waiter discussed the wine with Bella's husband, he 'bent his head as though stooping to the Papistical practice of receiving auricular confession', and that when a suggestion was made that did not meet his views, 'his face became overcast and reproachful, as enjoining penance'. It is in keeping with Dickens's habit of sustaining a joke that, on the strength of this comparison, the head waiter is afterwards described as 'the supervising dignitary, the Archbishop of Greenwich' and 'his Grace' (*OMF*, Bk IV, ch. 4).

Not all the similes are sustained; some of the most striking are the briefest. Mrs Hominy wore a large straw bonnet, 'in which she looked as if she had been thatched by an unskilful labourer' (*MC*, ch. 22). Mrs Skewton was prepared for repose by her maid, after which she 'tumbled into ruins like a house of painted cards' (*DS*, ch. 30). Mrs Gradgrind looked 'like an indifferently executed transparency of a small female figure, without enough light behind it' (*HT*, Bk I, ch. 4). John Willet's slight difficulties in breathing while asleep are said to resemble those which a carpenter meets with when he is planing and comes to a knot (*BR*, ch. 33). Tony Weller has 'a hoarse voice, like some strange effort of ventriloquism' (*PP*, ch. 20). Tite Barnacle's house has 'a little, dark area, like a damp waistcoat pocket' (*LD*, Bk I, ch. 10). Mrs Gowan's servant is 'a smiling man like a reformed assassin' (*LD*, Bk II, ch. 6).

Sometimes a simile is condensed into a metaphor or succession of metaphors. The props supporting Mrs Clennam's half-ruined house are 'gigantic crutches' and a 'gymnasium for the

neighbouring cats' (*LD*, Bk I, ch. 3). Pancks is repeatedly
spoken of as a steamer or tug. Lord Decimus Barnacle, standing
in front of a painting of two cows after Cuyp is described as
making a third cow in the group (*LD*, Bk II, ch. 12). Sometimes the metaphor is rather technical. Mrs Varden is so
capricious that she

> would sometimes ring the changes backwards and forwards on all
> possible moods and flights in one short quarter of an hour; perform-
> ing, as it were, a kind of triple bob major on the peal of instruments
> in the female belfry, with a skilfulness and rapidity of execution
> that astonished all who heard her. (*BR*, ch. 7)

Metaphors and similes may be combined to present a series
of images developing a single theme. Lord Lancaster Stiltstalk-
ing in *Little Dorrit* is described as a noble Refrigerator who
'had iced several European courts in his time' with such
success 'that the very name of Englishman yet struck cold to
the stomachs of foreigners who had the distinguished honour
of remembering him, at a distance of a quarter of a century'.
He is described as having a ponderous white cravat, like a stiff
snow-drift, and at a dinner party he 'shaded the dinner, cooled
the wines, chilled the gravy, and blighted the vegetables' (*LD*,
Bk I, ch. 26). This is a comparison which Dickens uses elsewhere to describe the behaviour of the aristocracy: Sir Leicester
Dedlock 'moves among the company, a magnificent refrigerator'
(*BH*, ch. 9).

Dickens was fond of one particular type of comparison, which
might be called the fanciful 'as if'.[1] It generally takes the form
of the invention of some improbable but amusing explanation
of the appearance or behaviour of one of the characters in a
novel. In *Great Expectations*, Jaggers and Wemmick, who
pride themselves on their toughness, are betrayed into
expressing feelings of sympathy, and are, in consequence, very
suspicious and quarrelsome with each other until they are able
to round on a complaining client: 'Mr Jaggers and Wemmick
appeared to have re-established their good understanding, and
went to work again with an air of refreshment upon them as if

---

[1] On Dickens's use of this type of comparison see J. Hillis Miller,
Charles Dickens: The World of his Novels (Cambridge, Mass., 1965),
p. 152.

B

they had just had lunch' (*GE*, ch. 51). Similar examples are very numerous; the following are only a selection from two of the novels:

In *Our Mutual Friend* Alfred Lammle at his wedding is said 'to make a pasty sort of glitter, as if he were constructed for candlelight only, and had been let out into daylight by some grand mistake' (Bk I, ch. 10). George Sampson is received by Mrs Wilfer 'as if admitted to the honour of assisting at a funeral in the family' (Bk IV, ch. 16). In *Little Dorrit* Edmund Sparkler's gondola pursues that of Fanny Dorrit 'as if she were a fair smuggler and he a custom-house officer' (Bk II, ch. 7). Mrs General retires for the night frostily 'as if she felt it necessary that the human imagination should be chilled into stone to prevent its following her' (Bk II, ch. 15). Mr Merdle stands up suddenly 'as if he had been waiting in the interval for his legs, and they had just come' (Bk II, ch. 16). A woman at the theatre where Fanny Dorrit was employed 'was in such a tumbled condition altogether, that it seemed as if it would be an act of kindness to iron her' (Bk I, ch. 20). The Sparklers' house was 'at all times stuffed and close as if it had an incurable cold in its head' (Bk II, ch. 24).

The fanciful comparison is not always introduced by 'as if'. Mrs Wilfer speaks to her husband about their daughter 'with a lofty air of never having had the least co-partnership in that young lady: of whom she now made reproachful mention as an article of luxury which her husband had set up entirely on his own account and in direct opposition to her advice' (*OMF*, Bk IV, ch. 12). When Lammle and his wife quarrelled, 'they never addressed each other, but always some invisible presence that appeared to take a station about midway between them'. The author adds the comment: 'Perhaps the skeleton in the cupboard comes out to be talked to, on such domestic occasions?' (*OMF*, Bk III, ch. 12).

Dickensian similes are sometimes both fanciful and ingenious. Mr Mould's men, drinking before a funeral,

> found it necessary to drown their grief, like a young kitten in the morning of its existence; for which reason they generally fuddled themselves before they began to do anything, lest it should make head, and get the better of them. (*MC*, ch. 19)

Mr Pecksniff, locked in a church, opens a cupboard and is startled by the sight of 'a black and white surplice dangling against the wall; which had very much the appearance of two curates who had committed suicide by hanging themselves' (*MC*, ch. 31).

One of Dickens's favourite devices is the attribution of human emotions and powers to inanimate objects or to non-human living creatures. Many examples may be quoted from a single novel. On the first page of *Bleak House* flakes of soot are said to be as big as snow-flakes 'gone into mourning, one might imagine, for the death of the sun'. On the next page the shops are said to be lighted two hours before their time, 'as the gas seems to know, for it has a haggard and unwilling look'. The smooth round trees and the smooth round blocks of stone at Chesney Wold are said to look as if the trees were going to play at bowls with the stones (ch. 7); the stiff courtly chairs in Ada Clare's bedroom are said to be each attended by a little page of a stool (ch. 6); the rooks at Chesney Wold seem to discuss who is in the carriage that passes beneath (ch. 12). The setting sun, shining on the portraits at Chesney Wold, brings them to life:

> Then do the frozen Dedlocks thaw. Strange movements come upon their features, as the shadows of leaves play there. A dense Justice in a corner is beguiled into a wink. A staring Baronet, with a truncheon, gets a dimple in his chin. Down in the bosom of a stony shepherdess there steals a fleck of light and warmth, that would have done it good, a hundred years ago. One ancestress of Volumnia, in high-heeled shoes, very like her – casting the shadow of that virgin event before her full two centuries – shoots out into a halo and becomes a saint. A maid of honour of the court of Charles the Second, with large round eyes (and other charms to correspond), seems to bathe in glowing water, and it ripples as it glows. (ch. 40)

There are many examples of this animism in other novels. In *Great Expectations* Pip, seeing the seeds in Mr Pumblechook's shop, wonders 'whether the flower-seeds and bulbs ever wanted of a fine day to break out of those jails and bloom' (ch. 8). The lock on a door and the iron nails with which it is studded are said to give the door the appearance of being subject to warts (*SB, Tales*, ch. 10), and a large, flat stone bottle is said to look 'like a half-gallon jar that had been successfully tapped for the dropsy' (*SB, Tales*, ch. 10). Charity Pecksniff asks 'Who's there ?' through a key-hole 'in a shrill voice which might have belonged to a wind in its teens' (*MC*, ch. 2). In *Little Dorrit* the position of Mr Casby's house is described:

> Mr Casby lived in a street in Gray's Inn Road, which had set off from that thoroughfare with the intention of running at one heat down into the valley, and up again to the top of Pentonville Hill; but which had run itself out of breath, in twenty yards, and had stood still ever since. (Bk I, ch. 13)

We find also many examples of the converse process, by which living creatures are described as though they were inanimate. In *Great Expectations* Drummle is described as 'an old-looking young man of a heavy order of architecture' (ch. 23) and Wemmick is 'a dry man, rather short in stature, with a square, wooden face, whose expression seemed to have been imperfectly chipped out with a dull-edged chisel' (ch. 21). This impression of lack of animation is confirmed by the author's habit of describing his mouth as a post office. In one passage in *Pickwick Papers* there is an exchange between the roles of the living and the inanimate contents of a room at an inn:

> It is the right-hand parlour, into which an aspiring kitchen fire-place appears to have walked, accompanied by a rebellious poker, tongs and shovel. It is divided into boxes, for the solitary confinement of travellers, and is furnished with a clock, a looking-glass, and a live waiter: which latter article is kept in a small kennel for washing glasses, in a corner of the apartment. (ch. 35)

The human emotions of the fire-irons are emphasized by the description of the waiter, the only human being in the scene, as though he were a lifeless object, an 'article'.

Dickens was never afraid of making excessive use of a way of writing that happened to appeal to him. In the opening paragraph of *A Tale of Two Cities* he uses antithesis to indicate the contrasting ways in which it is possible to regard the state of England and France in 1775 – 'It was the best of times; it was the worst of times; it was the age of wisdom; it was the age of foolishness . . . ' but he goes on piling up the contrasts long after the point is made. He was never afraid of repetition. A phrase, either descriptive or conversational, once associated with a particular character, will be repeated at intervals throughout a novel whenever that character is introduced. Within a single paragraph one word may be repeated again and again, and such repetition is particularly liable to occur in the early chapters of the novels. The first chapter of *Hard Times* opens with Mr Gradgrind saying 'Now, what I want is Facts', and this sentence is followed by half a dozen other short sentences in which the same idea is expressed in slightly different words. In the first chapter of *Little Dorrit* Dickens is trying to emphasize the heat of Marseilles in August. In the first ten lines of the novel the word *stared* occurs three times and the word *staring* seven times, and then, after an intervening paragraph, the repetition of *stare* and *staring* begins again. The intervening paragraph illustrates another variety of Dickensian repetition, not of a word but of a category, resulting in an enumeration: 'Hindoos, Russians, Chinese, Spaniards, Portuguese, Englishmen, Frenchmen, Genoese, Neapolitans, Venetians, Greeks, Turks, descendants from all the builders of Babel, come to trade at Marseilles, sought the shade alike.' Having made it sufficiently clear that it was a hot day, Dickens uses similar methods to introduce the idea of imprisonment, which is, of course, one of the main themes of the book:

> A prison taint was on everything there. The imprisoned air, the imprisoned light, the imprisoned damps, the imprisoned men, were all deteriorated by confinement.

When Littimer is first introduced, at the beginning of chapter 21 of *David Copperfield*, Dickens emphasizes his respectability. The words *respectable* or *respectability* are used fifteen times in two pages.

In some contexts enumeration can be a very good way of bringing an idea home to the reader. The patience of Little Dorrit in finding jobs for her feckless brother Tip is emphasized in a single paragraph which could have been expanded to fill several chapters without any gain in effectiveness. The list is divided into stanzas by the use of the refrain 'into the law again':

> Tip tired of everything. With intervals of Marshalsea lounging, and Mrs Bangham succession, his small second mother, aided by her trusty friend, got him into a warehouse, into a market garden, into the hop trade, into the law again, into an auctioneer's, into a brewery, into a stockbroker's, into the law again, into a coach office, into a waggon office, into the law again, into a general dealer's, into a distillery, into the law again, into a wool house, into a dry goods house, into the Billingsgate trade, into the foreign

fruit trade, and into the docks. But whatever Tip went into, he came out of tired, announcing that he had cut it. (*LD*, Bk I, ch. 7)

Repetition is sometimes used to describe a character's thoughts. When Lizzie Hexam is told that her father is suspected of murder, the author's comment is: 'Of her father's being groundlessly suspected, she felt sure. Sure. Sure'. (*OMF*, Bk I, ch. 6). The repetition is not so much for emphasis as to show Lizzie trying to reassure herself.

Many other examples of repetition could be given from any of the novels. It is particularly frequent in *Our Mutual Friend*:

> Mr and Mrs Veneering were bran-new people in a bran-new house in a bran-new quarter of London. Everything about the Veneerings was spick and span new. All their furniture was new, all their friends were new, all their servants were new, their plate was new, their carriage was new, their harness was new, their horses were new, their pictures were new, they themselves were new, they were as newly-married as was lawfully compatible with their having a bran-new baby, and if they had set up a great-grandfather, he would have come home in matting from the Pantechnicon, without a scratch upon him, French-polished to the crown of his head. (Bk I, ch. 2)

> Bradley Headstone, in his decent black coat and waistcoat, and decent white shirt, and decent formal black tie, and decent pantaloons of pepper and salt, with his decent silver watch in his pocket and its decent hair-guard round his neck, looked a thoroughly decent young man of six-and-twenty. (Bk II, ch. 1)

Sometimes the repetition takes a different form. Instead of the repetition of the same word many times in a few successive sentences, we find a longer unit repeated, often after a considerable interval. More than two hundred pages separate the following two passages, but the resemblance between them is so close that it is clear that the second is a deliberate echo of the first:

> There were friends who seemed to be always coming and going across the Channel, on errands about the Bourse, and Greek and Spanish and India and Mexican and par and premium and discount and three quarters and seven eights. (*OMF*, Bk II, ch. 4)

> Fitting occasion made, Mrs Lammle accordingly produced the most passable of those feverish, boastful, and indefinably loose gentlemen who were always lounging in and out of the City on questions of the Bourse and Greek and Spanish and India and Mexican and par and premium and discount and three-quarters and seven-eighths. (Bk III, ch. 5)

There is another instance of the same sort of repetition, this time without the wide separation, in the passage, too long to quote, describing Mr Podsnap's habits, with the refrain 'getting up at eight, shaving close at a quarter-past, breakfasting at nine, going to the City at ten, coming home at half-past five, and dining at seven' (*OMF*, Bk I, ch. 11).

Dickens realized that spoken language has a wider range of ways of expressing meaning and emotion than written language, and he makes an attempt to overcome the shortcomings of the written language by giving the reader fairly frequent descriptions of the way in which characters speak. In *Bleak House* a speech by Conversation Kenge is followed by Esther Summerson's comment:

> He appeared to enjoy beyond everything the sound of his own voice. I couldn't wonder at that, for it was mellow and full, and gave great importance to every word he uttered. He listened to himself with obvious satisfaction, and sometimes gently beat time to his own music with his head, or rounded a sentence with his hand. I was very much impressed by him – even then, before I knew that he formed himself on the model of a great lord who was his client, and that he was generally called Conversation Kenge. (ch. 3)

Miss Knag, in *Nicholas Nickleby*, has a mannerism which is described at some length:

> Here Miss Knag paused to take breath, and while she pauses it may be observed – not that she was marvellously loquacious and marvellously deferential to Madame Mantalini, since these are facts which require no comment; but that every now and then, she was accustomed in the torrent of her discourse, to introduce a loud, shrill, clear, 'hem!' the import and meaning of which, was variously interpreted by her acquaintance; some holding that Miss Knag dealt in exaggeration, and introduced the monosyllable, when any fresh invention was in course of coinage in her brain; others, that when she wanted a word, she threw it in to gain time, and prevent anybody else from striking into the conversation. (ch. 17)

Usually descriptions of speech are briefer, but they contribute a good deal to the life-like portrayal of the character in question. Mrs Pardiggle and Mr Boythorn have loud voices (*BH*, chs. 8, 9). The Cheeryble Brothers have a very emphatic and earnest delivery and speak as though they had plums in their mouths (*NN*, ch. 35). Mrs General speaks 'in her emotionless and expressionless manner' (*LD*, Bk II, ch. 5). When Joe

Gargery describes his wife as 'a Buster', he pronounces the word 'as if it began with at least twelve capital Bs' (*GE*, ch. 7). Miss Peecher, the schoolmistress, addresses her favourite pupil 'in a tunefully instructive voice' (*OMF*, Bk II, ch. 11). Rokesmith speaks to Riderhood 'in a tone which seemed to leave some such words as "you dog", very distinctly understood', and he goes on 'in a low voice, this time with a grim sort of admiration of him as a perfect piece of evil' (*OMF*, Bk II, ch. 12). Mrs Wilfer speaks 'in her monotonous Act of Parliament tone' (*OMF*, Bk IV, ch. 5), and she delivers 'a few remarks from the throne' (Bk IV, ch. 16). Sleary, in *Hard Times*, has a voice 'like the efforts of a broken old pair of bellows' (Bk I, ch. 6), but the most noticeable feature of his speech is his lisp, which is reproduced with such thoroughness as to slow down the reader a good deal in the chapters in which Sleary plays a part. His first words in the novel set the pattern for what is to come:

> 'Thquire!' said Mr Sleary, who was troubled with asthma, and whose breath came far too thick and heavy for the letter *s*, 'your thervant! Thith ith a bad piethe of bithnith, thith ith.' (Bk I, ch. 6)

Dickens shows skill in the use of punctuation to overcome some of the difficulties that inevitably arise when written language is used to represent the much wider range of devices that can be used by a speaker. To indicate jerky speech he uses both hyphens and full-stops. When Silas Wegg is given a lift in a donkey-cart on his way to Boffin's Bower, we are told that 'conversation was jolted out of him in a most dislocated state', and hyphens are used to indicate the jerks: 'Was – it – Ev – verajail?', 'And – why – did – they – callitharm – Ony?', 'Do you know – Mist – erboff – in?' (*OMF*, Bk I, ch. 5). An example of the use of the full-stop to indicate jerky speech is the speech of Miss Flite in *Bleak House*. Her sentences are usually short, but, even when they are not, they are split up by punctuation that is rhetorical rather than logical:

> 'I was a ward myself. I was not mad at that time', curtseying low and smiling between every little sentence. 'I had youth and hope . . . I believe, beauty. It matters very little now. Neither of the three served or saved me. I have the honour to attend Court regularly. With my documents. I expect a judgment. Shortly. On the Day of Judgment . . . ' (ch. 3)

The same device is used in *David Copperfield* to represent the words of Peggotty speaking to David through a keyhole, 'shooting in each broken little sentence in a convulsive little burst of its own':

> 'Davy, dear. If I ain't been azackly as intimate with you. Lately, as I used to be. It ain't because I don't love you. Just as well and more, my pretty poppet. It's because I thought it better for you. And for some one else besides.' (ch. 4)

Full-stops indicate the military abruptness of Matthew Bagnet's speech:

> 'You're right. The old girl,' says Mr Bagnet. 'Is as quick. As powder.' (*BH*, ch. 49)

In *Bleak House* full-stops are used with another function:

> Mr Skimpole laughed at the pleasant absurdity, and lightly touched the piano by which he was seated.
>
> 'And he told me,' he said, playing little chords where I shall put full stops, 'That Coavinses had left. Three children. No mother. And that Coavinses' profession. Being unpopular. The rising Coavinses. Were at a considerable disadvantage.' (ch. 15)

Commas are used to represent the ticking of a clock when Paul Dombey has been introduced to Doctor Blimber:

> Grave as an organ was the Doctor's speech; and when he ceased, the great clock in the hall seemed (to Paul at least) to take him up, and to go on saying, 'how, is, my, lit, tle, friend? how, is, my, lit, tle, friend?' over and over and over again. (*DS*, ch. 11)

Dickens sometimes uses length-marks to indicate stress. In writing to Forster he quotes his French courier Louis Roche: 'What does master think of datter 'rangement? Is he cŏntĕnt?' (Forster, IV, 6). Elsewhere he makes exuberant use of punctuation. His emotion, when he conveys the news that seventeen hundred copies of the *Life of Grimaldi* were sold in the first week requires thirty exclamation marks to express it (Forster, II, 2). In contrast to this excessive punctuation, the long speeches of Flora Finching in *Little Dorrit* are under-punctuated. The author's comment is that she is 'running on with astonishing speed, and pointing her conversation with nothing but commas and very few of them' (Bk I, ch. 13); the impression that she makes on Clennam is one of 'disjointed

volubility'. The lack of punctuation gives the effect of breath-
lessness and increases the inconsequential effect as her mind
darts about from one parenthesis to another:

> 'Dear dear,' said Flora, 'only to think of the changes at home
> Arthur – cannot overcome it, seems so natural, Mr Clennam far
> more proper – since you became familiar with the Chinese customs
> and language which I am persuaded you speak like a native if not
> better for you were always quick and clever though immensely
> difficult no doubt, I am sure the tea chests alone would kill *me* if I
> tried, such changes Arthur – I am doing it again, seems so natural,
> most improper – as no one could have believed, who could have
> ever imagined Mrs Finching when I can't imagine it myself!' (Bk
> I, ch. 13)

Lack of punctuation serves to indicate the way in which a bored
and overworked clerk administers an oath:

> 'Take the book in your right hand this is your name and hand-
> writing you swear that the contents of this your affidavit are true
> so help you God a shilling you must get change I haven't got it.'
> (*PP*, ch. 40)

Initial capitals are used to indicate over-emphatic speech.
They are used, for example, to mark the pompous self-
importance of Mr Podsnap when trying to impress 'the foreign
gentleman' (*OMF*, Bk I, ch. 11), and to indicate the emphasis
with which Toots describes himself as a Brute and his guardian
as a Pirate and a Corsair (*DS*, ch. 60). They are used to
represent the rapture with which Maggy in *Little Dorrit*
describes the pleasures of being a patient in a hospital: 'a
Ev'nly place' (Bk I, ch. 9) where it is possible to have 'lots of
Chicking' (Bk I, ch. 24).

Dickens occasionally uses variations of spelling to represent
unusual pronunciations, as when he writes *drayma* in a letter to
Forster (Forster, II, 1), but his mis-spellings are generally
intended as a form of class dialect. Thackeray made frequent
use of such mis-spellings in *The Yellowplush Papers* and
elsewhere, and in doing so he was merely following a fashion
that had been set by eighteenth-century novelists. Dickens
makes use of mis-spellings in a way that is less easy to defend,
namely, as eye-dialect to record the speech of his lower-class
characters. The mis-spelling does not represent a vulgar
pronunciation, but is simply a more phonetic representation of

normal English. Examples are *sed* for *said*, *wos* for *was*, and *aukshneer* for *auctioneer*.

Dickens made frequent use of a device, much used by Flaubert, which has been described as 'le style indirect libre'. This device is reported speech which not only summarizes what is said but also manages to call attention to the linguistic characteristics and the unspoken thoughts of the speaker. Professor Randolph Quirk says of it:

> The value of the technique lies not only in the subtlety with which fast flowing narrative can be coloured by the characteristic idiom of a particular speaker, but also in the ability to convey the unspoken reflection of the speaker in the suggested language of his reflection – and even the suggested impact of one speaker upon another – without the clumsiness of explanation which would coarsen and over-sharpen the impression, and fatally simplify what the author would prefer to leave equivocal.[1]

Mrs Micawber reports 'that even the revengeful bootmaker had declared in open court that he bore him [i.e. Mr Micawber] no malice, but that when money was owing to him he liked to be paid. He said he thought it was human nature'(*DC*, ch. 12). The use of indirect speech can provide examples of the poly-syllabic humour for which Victorian novelists are so often condemned. When Mrs Clennam, looking for the Marshalsea, antagonizes the crowd, we are told that they were 'recommending an adjournment to Bedlam' (*LD*, Bk II, ch. 31). There is a deliberate contrast between the pedantic literary style of the indirect speech and the direct, forceful language that the crowd may be assumed to have actually used. In *Martin Chuzzlewit* we find a sentence in reported speech which shows the omniscient narrator speaking in the manner of Mr Jinkins: 'Oh, Todgers's could do it when it chose! Mind that' (ch. 9). Another example occurs in *Dombey and Son*. The thoughts of Briggs, one of Dr Blimber's pupils, are described in reported speech that preserves many of the colloquial idioms that Briggs would have used:

> After Briggs had got into bed, he lay awake for a long time, still bemoaning his analysis, and saying he knew it was all wrong, and they couldn't have analysed a murderer worse, and how would Doctor Blimber like it if his pocket-money depended on it? It was

[1] Randolph Quirk, *The Use of English* (Longmans, 1962), p. 247.

very easy, Briggs said, to make a galley-slave of a boy all the half-year, and then score him up idle; and to crib two dinners a-week out of his board, and then score him up greedy; but that wasn't going to be submitted to, he believed, was it? Oh! Ah! (ch. 14)

In the mixture of direct and indirect speech substandard pronunciations and syntactic features are introduced into a piece of recorded speech, contrary to the usual practice, which is to put recorded speech into standard English, even if the speaker would not habitually use standard English. There are many examples in *Little Dorrit*: the turnkey at the Marshalsea, when asked whether the wives of debtors were shocked by their experiences, 'gave it as the result of his experience that some of 'em was and some of 'em wasn't' (Bk I, ch. 6). A longer example is the summary of the account which Plornish gives to Arthur Clennam of life in Bleeding Heart Yard, of which the following passage is a brief extract:

They was all hard up there, Mr Plornish said, uncommon hard up, to be sure. Well, he couldn't say how it was; he didn't know as anybody *could* say how it was; all he know'd was, that so it was. When a man felt, on his own back and in his own belly, that poor he was, that man (Mr Plornish gave it as his decided belief) know'd well that he was poor somehow or other, and you couldn't talk it out of him, no more than you could talk Beef into him. Then you see, some people as was better off said, and a good many such people lived pretty close up to the mark themselves if not beyond it so he'd heerd, that they was 'improvident' (that was the favourite word) down the Yard. (Bk I, ch. 12)

There seems to be something about Bleeding Heart Yard which encourages Dickens to indulge in these long passages of substandard direct and indirect speech mixed together. The spread of the speculation mania triggered off by Mr Merdle is described in similar terms. The following is a typical sentence:

The female Bleeding Hearts, when they came for ounces of tea and hundred weights of talk, gave Mrs Plornish to understand, That how, ma'am, they had heard from their cousin Mary Anne, which worked in the line, that his lady's dresses would fill three waggons. (Bk II, ch. 13)

Another example is:

Mr Plornish amiably growled, in his philosophical but not lucid manner, that there was ups you see, and there was downs. It was in wain to ask why ups, why downs; there they was, you know. He had heerd it given for a truth that accordin' as the world went round, which round it did rewolve undoubted, even the best of gentlemen must take his turn of standing with his ed upside down and all his air a flying the wrong way into what you might call Space. Wery well then. What Mr Plornish said was, wery well then. That gentleman's ed would come up'ards when his turn come, that gentleman's air would be a pleasure to look upon being all smooth again, and wery well then! (Bk II, ch. 27)

The evidence given by Mrs Piper at the inquest on Captain Hawdon in *Bleak House* is summarized in the manner of a newspaper report, but with Mrs Piper's distinctive turns of phrase preserved so that it is an easy matter for the reader to reconstruct the evidence in the style which Mrs Piper would have used:

Why, Mrs Piper has a good deal to say, chiefly in parentheses and without punctuation, but not much to tell. Mrs Piper lives in the court (which her husband is a cabinet-maker), and it has long been well beknown among the neighbours (counting from the day next but one before the half-baptising of Alexander James Piper aged eighteen months and four days old on accounts of not being expected to live such was the sufferings gentlemen of that child in his gums) as the Plaintive – so Mrs Piper insists on calling the deceased – was reported to have sold himself. Thinks it was the Plaintive's air in which that report originatinin. See the Plaintive often and considered as his air was feariocious and not to be allowed to go about some children being timid (and if doubted hoping Mrs Perkins may be brought forard for she is here and will do credit to her husband and herself and family.) . . . (ch. 11)

A similar kind of reported speech is used to describe the evidence given by Jo at the same inquest:

Name, Jo. Nothing else that he knows on. Don't know that everybody has two names. Never heerd of sich a think. Don't know that Jo is short for a longer name. Thinks it long enough for *him*. *He* don't find no fault with it. Spell it? No. *He* can't spell it. No father, no mother, no friends. Never been to school. What's home? Knows a broom's a broom, and knows it's wicked to tell a lie. Don't recollect who told him about the broom, or about the lie, but knows both. Can't exactly say what'll be done to him arter he's dead if he tells a lie to the gentlemen here, but believes it'll be something wery bad to punish him, and serve him right – and so he'll tell the truth. (ch. 11)

It is not only substandard speech that is treated in this way. When the Barnacles gather in force for the wedding of Henry

Gowan, a specimen of the eloquence of a public speaker is presented in much the same way:

> Yes, there was Lord Decimus Tite Barnacle, who had risen to official heights on the wings of one indignant idea, and that was, My Lords, that I am yet to be told that it behoves a Minister of this free country to set bounds to the philanthropy, to cramp the charity, to fetter the public spirit, to contract the enterprise, to damp the independent self-reliance of the people. (*LD*, Bk I, ch. 34)

At the same wedding the conversation of a less important Barnacle is described:

> Barnacle Junior did, with indignation, communicate to two vapid young gentlemen his relatives, that there was a feller here, look here, who had come to our Department without an appointment, and said he wanted to know, you know. (Bk I, ch. 34)

The same effect is sometimes achieved by the introduction of many slang words into a piece of reported speech. In the following passage a prize-fighter is explaining his rather battered appearance:

> The Chicken himself attributed this punishment to his having had misfortune to get into Chancery early in the proceedings, when he was severely fibbed by the Larkey one, and heavily grassed. But it appeared from the published records of that great contest that the Larkey Boy had had it all his own way from the beginning, and that the Chicken had been tapped, and bunged, and had received pepper, and had been made groggy, and had come up piping, and had endured a complication of similar strange inconveniences, until he had been gone into and finished. (*DS*, ch. 44)

From the first Dickens has had detractors as well as enthusiastic admirers, and his detractors have made much of his faults of style. Forster devoted several pages of his *Life* to a defence of Dickens's style against the attacks of Taine. Some of the adverse criticism is the result of judging him by irrelevant standards: it amounts to saying that he wrote like a nineteenth-century, not a twentieth-century, author. Nevertheless, it must be admitted that some of the characteristics of the style of Dickens are likely to lessen, rather than to increase, a twentieth-century reader's enjoyment of his work.

There is, first of all, the lack of restraint. Dickens sometimes made too strong an appeal to the emotions. The result is that

the reader is liable to feel that he is 'piling it on' and to offer
some resistance to the assault on his emotions of the kind
represented by the last three words of the following paragraph,
describing Arthur Clennam's imprisonment in the Marshalsea:

> The autumn days went on, and Little Dorrit never came to the
> Marshalsea now, and went away without seeing him. No, no, no.
> (*LD*, Bk II, ch. 34)

The idea of a public execution is horrible enough without any
heightening of effects, and probably many readers will feel that
the following vivid description of Newgate would have been
more, and not less, effective without the emotional repetition in
the last two lines:

> . . . in that crowded street on which it frowns so darkly – within a
> few feet of squalid tottering houses – upon the very spot on which
> the venders of soup and fish and damaged fruit are now plying
> their trades – scores of human beings, amidst a roar of sounds to
> which even the tumult of a great city is nothing, four, six, or eight
> strong men at a time, have been hurried violently and swiftly from
> the world, when the scene has been rendered frightful with excess
> of human life; when curious eyes have glared from casement, and
> house-top, and wall and pillar; and when, in the mass of white and
> upturned faces, the dying wretch, in his all-comprehensive look of
> agony, has met not one – not one – that bore the impress of pity or
> compassion. (*NN*, ch. 4)

Another of Dickens's stylistic devices that tends to jar on a
reader of today is apostrophe, like the one which the author
addresses to Twemlow in *Our Mutual Friend*.

> Ah! my Twemlow! Say, little feeble grey personage, what thoughts
> are in thy breast today, of the Fancy – so still to call her who
> bruised thy heart when it was green and thy head brown – and
> whether it be better or worse, more painful or less, to believe in
> the Fancy to this hour, than to know her for a greedy armour-plated
> crocodile, with no more capacity of imagining the delicate and
> sensitive and tender spot behind thy waistcoat, than of going
> straight at it with a knitting-needle. Say likewise, my Twemlow,
> whether it be the happier lot to be a poor relation of the great, or
> to stand in the wintry slush giving the hack horses to drink out of the
> shallow tub at the coach-stand, into which thou hast so nearly set thy
> uncertain foot. Twemlow says nothing, and goes on. (Bk II, ch. 16)

When Mrs General complains to Mr Dorrit that his daughter
Amy has no force of character, Dickens is not content to leave

the reader to appreciate for himself what a foolish observation
this is; he inserts an apostrophe to Mrs General to underline
the absurdity of the criticism, making things harder for the
reader by putting it in the mouth of Mr Dorrit and then saying
that it never occurred to him:

> None? O Mrs General, ask the Marshalsea stones and bars. O
> Mrs General, ask the milliner who taught her to work, and the
> dancing-master who taught her sister to dance. O Mrs General,
> ask me, her father, what I owe to her; and hear my testimony
> touching the life of this slighted little creature, from her childhood
> up!
>
> No such adjuration entered Mr Dorrit's head. (*LD*, Bk II, ch. 5)

An apostrophe very much in the manner of Carlyle is
addressed to the schoolmaster McChoakumchild in *Hard Times*:

> He went to work in the preparatory lesson, not unlike Morgiana
> in the Forty Thieves – looking into all the vessels ranged before
> him, one after another, to see what they contained. Say, good
> McChoakumchild: when from thy boiling store thou shalt fill each
> jar brim full by-and-by, dost thou think that thou wilt always kill
> outright the robber Fancy lurking within – or sometimes only
> maim him and distort him! (Bk I, ch. 2)

The death of Jo in *Bleak House* provokes another very
emotional apostrophe:

> The light is come upon the dark benighted way. Dead!
> Dead, your Majesty. Dead, my lords and gentlemen. Dead,
> Right Reverends and Wrong Reverends of every order. Dead, men
> and women, born with Heavenly compassion in your hearts. And
> dying thus around us every day. (ch. 47)

This apostrophe occurs at the end of a chapter, and that is a
position where general reflections, embodied in pieces of 'fine
writing', are liable to occur. We may compare the second
chapter of *Little Dorrit*, which ends with the words:

> The day passed on; and again the wide stare stared itself out;
> and the hot night was on Marseilles; and through it the caravan of
> the morning, all dispersed, went their appointed ways. And thus
> ever, by day and night, under the sun and under the stars, climbing
> the dusty hills and toiling along the weary plains, journeying by
> land and journeying by sea, coming and going so strangely, to
> meet and to act and react on one another, move all we restless
> travellers through the pilgrimage of life.

One of the rather surprizing effects of emotion on some writers is to make them write prose that can be scanned as if it were blank verse. There are many examples in *The Old Curiosity Shop*:

I have been sexton here, good fifty years. (ch. 70)

Why dost thou lie so idle there, dear Nell, when there are bright red berries out of doors, waiting for thee to pluck them. (ch. 71)

The use of blank verse is not confined to speeches; there are examples too in descriptive and narrative passages:

Kit often tried to catch the earliest glimpse of twinkling lights denoting their approach to some not distant town. (ch. 70)

The old church tower, clad in a ghostly garb. (ch. 70)

Kit tried to speak, and did pronounce some words. (ch. 71)

Occasional examples might be the result of accident, but in some of these examples it is clear that the metrical effect is the result of the choice of some slightly unidiomatic or archaic turn of phrase, like 'not distant' or the elliptic phrase 'good fifty years'. Dickens did not set out to achieve lines of blank verse and, indeed, he fought against the tendency. In sending Forster a set of proofs of *The Battle of Life*, he wrote:

If in going over the proofs you find the tendency to blank verse (I *cannot* help it, when I am very much in earnest) too strong, knock out a word's brains here and there. (Forster, V, 6)

Some authors are content to stand aside unobtrusively but Dickens was not of their number. It is always clear where his own sympathies lie. We soon realize, for example, that he likes Walter Gay and that he does not like Charlie Hexam. His affection for Sam Weller is unbounded. In spite of Sam Weller's faithful affection for Mr Pickwick, the careful reader cannot help noticing that, especially in the early part of the book, he is the cause of many of his master's misadventures. When Mr Pickwick is left unattended with the result that he is taken to the village pound, there is no hint of Sam's share in his misfortunes; the day ends with 'a magnum of extra strength for Mr Samuel Weller'.

Dickens gives the reader a lead by his choice of adjectives. When he says of Little Nell that 'one of her little feet was blistered and sore' (*OCS*, ch. 15), the adjective 'little' is a direct appeal for the reader's sympathy, and similarly Paul Dombey is 'poor' or 'little', Walter Gay is 'the generous, handsome, gallant-hearted youth' (*DS*, ch. 32), whereas Tom Gradgrind is 'the villainous whelp, sulky to the last' (*HT*, Bk III, ch. 7), and Blandois is said to have dropped whatever thin disguise he had worn and to have 'faced it out, with a bare face, as the infamous wretch he was' (*LD*, Bk II, ch. 28).

For many readers such partisanship fails of its effect. Dickens is determined that his readers shall admire Mark Tapley, and probably most readers do find him an attractive character, but at least one of his admirers would like him even better if he were not quite so persistent in declaring his desire to acquire merit by being jolly in difficult circumstances.

The author's intervention sometimes leads to confusion between the opinions of the author and those of his characters. When Mr Gregsbury in *Nicholas Nickleby* is explaining to Nicholas the sort of speech that he would be expected to prepare, he gives an example:

> For instance, if any preposterous bill were brought forward, for giving poor grubbing devils of authors a right to their own property . . . (ch. 16)

Here the adjective 'preposterous' is Mr Gregsbury's contribution, but in the rest of the quotation the speaker is Charles Dickens, expressing his views on a subject that he had very much at heart. Again, in *Pickwick Papers* Stiggins delivers 'an edifying discourse' to the Weller family. The summary of this homily is followed by a *précis* of what Stiggins did not say, and here Dickens is unashamedly interposing his own views:

> Mr Stiggins did not desire his hearers to be upon their guard against those false prophets and wretched mockers of religion, who, without sense to expound its first doctrines, or hearts to feel its first principles, are more dangerous members of society than the common criminal; imposing, as they necessarily do, upon the weakest and worst informed, casting scorn and contempt on what should be held most sacred, and bringing into partial disrepute large bodies of virtuous and well-conducted persons of many excellent sects and persuasions. But as he leant over the back of the chair for a considerable time, and closing one eye, winked a good deal with the other, it is presumed that he thought all this, but kept it to himself. (ch.45)

Many readers find such interventions unwelcome, regarding them as self-conscious interruptions of the illusion. The practice was more common in the Victorian novel than it is today, and the reader of Dickens has to be prepared to accept such remarks as 'But bless our editorial heart, what a long chapter we have been betrayed into' (*PP*, ch. 28).

At the end of *Pickwick Papers* the author complains about the convention that a novel should conclude with an account of what happened to the various characters in the novel. Dickens protests but complies:

> In compliance with this custom – unquestionably a bad one – we subjoin a few biographical words. (ch. 57)

In exactly the same way Charles Reade was later to protest against the convention in the last chapter of *The Cloister and the Hearth*:

> In accordance with a custom I despise, but have not the spirit to resist, I linger on the stage to pick up the smaller fragments of humanity I have scattered about.

Sometimes Dickens's interest in language combined with his natural exuberance to make him indulge in linguistic word-play. Today puns are tolerated in a few specialized contexts, as in radio word games, but they are not as a rule indulged in by writers even of light fiction, except occasionally and defiantly. Dickens does not hesitate to hold up his narrative in order to insert a facetious parenthesis that is a mere play upon words. When Ben Allen asks Bob Sawyer how long his landlady's bill has been running, the author interposes a comment of his own between the question and the reply:

> A bill, by the bye, is the most extraordinary locomotive engine that the genius of man ever produced. It would keep on running during the longest lifetime, without ever once stopping of its own accord. (*PP*, ch. 32)

In much the same way Mr Pickwick soliloquizes on a fine morning at Dingley Dell:

> 'Who could continue to exist, where there are no cows but the cows on the chimney-pots; nothing redolent of Pan but the pan-tiles; no crop but stone-crop?' (*PP*, ch. 7)

Sometimes pun combines with metaphor. The prize-fighter who acts as attendant to Toots in *Dombey and Son* has the nickname Game Chicken and the nickname causes the author to say that he 'dips his beak into a tankard of strong beer, in Mr Toots's kitchen, and pecks up two pounds of beefsteaks' (ch. 31).

Misunderstandings that are little more than puns can be tiresome enough, as when Bill Simmons, giving Martin Chuzzlewit a lift to London, says of Ned of the Light Salisbury 'He *was* a guard. What you may call a Guard'an Angel, was Ned' (*MC*, ch. 13), and that when he went to America he must have been 'something in the public line' because 'he wrote home that him and his friends was always a-singing, Ale Columbia' (*MC*, ch. 13). But such misunderstandings can be used in a manner both pathetic and realistic, as in the reply of Chuffey, the old clerk, half-crazy with age and grief at the death of his master:

> 'Come, Mr Chuffey,' said Pecksniff, 'Come with me. Summon up your fortitude, Mr Chuffey.'
> 'Yes, I will,' returned the old clerk. 'Yes. I'll sum up my forty – How many times forty – Oh, Chuzzlewit and Son . . . ' (*MC*, ch. 19)

An effect similar to that of a pun can be gained by the deliberate confusion between two quite different senses of the same word. It is the concern of the etymologist to show that 'to draw one's salary' and 'to draw one's sword' illustrate different uses of the same word; the reader receives a shock of amused surprise when Dickens deliberately substitutes an unexpected sense in his reference to the holder of a sinecure who had died at his post 'with his drawn salary in his hand, nobly defending it to the last extremity' (*LD*, Bk I, ch. 17).

There are other figures of speech whose appeal is similar to that of the pun. Like puns, they can be regarded as playing with language and they are frowned upon by those who consider language a serious matter to be regarded only as a means to the expression of ideas. Such figures are to be found especially in the writings of young men, who are just becoming conscious of the enormous potentialities of language. One of these figures is syllepsis, often confused with zeugma.[1] An example from *Pickwick Papers* is often quoted: while at Bath Mr Pickwick played at cards so badly that his partner, Miss Bolo, 'rose from

---

[1] Both figures involve the use of a verb with two different objects; the difference between them is that in syllepsis the verb can properly govern both objects; in zeugma it cannot.

the table considerably agitated, and went straight home in a flood of tears and a sedan-chair'. (ch. 35). There are several other instances. For example, Bob Sawyer 'threw off his green spectacles and his gravity together' (*PP*, ch. 50). When Mr Pickwick had drunk too much cold punch after being pushed along in a wheelbarrow because he was unfit to walk, he 'fell into the barrow, and fast asleep, simultaneously' (*PP*, ch. 19). Syllepsis is very common in *Sketches by Boz*: 'a child in a braided frock and high state of astonishment' (*Scenes*, ch. 11), 'Mr Barker entered into a new suit of clothes, and on a new sphere of action' (*Scenes*, ch. 17), 'they . . . were carried to their respective abodes in a hackney-coach and a state of insensibility' (*Characters*, ch. 4), Mr Simon Tuggs 'kept his father's books, and his own counsel' (*Tales*, ch. 4).

The exuberance that gives rise to jokes of this kind sometimes takes other forms. By a parody of the phrase 'of the earth, earthy', E. W. B. Childers is described as being 'of the Turf, turfy' (*HT*, Bk I, ch. 6). In the same novel, after describing the collections of shells and minerals which served the Gradgrind children instead of toys, Dickens suddenly indulges in a parody of a well-known alliterative nursery rhyme:

> to paraphrase the idle legend of Peter Piper, who had never found his way into *their* nursery, if the greedy little Gradgrinds grasped at more than this, what was it for good gracious goodness' sake that the greedy little Gradgrinds grasped at! (Bk I, ch. 3)

There are other devices which now seem facetious rather than funny. One of these is the unnecessary parenthesis. It shows a straining after comic effect when an author thinks it necessary to warn his readers against a misunderstanding of which no one but a fool would be guilty, as in the passage in *Pickwick Papers* where Captain Boldwig is described as walking about his property 'in company with a thick rattan stick with a brass ferrule, and a gardener and a sub-gardener with meek faces, to whom (the gardeners, not the stick) Captain Boldwig gave his orders with all due grandeur and ferocity' (ch. 19). Again, in *Nicholas Nickleby* Miss La Creevy is described as wearing a yellow turban when a coach arrives for Mrs Nickleby and Kate. The author thinks it necessary to add a parenthesis that it is the coach, and not the turban, that goes away with the two ladies and their luggage inside it (ch. 11).

2

CLASS DIALECTS

The most interesting feature of the language used by the characters of Dickens is the wide variety of class dialects. One dialect – that of poor people living in London – is so important that it is discussed more fully elsewhere in this book (Chapter III and Appendix); the purpose of the present chapter is to illustrate the other class and occupational dialects used by characters in the novels of Dickens.

Dickens's references to upper-class speech are generally uncomplimentary. A typical comment is his reference in *Hard Times* to fine gentlemen who 'yaw-yawed in their speech' (Bk II, ch. 2). In matters of class dialect extremes often meet, and the broker's man 'Coavinses', who comes to arrest Harold Skimpole for debt, shares with the debilitated cousin of Sir Leicester Dedlock a tendency to omit lightly-stressed syllables, as in 'yes'day aft'noon' (*BH*, chs. 6, 40). A similar process can be observed in the development of vocabulary and idiom. Old-fashioned expressions of politeness struggle on among people with no pretensions to fashion long after they have passed out of upper-class use. The one-time fashionable greeting 'Your servant' occurs frequently in Dickens in the mouths of unfashionable characters. Mr Omer the undertaker greets David Copperfield 'Servant, sir' (*DC*, ch. 21) and Mr Micawber says 'Your servant' to Uriah Heep's mother (*DC*, ch. 17). When John Browdie and Nicholas Nickleby are introduced to each other, Browdie says 'Servant, sir' and Nicholas replies 'Yours to command, sir' (*NN*, ch. 9). The greetings are repeated in a somewhat abridged form when the two meet again after a quarrel and after Nicholas has left Dotheboys Hall:

'Servant, young genelman,' said John. 'Yours,' said Nicholas. (*NN*, ch. 13)

Ernest Weekley has shown[1] that some of the substandard
features that occur in the speech of characters like Mrs Gamp
were originally features of upper-class speech that have come
down in the world, their use by upper-class speakers giving
them a prestige which led the middle and lower classes to
imitate them.

The most sustained representation of upper-class speech in
Dickens is that of Lord Frederick Verisopht, and the characteristic of that speech that Dickens is at most pains to emphasize is
the lengthening of vowels. [æ] is represented by *a-a* (or *a-a-*
or *-a-a*), as in *pa-ack*, *wa-a-x*, *pla-an*, *ba-a-d*, *d-a-amn*, *ma-an*,
[e] by *ey*, *ay*, or *ea-a* as in *deyvle*, *deyvlish*, *playsure*, *nayver*,
jea-alous, [ei] by *a-a-y*, *a-ay* or *a-a*, as in *da-a-y*, *na-ay*, *a-age*
(chs. 19, 21, 32). This lengthening is shared by the debilitated
cousin in *Bleak House*, who thinks 'Country's going – *Dayvle'*
(ch. 40, cf. Gerson § 2.6). Verisopht's *ga-a-l* (*NN*, ch. 22)
suggests that *gal*, a variant of *girl*, has undergone lengthening,
and *a-ask* (ch. 19) suggests that the [ɑ:], already long in
Southern English, has been still further lengthened. Apart from
the lengthened vowels, Verisopht's speech has a few conventional upper-class features of a kind frequently used in novels
as class-indicators, such as *Gad* and *How de do?* (ch. 19).

The vowel-sound in the place-name *Bath* is today longer in
the South than in the North and it seems likely that the same
distinction existed in the days of Dickens. Most of the characters
in *Pickwick Papers* are Southerners, and therefore Angelo
Cyrus Bantam's pronunciation, represented by the spelling
Ba-ath (ch. 35), must be assumed to be something more than
the normal Southern pronunciation. No doubt he gave the
vowel an unusually long pronunciation as an individual
eccentricity.

It is not easy to see why aristocratic birth should lead to
difficulty in pronouncing the sound [r], but it is one of the
most firmly established conventions of the English stage and
novel that it does. The substitution of [w] for [r] is emphasized
in the speech of Lord Mutanhed at the Bath Assembly Rooms.
It almost seems as though the author, to emphasize this

---

[1] 'Mrs Gamp and the King's English' in *Adjectives and Other Words*
(John Murray, 1930), pp. 138–161.

characteristic, has gone out of his way to give Lord Mutanhed
speeches with as many *r*'s in them as possible:

> 'Gwacious heavens!' said his lordship, 'I thought evewebody had
> seen the new mail cart; it's the neatest, pwettiest, gwacefullest
> thing that ever wan upon wheels. Painted wed, with a cweam
> piebald.' (*PP*, ch. 35)

But Dickens goes too far when he makes Lord Mutanhed speak
of the cart having an 'iwon wail, for the dwiver'. It is hard to
believe that the *r* of *iron* was pronounced as a consonant during
the lifetime of Dickens; the spelling *iwon* is probably an example
of merely mechanical substitution. Verisopht has a similar
difficulty in pronouncing [r]; his solution is to leave it out, as
in *pitty* 'pretty' (*NN*, ch. 19).

A special variety of affected upper-class speech is that of Mr
Mantalini, who has developed a highly stylized manner of
speaking, of which the chief characteristic seems to be the
raising of [æ] to [e], especially in the words *demd, demmit* and
demnition, with which he interlards his speech. The first *i* in
demnition no doubt represents the diphthong [ai], as does the *i* in
outrigeously (ch. 17), which is printed in italics to call attention
to its pronunciation. Most of his remarks are addressed to his
wife or to some other woman whom he is trying to captivate,
and consequently terms of endearment enter largely into his
vocabulary. He addresses his wife as 'my heart's joy', 'my
senses' idol' and, on one occasion, 'my essential juice of
pine-apple' (chs. 10, 34). He sometimes resorts to baby-talk
('its own popolorum tibby', ch. 34), and to hyperbole ('Not
for twenty thousand hemispheres populated with – with – with
little ballet-dancers', ch. 10). In imitation of baby-talk he
addresses his wife as 'it' ('It shall be brought round in any way
it likes best'), and this form of address is combined rather
awkwardly with the imperative in 'Do not put itself out of
humour' (ch. 17).

Mr Turveydrop, in *Bleak House*, deliberately uses old-
fashioned language because he thinks of it as characteristic of
the aristocrats of the Regency. He uses *ye* for the lightly-stressed
pronoun *you* ('I have promised never to leave ye . . . Now,
bless ye!' (ch. 50), and his pronunciation of *woman* is another
old-fashioned affectation: 'But Wooman, lovely Wooman,
what a sex you are!' (ch. 14).

The servants of the upper classes are liable, consciously or unconsciously, to imitate the speech of their employers. Mrs Rouncewell is no doubt doing this when she says that a tall French clock has been 'placed there a purpose' (*BH*, ch. 7). The footmen of Bath, with whom Sam Weller fraternizes, make use of a parody of upper-class speech. It is a mixture of vulgarisms and affectations, and it is contrasted with the down-to-earth substandard speech of Sam Weller, who takes a delight in making fun of its pretentiousness. The ignorance on which it rests is made clear from the start in the invitation sent by Smauker to Sam Weller saying that 'the swarry will be on table at half-past nine o'clock punctually' (*PP*, ch. 37). Sam Weller's comment is typical of his attitude towards the Bath footmen and their language:

> 'Vell,' said Sam, 'this is comin' it rayther powerful this is. I never heerd a biled leg o' mutton called a swarry afore. I wonder wot they'd call a roast one.'

Smauker's pretentiousness is an obvious object of satire. He describes himself as a 'gentleman' and his employer as the 'mutual acquaintaince' of himself and Sam Weller. He is so anxious not to use the plebeian title 'Mr' that he addresses the letter to 'blank Weller, Esq'. The strain of keeping up the fashionable style is too much for Smauker: the letter written in the third person is signed, and the envelope bears the instruction 'airy bell', with the substandard spelling of *area*.

The speech of the footmen includes phrases and pronunciations that they may be assumed to have picked up from their employers, such as 'Have you drank the waters?', 'Your fin' for 'Your hand', and possibly the pronunciations represented by the spellings *killibeate*, *kiver* sb., *reskel*, *blaygaird*, *theayter*, *promese*, *uncauminly*, *gal*, *petticut*, *irrevokeable*, and *creechure*. These forms occur side by side with such normal substandard forms as *hobvus* for *obvious* and *raly* for *really* (ch. 37).

The friendly young member of the Barnacle family in *Little Dorrit* is a convincing example of one type of upper-class speaker with a limited vocabulary, which is nevertheless adequate to indicate his shocked sense of outraged decencies. Mr A. O. J. Cockshut says that in portraying this character 'Dickens hits off perfectly that subtle note of informal formality

of the English upper class at work ("You mustn't come here,
saying you want to know, you know").[1] Elsewhere the same
kind of language is caricatured in the speech of 'the simpering
fellow with the weak legs' in *David Copperfield*:

> 'Oh, you know, deuce take it,' said this gentleman, looking
> round the board with an imbecile smile, 'we can't forego Blood,
> you know. We must have Blood, you know. Some young fellows,
> you know, may be a little behind their station, perhaps, in point of
> education and behaviour, and may go a little wrong, you know, and
> get themselves and other people into a variety of fixes – and all
> that – but deuce take it, it's delightful to reflect that they've got
> Blood in 'em.' (ch. 25)

The chief characteristics of this kind of speech are its repetitive-
ness and the speaker's fondness for meaningless expletives. The
same chapter provides an example of one special variety of the
speech of the hangers-on of the upper classes, who shroud their
speech with mystery in the hope of creating a good effect. Mr
Henry Spiker and Mr Gulpidge 'entered into a defensive alliance
against us, the common enemy, and exchanged a mysterious
dialogue across the table for our defeat and overthrow':

> 'That affair of the first bond for four thousand five hundred pounds
> has not taken the course that was expected, Spiker,' said Mr Gulpidge.
> 'Do you mean the D. of A.'s?' said Mr Spiker.
> 'The C. of B.'s!' said Mr Gulpidge.
> Mr Spiker raised his eyebrows and looked much concerned.
> 'When the question was referred to Lord – I needn't name him,'
> said Mr Gulpidge, checking himself –
> 'I understand,' said Mr Spiker, 'N.'

There is a close parallel to this talking for effect in *Nicholas
Nickleby*, when Pyke and Pluck have undertaken the easy
assignment of impressing Mrs Wititterly:

> 'Is there anybody,' demanded Mr Pluck, mysteriously, 'anybody
> you know, whom Mrs Wititterly's profile reminds you of?'
> 'Reminds me of!' answered Pyke. 'Of course there is.'
> 'Who do you mean?' said Pluck, in the same mysterious manner.
> 'The D. of B.?'
> 'The C. of B.,' replied Pyke, with the faintest trace of a grin
> lingering in his countenance. 'The beautiful sister is the countess;
> not the duchess.' (ch. 28)

---

[1] A. O. J. Cockshut, *The Imagination of Charles Dickens* (Collins,
1961), p. 60.

Forster quotes from Dickens's note-book a memorandum on
the same lines:

> The mysterious character, or characters, interchanging confidences.
> 'Necessary to be very careful in that direction' – 'In what direc-
> tion?' – 'B' – 'You don't say so. What, do you mean that C—?' –
> 'Is aware of D. Exactly.' (IX, 7)

One of the characteristics of upper-class speech is a tendency
to drop lightly-stressed syllables, giving a clipped effect. The
best example in Dickens is the debilitated cousin of Sir Leicester
Dedlock who supposes that Mr Tulkinghorn must be "nor-
mously rich fler', and that an election defeat is 'sort of thing
that's sure tapn slongs votes – giv'n – Mob' (*BH*, ch. 40). His
speech is sometimes so curtailed as to make a gloss necessary.
With the contrast of styles of speech in which Dickens took a
delight, Inspector Bucket addresses him:

> ' . . . I'll go so far as to say that not even *you* have any idea, sir,
> what games goes on!'
>   The cousin, who has been casting sofa-pillows on his head, in a
> prostration of boredom, yawns, 'Vayli' – being the used-up for
> 'very likely'. (*BH*, ch. 53)

The vocabulary of upper-class speech is not so rich as that of
lower-class speech, but there are occasional examples of words
belonging to an upper-class dialect, as when Sir John Chester
speaks to Haredale, providing a translation of the word *hipped*:

> 'You will be hipped, Haredale; you will be miserable, melancholy,
> utterly wretched.' (*BR*, ch. 27)

Eugene Wrayburn uses the same word in complaining that
Mortimer Lightwood is too serious (*OMF*, Bk III, ch. 10).
The speech of these two young men does not show many
marked upper-class features, but Eugene's use of the language
of the hunting field, on realizing that Bradley Headstone is
following him, may perhaps be regarded as a class-indicator:

> 'Bravo!' cried Eugene, rising too. 'Or, if Yoicks would be in better
> keeping, consider that I said Yoicks. Look to your feet, Mortimer,
> for we shall try your boots. When you are ready I am – need I say
> with a Hey Ho Chivy, and likewise with a Hark Forward, Hark
> Forward, Tantivy?' (*OMF*, Bk III, ch. 10)

Many people are agreed that there are differences between the
language of women and that of men beyond the obvious one of

pitch of the voice, but there is less agreement about what those differences are. They can best be recognized by their absence: when a woman talks like a woman, no one is conscious of special characteristics, but when she uses expressions that are more often used by men, the reader realizes that these are not expressions that a woman would normally use. Mrs Bagnet, for example, addresses Mr George as 'old fellow' (*BH*, ch. 34). The masculinity of Sally Brass is indicated rather by the way in which she is addressed or described than by the language that she herself uses. Dick Swiveller calls her 'a dull dog', 'the old buck', and 'old boy', while her brother calls her an 'aggravating vagabond' and a 'malignant fellow' (chs. 58, 59, 66).

The insertion of 'oh' in the middle of a sentence to heighten the emotional effect is perhaps a feminine characteristic. When Mrs MacStinger complains to Florence Dombey and Susan Nipper of the behaviour of Captain Cuttle, she says:

'and when I let the upper floor to Cap'en Cuttle, oh, I do a thankless thing, and cast pearls before swine.' (*DS*, ch. 23)

Another complaining woman, Mrs Snagsby, reflecting on her husband's wickedness, says:

'and O you may walk a long while in your secret ways . . . but you can't blind ME!' (*BH*, ch. 25)

A very different kind of woman, Esther Summerson, indulges in the same mannerism:

'I felt in the same way towards my school companions; I felt in the same way towards Mrs Rachael, who was a widow; and oh, towards her daughter, of whom she was proud, who came to see her once a fortnight!' (*BH*, ch. 3)

Again, nearly at the end of the novel, after describing the death of Richard Carstone, she says 'Not this world, O not this!' (*BH*, ch. 65).

Mrs General's insistence upon the importance of genteel language, especially for young ladies, is famous, as is her advice that 'Papa, potatoes, poultry, prunes and prism' impart a becoming shape to the speaker's lips. She practises what she preaches, and concludes one of her own exhortations to Little Dorrit by saying:

A truly refined mind will seem to be ignorant of the existence of anything that is not perfectly proper, placid, and pleasant. (*LD*, Bk II, ch. 5)

Difficult wives play a prominent part in the novels of Dickens. An outstanding example is the wife of Gabriel Varden in *Barnaby Rudge*, but Mrs Pott in *Pickwick Papers* has the same unendearing habit of exploiting her real or fancied ill-health to make her husband miserable. Dickens clearly had little sympathy with hysterical attacks and he regarded them as a proper subject for comic treatment. When Lavinia Wilfer works herself up into a state of violent emotion, the author's comment is:

> The young lady, who, hysterically speaking, was only just come of age, and had never come off yet, here fell into a highly creditable crisis, which, regarded as a first performance, was very successful. (*OMF*, Bk IV, ch. 5)

George Sampson emphasizes the comedy of the episode by bending over Lavinia's body in a state of distraction and addressing to Mrs Wilfer the memorable words: 'Demon – with the highest respect for you – behold your work!' The author's comment continues to be unsympathetic:

> Among the most remarkable effects of this crisis may be mentioned its having, when peace was restored, an inexplicable moral influence, of an elevating kind, on Miss Lavinia, Mrs Wilfer, and Mr George Sampson, from which R.W. was altogether excluded, as an outsider and non-sympathiser. Miss Lavinia assumed a modest air of having distinguished herself; Mrs Wilfer, a serene air of forgiveness and resignation; Mr Sampson, an air of having been improved and chastened. (*OMF*, Bk IV, ch. 5)

Dickens saw the tyranny of unreasonable women as an abiding problem, and mockingly expresses alarm at any evidence that it is hereditary. Lavinia Wilfer addresses George Sampson 'in a sepulchral, warning voice, founded on her mother's' (*OMF*, Bk III, ch. 16), and the effect of the enforced marriage of Jack Bunsby on his bride's daughter is graphically described:

> One of the most frightful circumstances of the ceremony to the Captain, was the deadly interest exhibited therein by Juliana MacStinger; and the fatal concentration of her faculties with which that promising child, already the image of her parent, observed the whole proceedings. (*DS*, ch. 60)

The difficult women in the novels of Dickens often achieve their results not so much by what they say as by the nasty way in which they don't say it; they like to give the impression that they could say very much more if they were not so forbearing. Rosa Dartle conveys her hints by asking questions. Mrs Wickam is very good at conveying an atmosphere of ominous gloom. Berry's remark that Paul Dombey is a pretty fellow when asleep is enough to start her off:

> 'Ah!' sighed Mrs Wickam, 'He need be.'
> 'Why, he's not ugly when he's awake,' observed Berry.
> 'No, Ma'am. Oh, no. No more was my uncle's Betsey Jane,' said Mrs Wickam. (ch. 8)

This is worthy of Mr F's Aunt. Just as Clennam's inoffensive behaviour seems to enrage Mr F's Aunt, Mrs Wickam is able to work herself up into an injured state by replying to remarks that no one has made:

> You may say nonsense! I an't offended, Miss. I hope you may be able to think in your own conscience that it is nonsense; you'll find your spirits all the better for it in this – you'll excuse my being so free – in this burying-ground of a place; which is wearing o me down. (ch. 8)

Mrs Wilfer manages to impose on her family by a tacit assumption that she is ill-used but too forbearing to go into details. The chief characteristic of her speech is its stateliness. When urged by Lavinia to loll, she replies 'I hope I am incapable of it' (*OMF*, Bk IV, ch. 16), and in her speech too she never relaxes. In giving orders to a coachman she uses high style that would be more appropriate in a poetical account of a battle: 'Onward!' (Bk IV, ch. 16). She is genteel, and when Mr Boffin asks her if she has a lodger, she replies 'A gentleman undoubtedly occupies our first floor' (Bk I, ch. 9). The only character in *Our Mutual Friend* who seems impressed by her is George Sampson: 'I also respect you, ma'am, to an extent which must ever be below your merits, I am well aware, but still up to an uncommon mark' (Bk IV, ch. 16). Dickens describes her manner in some detail:

> Indeed, the bearing of this impressive woman, throughout the day, was a pattern to all impressive women under similar circumstances. She renewed the acquaintance of Mr and Mrs Boffin, as if

Mr and Mrs Boffin had said of her what she had said of them, and as if Time alone could quite wear her injury out. She regarded every servant who approached her as her sworn enemy, expressly intending to offer her affronts with the dishes, and to pour forth outrages on her moral feelings from the decanters. She sat erect at table, on the right hand of her son-in-law, as half suspecting poison in the viands, and as bearing up with native force of character against other deadly ambushes. Her carriage towards Bella was as a carriage towards a young lady of good position whom she had met in society a few years ago. Even when, slightly thawing under the influence of sparkling champagne, she related to her son-in-law some passages of domestic interest concerning her papa, she infused into the narrative such Arctic suggestions of her having been an unappreciated blessing to mankind, since her papa's days, and also of that gentleman's having been a frosty impersonation of a frosty race, as struck cold to the very soles of the feet of the hearers. (Bk IV, ch. 16)

Dickens was a careful observer of the speech of children. Baby-talk, the highly stylized form of language used by some adults in talking to babies, is for him, rightly, an object of satire. When Mrs Chick is talking to Mr Dombey about his newly-born son, she slips into baby-language:

'I thought I should have fallen out of the staircase window as I came down from seeing dear Fanny, and that tiddy ickle sing.' These last words originated in a sudden vivid reminiscence of the baby. (*DS*, ch. 1)

Mrs Veneering makes use of baby-talk and we may assume, from the reference to Lady Tippins and the appreciation of 'the four Buffers' that Dickens did not regard it with any great favour:

And then Mrs Veneering – for Lady Tippins's winning wiles are contagious – folds her hands in the manner of a supplicating child, turns to her left neighbour, and says, 'Tease! Pay! Man from Tumwhere!' At which the four Buffers again mysteriously moved all four at once, exclaim, 'You can't resist.' (*OMF*, Bk I, ch. 2)

It is Mrs Veneering's affectation rather than the use of baby-language in itself that is the object of mockery here, for later in the novel when Betty Higden takes leave of Bella Wilfer, addressing her in Johnny's phrase as 'the boofer lady' (Bk II, ch. 14), the treatment is entirely sympathetic. At the end of the novel Bella's baby is given imaginary speeches which include some conventional baby-talk, like 'ladies and gemplemorums', but for the most part the whole point of the speeches assigned to the baby is that they are in adult language, and assigning them to the baby is the author's joke:

> 'I won't,' said the inexhaustible baby, ' – allow – you – to make – game – of – my – venerable – Ma.' At each division administering a soft facer with one of the speckled fists. (*OMF*, Bk IV, ch. 12)

Dickens's representation of the speech of older children often carries conviction. There is something very convincing in the candour and seriousness with which Paul Dombey replies to Mrs Pipchin:

> 'Well, Sir,' said Mrs Pipchin to Paul, 'how do you think you shall like me?'
> 'I don't think I shall like you at all,' replied Paul. 'I want to go away. This isn't my house.' (*DS*, ch. 8)

Charlie Hexam's speech is a good reflexion of his complicated and unattractive character. When he is first introduced, Dickens comments on the 'curious mixture in the boy of uncompleted savagery and uncompleted civilisation'. This mixture is reflected in his speech, with its mixture of the colloquial, the stilted and the substandard all within the space of a few lines. His first speech of more than half a dozen words is:

> 'It's a goodish stretch, sir. I come up in a cab, and the cab's waiting to be paid. We could go back in it before you paid it, if you liked. I went first to your office, according to the direction of the papers found in the pockets, and there I see nobody but a chap of about my age who sent me on here.' (*OMF*, Bk I, ch. 3)

His next speech, in which he refers to Lazarus and to Pharaoh's army drowned in the Red Sea, may seem out of place, but it is really very true to life in showing the ambitious schoolboy's display of erudition, and the source of both allusions in the Bible is a reminder of the part played by the churches and Sunday schools in popular education in the nineteenth century. Another very natural touch is his contempt for his sister's more modest attainments, expressed in language which shows that he himself still has some way to go:

> 'She ain't half bad,' said the boy, 'but if she knows her letters it's the most she does – and them I learned her.' (Bk I, ch. 3)

When children in the novels of Dickens protest against ill-usage or misunderstanding, they are liable to do it in a number of short sentences or ejaculations. Esther Summerson rebukes Egbert Pardiggle, who accuses his mother of having 'boned' his pocket money. He replies:

'O then! Now! Who are you! *You* wouldn't like it, I think? What does she make a sham for, and pretend to give me money, and take it away again?' (*BH*, ch. 8)

The mistakes made by foreigners in the use of English have frequently been used with comic effect by novelists and play-wrights. Dickens was more aware than most novelists that the absurdities are not all on one side, but in *Pickwick Papers* he follows the conventional line in making fun of Count Smorltork's attempts to speak English (ch. 15). The Count experiences the difficulties that English pronunciation commonly presents to foreigners: *th* and *w* represent unfamiliar sounds and consequently *things* becomes *tings* and *Pickwick* becomes *Pig Vig*; confusion between voiced and voiceless consonants adds to his difficulty in pronouncing, *Pickwick* thus producing *Big Vig* beside *Pig Vig*; lightly-stressed syllables are not always heard, with the result that *very* becomes *ver* and *politics* becomes *poltics*; one unfamiliar word is easily confused with another, and *comprises* becomes *surprises* and *expiring frog* becomes *perspiring fog*. The degrees of formality appropriate to social occasions are very difficult for foreigners to master, and when the Count thinks that he has mastered the name of Mr Pickwick, to whom he has just been introduced ('Peek – christian name; Weeks – surname; good, ver good'), we have the sudden burst of informality: 'How you do, Weeks?'

It is not only to provide amusement that the mistakes of foreigners are recorded; they also serve as an aid to characterization. We are constantly reminded that Hortense, in *Bleak House*, is a foreigner, and her foreign birth is suggested as an adequate reason for her violent emotions and her readiness to resort to murder in pursuit of revenge. She consequently rolls her *r*'s in saying that she is en-r-r-r-raged, has difficulty with the *th* in *alltogezzer*, uses Gallicisms like *attrapped*, which she glosses as *catched*, and describes Lady Dedlock as 'a Ladyship so infame' and Sir Leicester as 'a poor abused' (chs. 42, 54).

C

Already as early as *Nicholas Nickleby* Dickens began to make fun of the insularity shown by Englishmen when confronted by a foreign language. Mr Lillyvick's reason for thinking French a dismal language because he had heard it used by prisoners-of-war is in the tradition of farce, as is his reason for continuing to think meanly of that language:

> 'What's the water in French, sir?'
> 'L'eau,' replied Nicholas.
> 'Ah!' said Mr Lillyvick, shaking his head mournfully, 'I thought as much. Lo, eh? I don't think anything of that language – nothing at all.' (ch. 16)

Especially in the later novels there are many more or less good-humoured attacks on the British attitude to foreigners. In *Little Dorrit* Cavalletto's difficulties in speaking English are mentioned, but the real object of satire is the attitude of Englishmen to foreigners and their attempts to speak English. Some of these attacks on xenophobia have a very modern application, as, for example, the account of the attitude of the inhabitants of Bleeding Heart Yard to Cavalletto:

> It was up-hill work for a foreigner, lame or sound, to make his way with the Bleeding Hearts. In the first place, they were vaguely persuaded that every foreigner had a knife about him; in the second, they held it to be a sound constitutional national axiom that he ought to go home to his own country. They never thought of inquiring how many of their own countrymen would be returned upon their hands from divers parts of the world, if the principle were generally recognised; they considered it practically and peculiarly British. (Bk I, ch. 25)

The characters in *Little Dorrit* whose attitude to foreign languages is satirized, Mr Meagles, Pancks and Mrs Plornish, are not on the whole unattractive characters, and it may be assumed that Dickens thought that their attitudes were a proper subject for good-humoured ridicule but not for strong condemnation.

Cavalletto makes the sort of mistakes that any foreigner might make in speaking English. Strong verbs present difficulties and it is therefore natural that Cavalletto should say *writed*, and, since the name *Pancks* contains a consonant-group strange to Italian ears, it is equally natural that he should call him Signor Panco (Bk II, ch. 28). Ignoring the irregularities of the

English comparison of adjectives, he speaks of 'a baddest man', and he occasionally uses words like *ricontrato* 'met' when he cannot think of their English equivalents (Bk II, ch. 13). He says *consequentementally*, *secrettementally* and *patientissamentally*, and the author adds the comment:

> it would have given Mrs Plornish great concern if she could have been persuaded that his occasional lengthening of an adverb in this way, was the chief fault of his English. (Bk II, ch. 28)

Dickens's attitude towards the inhabitants of Bleeding Heart Yard and their dealings with Cavalletto is one of affectionate mockery:

> They began to think that although he could never hope to be an Englishman, still it would be hard to visit that affliction on his head . . . They spoke to him in very loud voices as if he were stone deaf. They constructed sentences, by way of teaching him the language in its purity, such as were addressed to the savages by Captain Cook, or by Friday to Robinson Crusoe. Mrs Plornish was particularly ingenious in this art; and attained so much celebrity by saying 'Me ope you leg well soon', that it was considered in the Yard but a very short remove indeed from speaking Italian. (Bk I, ch. 25)

Many of Cavalletto's problems in speaking English arise from Mrs Plornish's well-intentioned attempts to make things easier for him. Her translations of straightforward English into a form that Cavalletto can be expected to understand bear a strong resemblance to Pidgin English: 'E please. E glad get money', 'E hope you leg well soon' (Bk I, ch. 25), 'Ow you know him bad?' (Bk II, ch. 13). Just as Englishmen who use Pidgin English sometimes imagine that they are using a foreign language, Dickens makes fun of Mrs Plornish's debased English by calling it Italian:

> 'Why,' inquired Mrs Plornish, reverting to the Italian language, 'why ope bad man no see.' (Bk II, ch. 13)

Later, Mrs Plornish describes a conversation she has had with Cavalletto, and she quotes herself as saying 'Mooshattonisha padrona'. The author keeps up the joke by adding the comment:

> Though not conceited, Mrs Plornish felt that she had turned this Tuscan sentence with peculiar elegance. Mr Plornish could not conceal his exultation in her accomplishments as a linguist. (Bk II, ch. 27)

Similarly, in *Bleak House*, Inspector Bucket admonishes Hortense: 'In short, the less you Parlay, the better, you know,' and he 'is very complacent over this French explanation' (ch. 54).

Dickens's travels in Italy had impressed him with the wide range of meanings of the Italian word *altro*. Cavalletto uses it in the first chapter of *Little Dorrit*, and the author adds the comment:

> The word being, according to its Genoese emphasis, a confirmation, a contradiction, an assertion, a denial, a taunt, a compliment, a joke, and fifty other things, became in the present instance, with a significance beyond all power of written expression, our familiar English 'I believe you'. (Bk I, ch. 1)

Mrs Plornish expresses the same idea with less detail in her reply to Pancks's query about the meaning of the word: 'It's a sort of general kind of expression, sir' (Bk I, ch. 25).

The same attitude towards foreigners and their attempts to speak English is shown in *Our Mutual Friend*. Mr Podsnap is a less sympathetic character than Mrs Plornish, but his attitude to his guest, the 'foreign gentleman', is very similar to hers:

> There was a droll disposition, not only on the part of Mr Podsnap, but of everybody else, to treat him as if he were a child who was hard of hearing.
>
> As a delicate concession to this unfortunately-born foreigner, Mr Podsnap, in receiving him, had presented his wife as Madame Podsnap; also his daughter as Mademoiselle Podsnap, with some inclination to add ma fille, in which bold venture, however, he checked himself. (Bk I, ch. 11)

In the conversation between Mr Podsnap and the foreign gentleman the latter's defective pronunciation of English is indicated, but this is balanced by the 'youngish sallowish gentleman in spectacles, with a lumpy forehead' who 'caused a profound sensation by saying, in a raised voice, "Esker", and then stopping dead', and the real object of satire is Mr Podsnap's patronizing correction of the foreigner's mistakes:

> ' . . . No Other Country is so Favoured as This Country.'
>
> 'And ozer countries?—' the foreign gentleman was beginning, when Mr Podsnap put him right again.
>
> 'We do not say Ozer; we say Other: the letters are "T" and "H"; you say Tay and Aish, You Know'; (still with clemency). 'The sound is "th" – "th!".'

'And other countries,' said the foreign gentleman. 'They do how?'
'They do, Sir,' returned Mr Podsnap, gravely shaking his head;
'they do – I am sorry to be obliged to say it – as they do.'

The helpfulness of Mrs Plornish and the schoolmasterish
disapproval of Mr Podsnap represent two attitudes towards
foreigners, but a more extreme example of British xenophobia
is the opinion of Towlinson, Mr Dombey's servant, who 'never
knew of any good that ever come of foreigners', and, when
taxed with prejudice, says, 'Look at Bonaparte who was the
head of 'em, and see what he was always up to!' (*DS*, ch. 31).
A more good-humoured attitude is the indifference of Tony
Weller. When he is urging on Sam the importance of an alibi
for Mr Pickwick, he says that without one Mr Pickwick will be
'what the Italians call reg'larly flummoxed' (*PP*, ch. 33).
There is no reason to suppose the word *flummoxed* to be of
Italian origin, but we are to assume that Tony Weller regarded
the attempt to distinguish between one foreign language and
another as splitting hairs.

Forster records that Dickens never spoke French very well,
but that, as the result of constant practice, he learnt to write it
with remarkable ease and fluency (Forster, V, 7). Dickens's
comment on one of the characters in *Somebody's Luggage* (*CS*)
could clearly be applied to himself:

> Mr. The Englishman was not particularly strong in the French
> language as a means of oral communication, though he read it very
> well. It is with languages as with people, – when you only know them
> by sight you are apt to mistake them; you must be on speaking terms
> before you can be said to have established an acquaintance. (ch. 2)

Dickens was amused by the English spoken by the French
courier Louis Roche: 'Datter chip is greatest tief – and you
know it you rascal – as never did en-razh me so, that I cannot
bear myself!' (Forster, IV, 6). There is more than a touch of
Dickens himself in Mr Meagles in *Little Dorrit*, but Dickens
would not go so far as Mr Meagles in regarding the use of
French by Frenchmen as a legitimate subject of complaint:
'Allong and marshong, indeed!' (Bk I, ch. 2). Mr Meagles
followed the example of Dr Johnson in firmly refusing to speak
French when in France.[1] His daughter has to act as interpreter,

---

[1] Cf. Boswell, *Life of Johnson* (ed. Birkbeck Hill), ii, 404.

and Dickens adds the comment that Mr Meagles 'never by any accident acquired any knowledge whatever of the language of any country into which he travelled' (*LD*, Bk I, ch. 2). He preserves this attitude to foreign languages to the end. At the end of the novel he sets out in search of the box which had fallen into Rigaud's hands:

> With no other attendant than Mother, Mr Meagles went upon his pilgrimage, and encountered a number of adventures. Not the least of his difficulties was, that he never knew what was said to him, and that he pursued his inquiries among people who never knew what he said to them. Still, with an unshaken confidence that the English tongue was somehow the mother tongue of the whole world, only the people were too stupid to know it, Mr Meagles harangued innkeepers in the most voluble manner, entered into loud explanations of the most complicated sort, and utterly renounced replies in the native language of the respondents, on the ground that they were 'all bosh'. Sometimes interpreters were called in; whom Mr Meagles addressed in such idiomatic terms of speech, as instantly to extinguish and shut up – which made the matter worse. (Bk II, ch. 33)

On the other hand, proficiency in foreign languages is sometimes regarded as having prestige value. Mrs Kenwigs is tremendously proud when Nicholas Nickleby gives French lessons to her children. When the turnkey of the Marshalsea is singing the praises of Mr Dorrit, he says:

> As to languages – speaks anything. We've had a Frenchman here in his time, and it's my opinion he know'd more French than the Frenchman did. We've had an Italian here in his time, and he shut *him* up in about half a minute. (*LD*, Bk I, ch. 6)

In *Bleak House* 'the fashionable intelligence' is described as using common French words and phrases like *élite* and *beau monde* and there follows the comment: 'the fashionable intelligence is weak in English, but a giant refreshed in French' (ch. 12). In the same novel Jobling's anxiety to use French phrases is greater than his proficiency:

> 'Ill fo manger, you know,' says Mr Jobling, pronouncing that word as if he meant a necessary fixture in an English stable. 'Ill fo manger. That's the French saying, and mangering is as necessary to me as it is to a Frenchman. Or more so.' (ch. 20)

When foreigners are speaking, even when the scene of a novel or story is set in a foreign country, Dickens makes free use of Gallicisms to remind us of the fact. Mr Meagles, following on the track of Rigaud, is denounced as 'a Knight of Industry' (*LD*, Bk II, ch. 33), a phrase clearly used in the sense of the French *chevalier d'industrie*. When Rigaud calls at the French inn, the Break of Day, both he and the landlady talk in language which reads like a bad, because over-literal, translation from the French:

'One can lodge here to-night, madame?' 'Perfectly.'

A Swiss visitor addresses the landlady:

'Doubtless you were enraged against that man, madame?'
'Ay, yes, then!' cried the landlady . . . 'Naturally, yes.'
'He was a bad subject.' (*LD*, Bk I, ch. 11)

Rigaud's speech abounds in Gallicisms: 'Holy blue', 'Death of my soul!', 'the ravishing little family history I go to commence', 'right to a marvel' (Bk I, ch. 30; Bk II, ch. 30). The second chapter of *Somebody's Luggage (CS)* is a story of an Englishman called Langley staying in a French town. His name has been misunderstood as *L'Anglais* and therefore throughout the chapter he is described as 'Mr The Englishman'. Similarly, both in direct and reported speech, the speeches of French-speaking characters are full of literal translations of French idioms. An example of direct speech is Madame Bouclet's: 'And her friend the corporal? Yes, yes, yes, yes! So genteel of him' (ch. 2). Another example is in the same chapter, where a French corporal, speaking to a child, says: 'Monsieur demands, what is this Bebelle?' An example of the use of Gallicisms in reported speech is:

But Madame Bouclet looking in apologetically one morning to remark that, O Heaven! she was in a state of desolation because the lamp-maker had not sent home that lamp confided to him to repair, but that truly he was a lamp-maker against whom the whole world shrieked out, Mr. The Englishman seized the occasion. (ch. 2)

Englishmen confronted with a foreign language are often ready to detect resemblances between the foreign words and certain English words. Soldiers during the First World War transformed *ça ne fait rien* into *san fairy Anne;* in much the same way, Miss Mowcher transforms *bon soir:*

'Bob swore!' – as the Englishman said for 'Good night', when he first learnt French, and thought it so like English. (*DC*, ch. 22)

The speech-habits of Jews are a frequent object of satire by English novelists. When Arthur Clennam is arrested for debt, he is taken to the Marshalsea by 'an elderly member of the Jewish persuasion, preserved in rum', who only speaks five words ('a tyfling madder ob bithznithz') but in them he manages to illustrate four or five mispronunciations which Dickens apparently regarded as typically Jewish: the loss of *r* after a consonant, the voicing of *t* between vowels, the assimilation of the final consonant of *of* to the initial *b* of the next word, and the lisping of *s* and *z* (*LD*, Bk II, ch. 26). Elsewhere difficulty in pronouncing nasal consonants is clearly regarded as the chief characteristic of Jewish speech. In *Oliver Twist* Barney, a Jewish youth, makes remarks like 'I'b dot certaid you cad', 'Ad rub uds too', and 'Frob the cuttry, but subthig in your way, or I'b bistaked' (ch. 42). A would-be client of Mr Jaggers in *Great Expectations*, who describes himself as 'hown brother to Habraham Latharuth', has quite different speech-habits, chief of which are a lisp and a fondness for inorganic initial *h*:

> 'Mithter Jaggerth! Half a moment! My hown cuthen'th gone to Mithter Wemmick at thirth prethenth minute to hoffer him any termth, Mithter Jaggerth! Half a quarter of a moment! If you'd have the condethenthun to be bought off from the t'other thide – at any thuperior prithe! – money no object! – Mithter Jaggerth – Mithter—!' (ch. 20)

Riah, in *Our Mutual Friend*, has a distinctive speech indicated not by his pronunciations but by his syntax and choice of words, as may be seen in his exhortation to Lizzie Hexam:

> 'He is a thankless dog,' said the Jew, angrily. 'Let him go. Shake the dust from thy feet and let him go. Come daughter! Come home with me – it is but across the road – and take a little time to recover your peace and to make your eyes seemly, and then I will bear you company through the streets. For it is past your usual time, and will soon be late, and the way is long, and there is much company out of doors to-night.' (Bk II, ch. 15)

The succession of short sentences joined by 'and' no doubt shows biblical influence, as does the phrase 'Shake the dust from thy feet'. There are many archaisms, such as the second person singular pronoun *thy*, *but* in the sense 'only', and phrases like *much company*, *bear you company* and *the way is long*. Elsewhere Riah uses archaisms like *damsel*, *therefrom*, *thereof*, *incline towards*, *counselled*, *fair* 'beautiful', *verily*, *indited*, and phrases like *mine own eyes*, and *bending my neck to the yoke* (Bk III, ch. 1; Bk IV, ch. 9).

Occupational dialects, especially those of the learned professions, are well represented in the novels of Dickens. Inevitably legal language is common in *Bleak House*. Even John Jarndyce, who hates lawyers, finds himself using legal language in his conversation with Guppy:

> 'Thank you, Mr Guppy,' returned my guardian. 'I am quite willing – I believe I use a legal phrase – to admit the certificate.' (ch. 64)

The pronunciation of lawyers, with a tendency to omit lightly-stressed syllables or whole groups of words, is illustrated in the first chapter of the novel by Mr Tangle. He is asked by the Lord Chancellor if he has nearly finished:

> 'Mlud, no – variety of points – feel it my duty t submit – ludship' is the reply that slides out of Mr Tangle.

Later the long vacation provides an opportunity for Dickens to describe various kinds of forensic eloquence:

> The very learned gentleman who has cooled the natural heat of his gingery complexion in pools and fountains of law, until he has become great in knotty arguments for term-time, when he poses the drowsy Bench with legal 'chaff', inexplicable to the uninitiated and to most of the initiated too, is roaming, with a characteristic delight in aridity and dust, about Constantinople. (ch. 19)

The unnecessary use of abbreviations in legal documents is satirised in the letter which Kenge and Carboy send to Esther Summerson. The letter satirizes the inhumanity of the lawyers who refer to Esther as though she were an inanimate object.

Old Square, Lincoln's Inn.

Madam,

> Our $\overline{\text{clt}}$ Mr Jarndyce being $\overline{\text{abt}}$ to $\overline{\text{rece}}$ into his house, under an Order of the $\overline{\text{Ct}}$ of $\overline{\text{Chy}}$, a $\overline{\text{Ward}}$ of the $\overline{\text{Ct}}$ in this cause, for whom he wishes to se*r*ure an $\overline{\text{elgble}}$ compn, directs us to inform you that he will be glad of your $\overline{\text{serces}}$ in the $\overline{\text{afsd}}$ capacity.

We have a̅r̅r̅n̅g̅d̅ for your being f̅o̅r̅d̅e̅d̅, carriage free, p^r eight
o'clock coach from Reading, on Monday morning next, to White
Horse Cellar, Piccadilly, London, where one of our c̅l̅k̅s̅ will be in
waiting to convey you to our o̅ff̅e̅ as above.

We are, Madam, Your obed^t Serv^{ts},

Kenge and Carboy.

Miss Esther Summerson.

(ch. 3)

The speech-habits of Dickensian lawyers illustrate the
principle of variety in uniformity. There are strong resemblances between the language of Conversation Kenge and that
of Vholes, but there are also differences. One characteristic that
they share is prolixity. Kenge uses long and involved sentences
which he is not always able to finish. Three times in chapter 3
his speeches include the words ' – the – a – ', which contribute
nothing to the meaning of the sentences in which they occur and
which may be assumed to represent the noises made by a
practised bore to prevent anyone else from interrupting while
he thinks what to say next. He has the orator's trick of piling
up a series of phrases each introduced by the same word or
phrase: 'every difficulty, every contingency, every masterly
fiction, every form of procedure known in that court' (ch. 3).
He affects to be fastidious about his choice of words and
introduces needless phrases like 'shall I say?' and 'I would say',
as if to apologize for the words that he chooses. Both of these
characteristics are illustrated in the following passage:

'Mr Jarndyce . . . being aware of the – I would say, desolate –
position of our young friend, offers to place her at a first-rate
establishment; where her education shall be completed, where her
comfort shall be secured, where her reasonable wants shall be
anticipated, where she shall be eminently qualified to discharge her
duty in that station unto which it has pleased – shall I say
Providence? – to call her.' (ch. 3)

Kenge's prolixity is reserved for those on whom he wishes to
make a good impression professionally; in dismissing Miss
Flite (ch. 3) he can be quite concise.

Vholes is introduced by a long preamble emphasizing his
respectability and the high opinion that Kenge and others have
of him. He achieves prolixity largely by repetition: 'That is
scarcely fair, sir, scarcely fair' and 'The question may branch

off into what is doing, what is doing?' (ch. 39); he shares this characteristic with Mr Casby in *Little Dorrit*.

In spite of the highly respectable build-up that he has been given, it is clear that Vholes is particularly detested by the author, who describes him as having a 'buttoned-up, half-audible voice, as if there were an unclean spirit in him that will neither come out nor speak out' (ch. 39). Vholes is guilty of vulgarisms, such as his habit of addressing Richard Carstone as Mr C., of which Kenge would never be guilty. From the speech of the lawyers in Dickens we may perhaps draw the conclusion that he was not greatly impressed by legal technicalities. It is Guppy, one of the most lowly, who makes most use of legal phrases; the more exalted Mr Tulkinghorn makes very little use of them. Guppy describes his proposal to Esther Summerson as 'filing a declaration' and hopes that it will be regarded as 'without prejudice' (ch. 9). His explanation of this phrase suggests that he has no great familiarity with the real meaning of the technical legal terms that he uses:

'What follows is without prejudice, miss?' said Mr Guppy, anxiously bringing a chair towards my table.
'I don't understand what you mean,' said I, wondering.
'It's one of our law terms, miss. You won't make any use of it to my detriment, at Kenge and Carboy's, or elsewhere. If our conversation shouldn't lead to anything, I am to be as I was, and am not to be prejudiced in my situation or worldly prospects. In short, it's in total confidence.' (ch. 9)

Dickens is fond of showing his lawyers carrying their habits of cross-examination into private life. In *Great Expectations* Jaggers is introduced as a stranger who causes the discomfiture of Mr Wopsle by cross-examining him in the Three Jolly Bargemen, but his adoption of similar methods with Joe Gargery is less successful (ch. 18). Guppy's cross-examination of Jo is described in general terms (*BH*, ch. 19), but his conversation with Mrs Chadband is worthy of Sergeant Buzfuz:

'Was you a party in anything, ma'am?' says Mr Guppy, trans-ferring his cross-examination.
'No.'
'*Not* a party in anything, ma'am?' says Mr Guppy.
Mrs Chadband shakes her head.
'Perhaps you were acquainted with somebody who was a party

in something, ma'am?' says Mr Guppy, who likes nothing better than to model his conversation on forensic principles.

'Not exactly that, either,' replies Mrs Chadband, humouring the joke with a hard-favoured smile.

'Not exactly that, either!' repeats Mr Guppy. 'Very good. Pray, ma'am, was it a lady of your acquaintance who had some trans-actions (we will not at present say what transactions) with Kenge and Carboy's office, or was it a gentleman of your acquaintance? Take time, ma'am. We shall come to it presently. Man or woman, ma'am?'

'Neither,' says Mrs Chadband, as before.

'Oh! A child!' says Mr Guppy, throwing on the admiring Mrs Snagsby the regular acute professional eye which is thrown on British jurymen. 'Now, ma'am, perhaps you'll have the kindness to tell us *what* child.' (ch. 19)

Sampson Brass provides a good parody of a prolix and unscrupulous lawyer putting a leading question to a witness who refuses to take a hint:

'Oh, this is the memorandum, is it?' said Brass, running his eye over the document. 'Very good. Now, Mr Richard, did the gentle-man say anything else?'

'No.'

'Are you sure, Mr Richard,' said Brass solemnly, 'that the gentleman said nothing else?'

'Devil a word, sir,' replied Dick.

'Think again, sir,' said Brass; 'it's my duty, sir, in the position in which I stand, and as an honourable member of the legal profession – the first profession in this country, sir, or in any other country, or in any of the planets that shine above us at night and are supposed to be inhabited – it's my duty, sir, as an honourable member of that profession, not to put to you a leading question in a matter of this delicacy and importance. Did the gentleman, sir, who took the first floor of you yesterday afternoon, and who brought with him a box of property – a box of property – say anything more than is set down in this memorandum?'

'Come, don't be a fool,' said Miss Sally.

Dick looked at her, and then at Brass, and then at Miss Sally again, and still said 'No'.

'Pooh, pooh! Deuce take it, Mr Richard, how dull you are!' cried Brass, relaxing into a smile. 'Did he say anything about his property? – there!'

'That's the way to put it,' said Miss Sally, nodding to her brother.

'Did he say, for instance,' added Brass, in a kind of comfortable, cosy tone – 'I don't assert that he did say so, mind; I only ask you, to refresh your memory – did he say, for instance, that he was a stranger in London – that it was not his humour or within his ability to give any references – that he felt we had a right to require them – and that, in case anything should happen to him, at any time, he particularly desired that whatever property he had upon the premises should be considered mine, as some slight recompense for the trouble and annoyance I should sustain – and were you, in short,' added Brass, still more comfortably and cosily than before, 'were you induced to accept him on my behalf, as a tenant, upon those conditions?'

'Certainly not,' replied Dick.

'Why then, Mr Richard,' said Brass, darting at him a supercilious and reproachful look, 'it's my opinion that you've mistaken your calling, and will never make a lawyer.' (*OCS*, ch. 35)

Another novel where legal language is freely used is *Pickwick Papers*. Some of the technical terms are used quite naturally in the course of the novel, as when Mrs Bardell's imprisonment results from her having given Dodson and Fogg a *cognovit* for the costs of the trial. Naturally, the trial scene provides many examples, all of which help in the creation of atmosphere. When it was discovered that only ten special jurymen were present, Sergeant Buzfuz 'prayed a *tales*', whereupon two of the common jurymen were pressed into the special jury (ch. 34). Sergeant Buzfuz's address to the jury is a good parody of the tricks of an unscrupulous barrister. Legal terms are freely used by Perker, Dodson and Fogg and their clerks: Mr Jackson says that Bardell and Pickwick will come on 'in the settens after Term' (ch. 31) and Dodson speaks of 'the *præcipe* book' (ch. 20). Abbreviation can make technical language more difficult. Perker speaks of 'the amount of the taxed costs and damages for which the ca-sa was issued' (ch. 40). A passage in Blackstone's *Commentaries* throws light on this passage:

What was formerly considered the most effectual writ of execution was that under which the *body* of the defendant was taken, viz, the *capias ad satisfaciendum*, so called to distinguish it from the *capias ad respondendum*, which lay to compel the defendant to give bail and enter an appearance at the beginning of a suit.[1]

[1] *The Commentaries on the Laws of England of Sir William Blackstone Knt*, . . . adapted to the present state of the Law by Robert Malcolm Kerr (fourth edition, John Murray, 1876), vol. III, p. 425. I am indebted to my colleague Professor P. M. Bromley for the explanation of this allusion.

Perker tries to impress his clients by using tags of legal Latin, such as *amicus curiae* and *ad captandum* (ch. 10), and, for the same reason, he is fond of quoting legal precedents, such as 'the well-known case in Barnwell and —' (ch. 10).

In *Little Dorrit* the unnamed barrister who is a guest of Mr Merdle carries into private life the mannerisms which he has found effective when addressing a jury:

> Bar was a man of great variety; but one leading thread ran through the woof of all his patterns. Every man with whom he had to do was a juryman; and he must get that juryman over, if he could. (Bk II, ch. 12)

There are many allusions to Bar's 'little jury droop'. He uses it, together with some technical legal language, in addressing the sprightly young Barnacle, Ferdinand:

> Bar, strengthened as usual with his double eye-glass and his little jury droop, was overjoyed to see the engaging young Barnacle; and opined that we were going to sit *in Banco*, as we lawyers called it, to take a special argument? (Bk II, ch. 12)

He later finds it necessary to add a gloss: 'meaning this to be a high and solemn occasion when, as Captain Macheath says, "the Judges are met; a terrible show!"' He goes on to speak of the sprightly young Barnacle as 'my learned friend'.

Legal language sometimes makes a strong impression on those who hear it chiefly from the dock and who ascribe to it an almost magical power. Rogue Riderhood, before giving information against Hexam, thinks that if he gives evidence on oath, his reward is secure:

> 'I am a man as gets my living, and as seeks to get my living, by the sweat of my brow. Not to risk being done out of the sweat of my brow, by any chances, I should wish afore going further to be swore in.' (*OMF*, Bk I, ch. 12)

He is fond of repeating the same phrase again and again within a single speech, and this repetition sometimes has the effect of an incantation:

> 'Tell us on what grounds you make this accusation,' said Mortimer Lightwood.
> 'On the grounds,' answered Riderhood, wiping his face with his sleeve, 'that I was Gaffer's pardner, and suspected of him many a long day and many a dark night. On the grounds that I knowed his

ways. On the grounds that I broke the pardnership because I see
the danger; which I warn you his daughter may tell another story
about that, for anythink I can say, but you know what it'll be
worth, for she'd tell you lies, the world round and the heavens
broad, to save her father. On the grounds that it's well understood
along the cause'ays and the stairs that he done it. On the grounds
that he's fell off from, because he done it. On the grounds that I
will swear he done it. On the grounds that you may take me where
you will, and get me sworn to it. I don't want to back out of the
consequences. I have made up my mind. Take me anywheres.'
    'All this is nothing,' said Lightwood. (Bk I, ch. 12)

Riderhood has all the veneration which the unbookish sometimes feel for the written word. He is most anxious to be 'took
down' and refuses even to give his name until Wrayburn is
prepared to write it down. The sort of incident that has given
Riderhood his confidence in the wonder-working properties of
'taking down' is illustrated in *Great Expectations*, where
Jaggers, the bullying lawyer, is examining a witness:

> my guardian had a woman under examination or cross-examination
> – I don't know which – and was striking her, and the bench, and
> everybody with awe. If anybody of whatsoever degree, said a word
> that he didn't approve of, he instantly required to have it 'taken
> down'. (ch. 24)

Riderhood's respect for the written word is probably the result
of frequent encounters with the law, and his use of the words
'him as I have made mention on' is described by the author as
'the dull Old Bailey evasion' (*OMF*, Bk II, ch. 12). When all
his requirements have been satisfied, he is willing to make a
declaration that achieves legal precision so far as names are
concerned, although it has all his habitual repetitive verbosity:

> 'I, Roger Riderhood, Lime'us Hole, Waterside character, tell
> you, Lawyer Lightwood, that the man Jesse Hexam, commonly
> called upon the river and along-shore Gaffer, told me that he done
> the deed. What's more, he told me with his own lips that he done the
> deed. What's more, he said that he done the deed. And I'll swear
> it!' (*OMF*, Bk I, ch. 12)

Magwitch has a similar confidence in the magical properties
of 'a greasy little clasped black Testament', and the suggestion
about its origin adds a pleasing touch of irony:

> To state that my terrible patron carried this little black book about
> the world solely to swear people on in cases of emergency, would

be to state what I never quite established – but this I can say, that I never saw him put it to any other use. The book itself had the appearance of having been stolen from some court of justice, and perhaps his knowledge of its antecedents, combined with his own experience in that wise, gave him a reliance on its powers as a sort of legal spell or charm. (*GE*, ch. 40)

Magwitch's respect for legal language does not enable him to remember the exact form of words to be used when he administers the oath to Herbert Pocket: 'Take it in your right hand. Lord strike you dead on the spot, if ever you split in any way sumever. Kiss it!' (ch. 40)

Captain Cuttle is proud of his legal-sounding language. He refuses to take back the sugar-tongs and tea-spoons he has given to Florence and Walter:

> 'I've made that there little property over, jintly.' These words he repeated with great unction and gravity, evidently believing that they had the virtue of an Act of Parliament, and that unless he committed himself by some new admission of ownership, no flaw could be found in such a form of conveyance. (*DS*, ch. 50)

The attraction of legal language is perhaps strongest for those who do not understand it. Mrs Chick, when complaining of Mr Dombey's refusal to leave his house, imagines what would happen if it were to be let:

> He couldn't remain here then. If he attempted to do so, there would be an ejectment, an action for Doe, and all sorts of things. (*DS*, ch. 59)

The habits of caution encouraged by daily contact with the law affect Wemmick's language even at home when Walworth sentiments would have been in order. His manner of identifying Magwitch shows elaborate circumlocution:

> 'I accidentally heard, yesterday morning,' said Wemmick, 'being in a certain place where I once took you – even between you and me, it's as well not to mention names when avoidable—'
> 'Much better not,' said I. 'I understand you.'
> 'I heard there by chance, yesterday morning,' said Wemmick, 'that a certain person not altogether of uncolonial pursuits, and not unpossessed of portable property – I don't know who it may really be – we won't name this person—'
> 'Not necessary,' said I.
> '—had made some little stir in a certain part of the world where

a good many people go, not always in gratification of their own inclinations, and not quite irrespective of the government expense—' (*GE*, ch. 45)

The distinctive language of members of religious sects has always been a favourite object of satire, and there are many examples in Dickens of the kind of language that was attributed to the dissenters whom he disliked so much. The chief characteristic of this kind of language is the frequent use of archaisms and of not very appropriate quotations from the Bible. Chadband speaks of 'corn and wine and oil or, what is much the same thing, money' (*BH*, ch. 54). Lord George Gordon says that he must not be a sluggard 'when the vineyard is menaced with destruction, and may be trodden down by Papist feet' (*BR*, ch. 37), and Stiggins uses 'man of wrath' as a term of abuse (*PP*, ch. 27). Great use is made of the word 'brother': Mr Honeythunder concludes a letter 'Your affectionate brother (In Philanthropy)' (*ED*, ch. 6), and at the Brick Lane Temperance meeting Mr Hamm reinforces the term by the use of archaic language:

'He may approach, I think,' said Mr Hamm, looking around him with a fat smile. 'Brother Tadger, let him come forth and greet us.' (*PP*, ch. 33)

Certain pronunciations seem to have been regarded as sanctimonious, particularly those which arise from the stressing of words which are normally lightly stressed. Chadband says *air* for *are*, *doe* for *do*, and *untoe* for *unto* (*BH*, ch. 54). It seems likely that the spelling *buzzim* for 'bosom' (Stiggins, *PP*, ch. 45) represents a pronunciation with [ʌ] in place of the standard English [u].

The most noticeable archaism is the use of *-eth* in the third singular of the present indicative. When Kit Nubbles rescues his mother from Little Bethel, the preacher feels bound to protest:

'Stay, Satan, stay!' roared the preacher again. 'Tempt not the woman that doth incline her ear to thee, but hearken to the voice of him that calleth. He hath a lamb from the fold!' cried the preacher, raising his voice still higher and pointing to the baby. 'He beareth off a lamb, a precious lamb! He goeth about, like a wolf in the night season, and inveigleth the tender lambs.' (*OCS*, ch. 41)

The prolixity of Chadband can no doubt be attributed to the practice of extempore preaching when the speaker had very little to say and when a long discourse was considered praiseworthy. The following is a specimen:

> 'My friends,' says Mr Chadband, 'Peace be on this house! On the master thereof, on the mistress thereof, on the young maidens, and on the young men! My friends, why do I wish for peace? What is peace? Is it war? No. Is it strife? No. Is it lovely, and gentle, and beautiful, and pleasant, and serene, and joyful? O yes! Therefore, my friends, I wish for peace, upon you and upon yours.' (*BH*, ch. 19)

This sort of thing could clearly go on indefinitely, and to many readers the satire no doubt seems to approach burlesque, but Dickens goes out of his way to say that it is based upon actual examples:

> it must be within everybody's experience, that the Chadband style of oratory is widely received and much admired. (ch. 19)

The language of the navy clearly appealed to Dickens, though the number of characters who use it is not large. Mrs Bayham Badger makes sentimental use of naval language in recalling her late husband, Captain Swosser:

> 'The dear old Crippler!' said Mrs Badger, shaking her head. 'She was a noble vessel. Trim, ship-shape, all a taunto, as Captain Swosser used to say. You must excuse me if I occasionally introduce a nautical expression; I was quite a sailor once. Captain Swosser loved that craft for my sake. When she was no longer in commission, he frequently said that if he were rich enough to buy her old hulk, he would have an inscription let into the timbers of the quarterdeck where we stood as partners in the dance, to mark the spot where he fell – raked fore and aft (Captain Swosser used to say) by the fire from my tops. It was his naval way of mentioning my eyes.' (*BH*, ch. 13)

In a later chapter she returns to the subject:

> 'Captain Swosser used to say of me that I was always better than land a-head and a breeze a-starn to the midshipmen's mess when the purser's junk had become as tough as the fore-topsel weather earrings. It was his naval way of mentioning generally that I was an acquisition to any society.' (ch. 17)

The Dickensian character who is most fond of using nautical imagery is Captain Cuttle in *Dombey and Son*. The following examples are only a selection:

Uncle much hove down? (ch. 9)
Lay your head well to the wind, and we'll fight through it (ch. 9)
Gills, what's the bearings of this business? (ch. 9)
Keep her off a point or so (ch. 15)
Take an observation of your nevy (ch. 17)
A man does get more way of himself (ch. 17)
Keep her free and ride easy (ch. 25)
You carry a weight of mind easy, as would swamp one of my tonnage soon (ch. 39)
The observation as I'm a-going to make is calc'lated to blow every stitch of sail as you can carry clean out of the bolt-ropes, and bring you on your beam-ends with a lurch (ch. 56)

Nautical imagery can be expressed in a single word. To a sailor *taut* is a term of high praise, and Captain Cuttle says of Jack Bunsby 'that he was a man as could give a pretty taut opinion too' (ch. 50).

Perhaps because he was so conscious that his own education had been neglected, Dickens took a keen interest in schools. School-teachers enter largely into *Our Mutual Friend*. The first school which Charlie Hexam attends is the subject of a long satirical description (Bk II, ch. 1) in the course of which some linguistic matters are mentioned. The over-careful speech of the schoolmaster is mimicked by the reference to 'the exponent drawling on to My Dearerr Childerrenerr', which in two words satirizes the rolling of the *r*'s and the addition of an off-glide resulting from excess of zeal in pronouncing final consonants clearly. Another linguistic feature satirized in this passage is the habit of using difficult and unfamiliar words in speaking to children. The teacher is described as 'repeating the word Sepulchre (commonly used among infants) five hundred times, and never once hinting what it meant' (Bk II, ch. 1).

Among the subjects taught at school, English grammar occupied an important place. When Mrs Jarley wants to attract visitors from boarding-schools to her waxworks, she does so 'by altering the face and costume of Mr Grimaldi as clown to represent Mr Lindley Murray as he appeared when engaged in the composition of his English Grammar' (*OCS*, ch. 29). The

influence of the teacher as prescriptive grammarian finding
fault with perfectly idiomatic expressions is to be seen in Miss
Peecher's admonition to her favourite pupil, Mary Anne, who
had allowed herself to say of Lizzie Hexam, 'They say she's
very handsome':

'Oh, Mary Anne, Mary Anne!' returned Miss Peecher, slightly
colouring and shaking her head, a little out of humour; 'how often
have I told you not to use that vague expression, not to speak in
that general way? When you say *they* say, what do you mean? Part
of speech They?'
Mary Anne hooked her right arm behind her in her left hand, as
being under examination, and replied:
'Personal pronoun.'
'Person, They?'
'Third person.'
'Number, They?'
'Plural number.'
'Then how many do you mean, Mary Anne? Two? Or more?'
'I beg your pardon, ma'am,' said Mary Anne, disconcerted now
she came to think of it; 'but I don't know that I mean more than
her brother himself.' As she said it, she unhooked her arm.
'I felt convinced of it,' returned Miss Peecher, smiling again.
'Now pray, Mary Anne, be careful another time. He says is very
different from they say, remember. Difference between he says and
they say? Give it me.'
Mary Anne immediately hooked her right arm behind her in her
left hand – an attitude absolutely necessary to the situation – and
replied: 'One is indicative mood, present tense, third person
singular, verb active to say. Other is indicative mood, present
tense, third person plural, verb active to say.'
'Why verb active, Mary Anne?'
'Because it takes a pronoun after it in the objective case, Miss
Peecher.'
'Very good indeed,' remarked Miss Peecher, with encouragement. 'In fact, could not be better.' (*OMF*, Bk II, ch. 1)

The most unexpected characters are liable to quote, more or
less inappropriately, from grammars which had obviously been
learned by rote. Mark Tapley comments on the warmth of
Tom Pinch's welcome by saying:

'It's a considerable invasion of a man's jollity to be made so
partickler welcome, but a Werb is a word as signifies to be, to do,
or to suffer (which is all the grammar, and enough too, as ever I
wos taught); and if there's a Werb alive, I'm it. For I'm always
a-bein', sometimes a-doin', and continually a-sufferin'.' (*MC*, ch. 48)

Tom Gradgrind, having told Harthouse that his sister 'never cared for old Bounderby', is provoked by his companion's reminder 'We are in the present tense now' into a parade of the jargon of a school grammar:

> 'Verb neuter, not to care. Indicative mood, present tense. First person singular. I do not care; second person singular, thou dost not care; third person singular, she does not care,' returned Tom· (*HT*, Bk II, ch. 3)

The amount of actual tuition going on at Dotheboys Hall is so slight that it hardly seems necessary for Squeers to have any knowledge of the subjects that he is supposed to teach, but English grammar is one subject of which he has at least a sketchy knowledge, although, by relying on verbal memory without comprehension, he gets the rules all wrong. When he calls on the deaf Peg Sliderskew, he replies to her query 'Is that you?' by saying:

> 'Ah! It's me, and me's the first person singular nominative case, agreeing with the verb "it's", and governed by Squeers understood, as a acorn, a hour; but when the h is sounded, the a only is to be used, as a and, a art, a ighway.' (*NN*, ch. 57)

The stage has for long had its special language, and it is only natural that the members of Vincent Crummles's company should use it freely both on and off the stage. When Folair and Lenville call on Nicholas Nickleby, they announce their arrival in accordance with stage conventions:

> 'House, house, house!' cried Mr Folair.
> 'What ho! within there!' said Mr Lenville, in a deep voice. (*NN*, ch. 24)

In the same chapter we find the technical language of the stage, like 'bespeak night', explained ostensibly for Nicholas's benefit but also for the reader's. Crummles defines 'a pretty good let' as four front places in the centre and the whole of the stage-box. There is also theatrical slang like 'Anything in the gruff and grumble way?' (ch. 24), and Lenville's nickname for Crummles, 'old bricks and mortar', because his style of acting is heavy (ch. 23). Some words had a distinctive pronunciation on the stage. Mrs Lenville appeals to her husband: 'forego all idle forms unless you would see me a blighted corse at your feet' (ch. 29). The reduction of *you* to *ye* is another example of a theatrical pronunciation. Lenville combines this pronunciation with a stage gesture:

'But they shall not protect ye!' said the tragedian, taking an upward look at Nicholas, beginning at his boots and ending at the crown of his head, and then a downward one, beginning at the crown of his head, and ending at his boots – which two looks, as everybody knows, express defiance on the stage. (ch. 29)

When Nicholas reports that Smike is ill, Mrs Crummles says 'How!' with a tragic recoil and, when she does not understand Nicholas's reply, she uses the language of the stage while Nicholas lapses into the stilted language of a circulating-library novel:

'What mean you?' rejoined Mrs Crummles, in her most popular manner. 'Whence comes this altered tone?'
'I mean that a dastardly enemy of mine has struck at me through him, and that while he thinks to torture me, he inflicts on him such agonies of terror and suspense as – You will excuse me, I am sure,' said Nicholas, checking himself. (ch. 48)

In *Sketches by Boz* Dickens includes a few brief but amusing parodies of stage language. After expressing a wish to see a play in which all the dramatis personae were orphans, he gives an example of a typical stage father helping along the dramatist's exposition: 'It is now nineteen years, my dear child, since your blessed mother . . . confided you to my charge. You were then an infant . . . ' Another parody is of a recognition scene:

Or else they have to discover, all of a sudden, that somebody whom they have been in constant communication with, during three long acts, without the slightest suspicion, is their own child: in which case they exclaim, 'Ah! what do I see? This bracelet! That smile! These documents! Those eyes! Can I believe my senses? – It must be! – Yes – it is, it is my child!' – 'My father!' exclaims the child; and they fall into each other's arms, and look over each other's shoulders, and the audience give three rounds of applause. (*Scenes*, ch. 11)

In another of these early 'Scenes' Dickens shows his knowledge of the technical language of the theatre and gives an example of the on-glides with which unskilful actors try to ensure clarity of articulation:

and then the wrongful heir comes in to two bars of soft music (technically called 'a hurry'), and goes on in the most shocking manner, throwing the young lady about as if she was nobody, and calling the rightful heir 'Ar – recreant – ar – wretch!' in a very loud voice. (*Scenes*, ch. 12)

One group of actors is of special interest: the circus performers in *Hard Times*. They appeal to an audience even less sophisticated than that which patronizes Vincent Crummles and they use the same turgid kind of English in advertizing their performances:

> Miss Josephine Sleary, as some very long and very narrow strips of printed bill announced, was then inaugurating the entertainments with her graceful equestrian Tyrolean flower-act . . . Signor Jupe was that afternoon to 'elucidate the diverting accomplishments oɪ his highly-trained performing dog Merrylegs' . . . The same Signor Jupe was to 'enliven the varied performances at frequent intervals, with his chaste Shakespearian quips and retorts'. (Bk I, ch. 3)

There is an amusing contrast between this inflated language for public use and the back-stage slang used by the actors when talking among themselves. Master Kidderminster, the child actor, is the one who uses the technical language of the circus most freely, and his companion, E. W. B. Childers, has to supply translations for Mr Gradgrind and Mr Bounderby:

> 'Kidderminster,' said Mr Childers, raising his voice, 'stow that! – Sir' to Mr Gradgrind, 'I was addressing myself to you. You may or may not be aware (for perhaps you have not been much in the audience) that Jupe has missed his tip very often lately.'
> 'Has – what has he missed?' asked Mr Gradgrind, glancing at the potent Bounderby for assistance.
> 'Missed his tip.'
> 'Offered at the Garters four times last night, and never done 'em once,' said Master Kidderminster. 'Missed his tip at the banners, too, and was loose in his ponging.'
> 'Didn't do what he ought to do, was short in his leaps and bad in his tumbling,' Mr Childers interpreted. (Bk I, ch. 6)

After Kidderminster has been turned out for being cheeky, Childers himself uses language that Mr Gradgrind finds hard to understand. He tells him that Jupe has cut (run away) because he has been repeatedly goosed (hissed) though he still has some future as a cackler (speaker). At the end of the novel

Sleary's lisp, combined with circus slang, produces another word that, naturally enough, Mr Gradgrind finds himself unable to understand: *a Jothkin* 'a carter'.

Commerce has its own stock of clichés, on which Dick Swiveller draws when he is involved in a scuffle with Quilp:

> 'There's plenty more of it at the same shop,' said Mr Swiveller, by turns advancing and retreating in a threatening attitude, 'a large and extensive assortment always on hand – country orders executed with promptitude and despatch.' (*OCS*, ch. 13)

Like many a later *entrepreneur*, Mrs Jarley has her doubts about prestige advertizing. She is tempted by Mr Slum's offer of verse to advertize her waxworks, but the five shillings demanded is a lot of money. 'It comes very expensive, sir, and I really don't think it does much good' (*OCS*, ch. 28). The pretentious language of advertizing has made great strides since the time of Dickens, but even in the eighteen-forties it was a legitimate object of parody. In *Dombey and Son* Miss Tox and Mrs Chick combine to recommend Mrs Pipchin's establishment to Mr Dombey:

> ' . . . It is not a Preparatory School by any means. Should I express my meaning,' said Miss Tox, with peculiar sweetness, 'if I designated it an infantine Boarding-House of a very select description?'
> 'On an exceedingly limited and particular scale,' suggested Mrs Chick, with a glance at her brother.
> 'Oh! Exclusion itself!' said Miss Tox. (*DS*, ch. 8)

Advertizers were already fond of superlatives. Jinkins comes to Charity Pecksniff's wedding wearing 'a bran new extra super double-milled blue saxony dress coat (that was its description in the bill)' (*MC*, ch. 54), and when David Copperfield decides to do himself well, he is told 'Twopence-halfpenny is the price of the Genuine Stunning ale' (*DC*, ch. 11). Gin-drinkers had the choice of a wide range of imaginatively-named brands. In an early essay on gin-shops Dickens described the dram-drinkers 'left in a state of pleasing hesitation between "The Cream of the Valley", "The Out and Out", "The No Mistake", "The Good for Mixing", "The real Knock-me-down", "The celebrated Butter Gin", "The regular Flare-up", and a dozen other, equally inviting and wholesome *liqueurs*' (*SB, Scenes*, ch. 22).

People of the same age and social class tend to talk alike, whatever their occupations. Simon Tappertit, greeting the members of the Protestant Association with the words 'My lord does me and you the honour to send his compliments per self' (*BR*, ch. 39), is using language of which William Guppy would have highly approved. Dickens is fond of making fun of the grandiloquent phrases encouraged by the societies which young men founded or joined. Dick Swiveller is 'the Perpetual Grand Master of the Glorious Apollers' (*OCS*, ch. 13) and Tappertit is the 'mighty captain' of the secret society of 'Prentice Knights (*BR*, ch. 8).

Those who are most impressed by the importance of their occupation are most likely to use its language unseasonably, and it is not surprising that Mr Lillyvick, the self-important collector of water-rates, should make free use of imagery drawn from his occupation. In expressing his indignation at the loss of his glass of punch, he complains 'I consider the way in which that punch was cut off, if I may use the expression, highly disrespectful to this company'. (*NN*, ch. 15). On another occasion he describes himself as 'the head of the family, or, as it may be, the main from which all the other little branches are turned on' (ch. 25), and when in dejection after his wife's desertion, he says 'The plug of life is dry, sir, and but the mud is left' (ch. 25). This remark provides another example of occupational dialect, since Newman Noggs, to whom it is addressed, attributes the style to the influence of the theatrical circles in which Mr Lillyvick had been moving, and the same influence no doubt accounts for the tragic weight which he manages to impart to the command 'Let me be shaved' (ch. 52).

Tony Weller's occupation can very easily be deduced from his imagery. When Sam reproaches him for his slowness in asking Mr Pickwick to take care of his money, he replies indignantly:

'You might ha' seen I warn't able to start . . . I'm on the wrong side of the road, and backin' into the palins and all manner of unpleasantness, and yet you won't put out a hand to help me.' (*PP*, ch. 56)

The source of Tony Weller's imagery is sometimes more obvious than his exact meaning. He greets a friend: 'Vell, George, . . . how is it? All right behind and full inside?' This calls for no translation, but when he goes on 'Is the vaybill all clear and straight for'erd?', the lawyer thinks it necessary to translate:

> 'The schedule, sir,' said Pell, guessing at Mr Weller's meaning, 'the schedule is as plain and satisfactory as pen and ink can make it.' (ch. 43)

Tony Weller's manner of asking when a case is to be heard is to point to the person chiefly concerned and say 'Ven do you take his cloths off?' (ch. 43). When Sam Weller asks where is the money that he wants to borrow, his father replies 'In the boot'. It is clear from the context that this is a picturesque way of referring to a rather inaccessible trousers pocket (ch. 43). The most sustained example of Tony Weller's use of the language of his trade is the letter which he caused to be written to Sam Weller to inform him of his stepmother's death. The authorship of the letter is rather complicated, but Tony Weller's share is easy to recognize. Sam Weller applies a little textual criticism to the letter and his conclusion is:

> The gen'l'm'n as wrote it wos a tellin' all about the misfortun' in a proper vay, and then my father comes a lookin' over him, and complicates the whole concern by puttin' his oar in. That's just the wery sort o' thing he'd do.

The account of Mrs Weller's death runs:

> her veels wos immedetly greased and everythink done to set her agoin as could be inwented your farther had hopes as she vould have vorked round as usual but just as she wos a turnen the corner my boy she took the wrong road and vent down hill with a welocity you never see and notvithstandin that the drag wos put on drectly by the medikel man it wornt of no use at all for she paid the last pike at twenty minutes afore six o'clock yesterday evenin havin done the journey wery much under the reglar time vich praps was partly owen to her haven taken in wery little luggage by the vay your father says that if you vill come and see me Sammy he vill take it as a wery great favor for I am wery lonely Samivel. (ch. 52)

When coaches give way to railways a new group of images becomes available, and Toodle, the engine-driver in *Dombey and Son*, draws on it freely when admonishing his children:

> 'If you find yourselves in cutting or in tunnels, don't you play no secret games. Keep your whistles going, and let's know where you are.'

The rising Toodles set up a shrill murmur, expressive of their resolution to profit by the paternal advice.

'But what makes you say this along of Rob, father?' asked his wife, anxiously.

'Polly, old 'ooman,' said Mr Toodle, 'I don't know as I said it partickler along o' Rob, I'm sure. I starts light with Rob only; I comes to a branch; I takes on what I finds there; and a whole train of ideas gets coupled on to him afore I knows where I am, or where they comes from. What a Junction a man's thoughts is,' said Mr Toodle, 'to-be-sure!' (ch. 38)

Joe Gargery makes his contribution to the occupational dialects in the novels of Dickens. As a blacksmith, he tentatively suggests that Pip might show his gratitude to Miss Havisham by turning her out 'a set of shoes all four round', but has to admit that such a present 'might not act acceptable as a present in a total wacancy of hoofs' (*GE*, ch. 15).

Dickens's early experiences as a newspaper reporter made him familiar with the occupational dialect of journalists. Like all dialects, journalese can be subdivided into many different categories. At least two kinds are illustrated in the novels of Dickens: the vituperative editorial of the *Eatanswill Gazette* and the rather fulsome gossip paragraph, which provided the staple diet of the readers of provincial newspapers. An example of the first kind, too long to quote, occurs in chapter 51 of *Pickwick Papers*. An example of the second kind is the paragraph which announces the retirement of Vincent Crummles from the English stage:

The talented Vincent Crummles, long favourably known to fame as a country manager and actor of no ordinary pretensions, is about to cross the Atlantic on an histrionic expedition. Crummles is to be accompanied, we hear, by his lady and gifted family. We know no man superior to Crummles in his particular line of character, or one who, whether as a public or private individual, could carry with him the best wishes of a larger circle of friends. Crummles is certain to succeed. (*NN*, ch. 48)

The characteristics of this kind of writing are verbosity, fondness for clichés, and an inflated diction designed to make unimportant people seem important. Sometimes puffs of this kind are inserted under the guise of Answers to Correspondents:

Philo-Dramaticus. Crummles, the country manager and actor, cannot be more than forty-three, or forty-four years of age. Crummles is NOT a Prussian, having been born at Chelsea. (*NN*, ch. 48)

Another good parody of gossipy journalism occurs in *Great Expectations*:

Our readers will learn, not altogether without interest, in reference to the recent romantic rise in fortune of a young artificer in iron of this neighbourhood (what a theme, by the way, for the magic pen of our as yet not universally acknowledged townsman TOOBY, the poet of our columns!) that the youth's earliest patron, companion, and friend, was a highly-respected individual not entirely unconnected with the corn and seed trade, and whose eminently convenient and commodious business premises are situate within a hundred miles of the High-street. It is not wholly irrespective of our personal feelings that we record HIM as the Mentor of our young Telemachus, for it is good to know that our town produced the founder of the latter's fortunes. Does the thought-contracted brow of the local Sage or the lustrous eye of local Beauty inquire whose fortunes? We believe that Quintin Matsys was the BLACKSMITH of Antwerp. VERB. SAP. (ch. 28)

Dickens has here admirably caught the wordy, allusive style of the journalist of his time and the coy hints of the gossip columnist.

It is in his early novels and sketches, written when his experience as a reporter was still fresh in his memory, that Dickens's satire of journalese occurs most frequently. The despair of the reporter who is required to write a bright and interesting report when virtually nothing has happened is portrayed in the Report of the First Meeting of the Mudfog Association:

Eleven o'clock
I open my letter to say that nothing whatever has happened since I folded it up.

The need to make much out of little produces pieces of padding, unnecessary detail and commonplace reflection:

'When I left New Burlington Street this evening in the hackney cabriolet, number four thousand two hundred and eighty-five, I experienced sensations as novel as they were oppressive. A sense of the importance of the task I had undertaken, a consciousness that I was leaving London, and, stranger still, going somewhere else, a feeling of loneliness and a sensation of jolting, quite bewildered my thoughts, and for a time rendered me even insensible to the presence of my carpet-bag and hat-box . . . ' (*SB, The Mudfog Papers*)

It is not only in newspapers that bad writing is to be found. In *Nicholas Nickleby* there is an excellent parody of the kind of novel which appealed to the less intelligent subscribers to circulating libraries:

> At this instant, while the Lady Flabella yet inhaled that delicious fragrance by holding the *mouchoir* to her exquisite, but thought-fully-chiselled nose, the door of the *boudoir* (artfully concealed by rich hangings of silken damask, the hue of Italy's firmament) was thrown open, and with noiseless tread two valets-de-chambre, clad in sumptuous liveries of peach-blossom and gold, advanced into the room followed by a page in *bas de soie* – silk stockings – who, while they remained at some distance making the most graceful obeisances, advanced to the feet of his lovely mistress, and dropping on one knee presented, on a golden salver gorgeously chased, a scented *billet*.
>
> The Lady Flabella, with an agitation she could not repress, hastily tore off the envelope and broke the scented seal. It *was* from Befillaire – the young, the slim, the low-voiced – *her own* Befillaire.
>
> 'Oh, charming!' interrupted Kate's patroness, who was sometimes taken literary; 'Poetic, really. Read that description again, Miss Nickleby.' (ch. 28)

One linguistic habit satirized in this passage is the excessive use of French loan-words. This was a practice on which Dickens held strong views. In describing the preparations for Fanny Dorrit's wedding, he goes to great lengths to avoid using the word *trousseau:*

> The preparation consisted in the despatch of her maid to Paris under the protection of the Courier, for the purchase of that outfit for a bride on which it would be extremely low, in the present narrative, to bestow an English name, but to which (on a vulgar principle it observes of adhering to the language in which it professes to be written) it declines to give a French one. (*LD*, Bk II, ch. 15)

3

SUBSTANDARD SPEECH

Dickens was very responsive to the substandard speech of his time. He found it amusing, and in his letters he often deliberately used vulgarisms as a sort of private joke, shared with his correspondent. Sometimes he uses substandard forms of single words, such as *wollum* for *volume* (Forster, II, 4) or *enthoozymoosy* for *enthusiasm* (VI, 1); sometimes he uses phrases, such as *your kind invite* (II, 1); *I knows a good 'ous* (II, 1); *who can be of any use whatsomdever* (II, 1); *I done it though* (II, 1); *let us have 'a bit o' talk' before we have a bit o' som'at else* (II, 3); *if you was a real gent* (IV, 5).

The substandard speech of characters in the novels is far from homogeneous, and the lack of homogeneity makes it all the more convincing. Substandard speech in its most extreme form is represented by the speech of Jo in *Bleak House*, of which the following is a typical specimen:

'They're wot's left, Mr Snagsby,' says Jo, 'out of a sov'ring as wos give me by a lady in a wale as sed she wos a servant and as come to my crossin one night and asked to be showd this 'ere ouse and the ouse wot him as you giv the writin to died at, and the berrin-ground wot he's berrid in. She ses to me, she ses, 'are you the boy at the Inkwhich?' she ses. I ses, 'yes,' I ses. She ses to me, she ses, 'can you show me all them places?' I ses, 'yes, I can,' I ses. And she ses to me 'do it,' and I dun it, and she giv me a sov'ring and hooked it.' (ch. 19)

This is a convincing example. It is made up of simple words, mainly monosyllabic; the frequent repetition of 'she ses' and 'I ses' can be paralleled in vulgar speech today, as can the attempt at an adjectival clause: 'this 'ere ouse wot him as you giv the writin to died at.' In its own way the passage is effective. Like most genuine dialect speakers, Jo does not realize that he is using a dialect, and when he needs a gloss for 'Fen larks', the best that he can provide is 'Stow hooking it', with 'Stow cutting away' as an alternative (ch. 16).

Joe Gargery provides rather more sophisticated examples, in which the substandard quality of the speech is emphasized by attempts at eloquence:

'The king upon his throne, with his crown upon his 'ed, can't sit and write his acts of Parliament in print, without having begun, when he were a unpromoted Prince, with the alphabet – Ah!' added Joe, with a shake of the head that was full of meaning, 'and begun at A too, and worked his way to Z. And I know what that is to do, though I can't say I've exactly done it.' (GE, ch. 9)

When Joe is ill at ease on visiting Pip in London, his embarrassment causes him to combine substandard with formal speech:

'Next day, Sir,' said Joe, looking at me as if I were a long way off, 'having cleaned myself, I go and I see Miss A.'
'Miss A., Joe? Miss Havisham?'
'Which I say, Sir,' replied Joe, with an air of legal formality, as if he were making his will, 'Miss A., or otherways Havisham. Her expression air then as follering: "Mr Gargery. You air in correspondence with Mr Pip?" Having had a letter from you, I were able to say "I am". (When I married your sister, Sir, I said, "I will"; and when I answered your friend, Pip, I said, "I am".) "Would you tell him, then," said she, "that which Estella has come home, and would be glad to see him." ' (ch. 27)

Another variety of substandard English is the genteel. Mrs Todgers is careful to call her boarding-house an 'establishment', and she is careful not to call her lodgers by any such vulgar term: 'There is no such passion in human nature as the passion for gravy among commercial gentlemen' (MC, ch. 9). There is similar anticlimax in the words which she imagines as those which any of her lodgers might use in giving notice: 'Mrs Todgers, this day week we part, in consequence of the cheese' (ch. 9). Rather surprisingly, in view of his honest and forthright nature, Mr Boffin's language is not completely free from the influences of commercial genteelism. He tells Silas Wegg that Mrs Boffin's father was engaged in the 'Canine Provision Trade' (OMF, Bk I, ch. 5). Genteel euphemisms come more appropriately from Mrs Wilfer:

'By-the-by, ma'am,' said Mr Boffin, turning back as he was going, 'you have a lodger?'
'A gentleman,' Mrs Wilfer answered, qualifying the low expression, 'undoubtedly occupies our first floor.' (OMF, Bk I, ch. 9)

Substandard English is sometimes the result of an attempt to make the language do too much. The mistake made by John Chivery is that he is too anxious to speak the exact truth:

> The world may sneer at a turnkey, but he's a man – when he isn't a woman, which among female criminals he's expected to be. (*LD*, Bk II, ch. 27)

John's point is adequately made in the first twelve words of this sentence, but unfortunately he remembers that there are women turnkeys.

Another kind of substandard speech which finds its way into some of the novels is the language of the underworld, technically but ambiguously known as cant, which had its origin in a desire for secrecy. In *Oliver Twist* the two Bow Street Runners Blathers and Duff, who are sent to investigate the burglary at Mrs Maylie's, speak a distinctive dialect, with a plentiful mixture of cant (ch. 31). Cant is used at the very beginning of the chapter when Blathers says that Duff is 'in the gig, a-minding the prad'. *Prad*, from Dutch *paard*, is a cant word for a horse, commonly used in the nineteenth century. Later Duff uses *crack* as a term for a burglary and Blathers speaks of *blunt* in the sense 'money'. Both words are common in nineteenth-century thieves' slang. Much is made of the necessity for translating the language of Blathers and Duff, sometimes when the need for translation is not apparent; it seems likely that some of these cant terms have passed into more general use since the time of Dickens. It is agreed that the burglary was not committed by a yokel, whereupon the doctor Mr Losberne thinks it necessary to say, 'And, translating the word yokel for the benefit of the ladies, I apprehend your meaning to be, that this attempt was not made by a countryman?' A little later the doctor finds himself unable to translate:

> 'Well, master,' said Blathers, . . . 'This warn't a put-up thing.'
> "And what the devil's a put-up thing?' demanded the doctor, impatiently.
> 'We call it a put-up robbery, ladies,' said Blathers, turning to them, as if he pitied their ignorance, but had a contempt for the doctor's, 'when the servants is in it.'

Blathers and Duff refer to well-known criminals affectionately by their nicknames. They disagree on the question whether a particular job was done by the Family Pet or Conkey Chick-weed, and Duff explains that Conkey means Nosey. This explanation arouses the contempt of Blathers: 'Of course the lady knows that, don't she?' (ch. 31).

Cant is merely one kind of slang; there is a fair amount of slang of a less specialized kind in the novels of Dickens. When Dickens uses slang he sometimes seems to feel that an apologetic or playful comment is called for, as when, in *Martin Chuzzlewit*, the Man in the Monument says that the charge for admission is 'a Tanner'; the author adds the comment 'It seemed a low expression, compared with the Monument' (ch. 36). Again, when Bob Sawyer uses the slang expression 'getting the steam up' the author calls attention to the slang by saying that Bob made the remark 'in a style of eastern allegory' (*PP*, ch. 32).

The three clerks in *Bleak House*, Guppy, Jobling and Small-weed, make free use of slang. When they set out to have a meal together, Smallweed suggests that they should 'make them-selves scarce'. Guppy reminds Jobling that he had once been 'on the wrong side of the post' (i.e. in debt), and Jobling points out that if this fact were known when he applied for a job it would 'sew him up' (ch. 20). He brushes aside attempts at polite paraphrase and declares roundly that he has 'got the sack'. The phrase has defied the normal rule that slang expres-sions soon either pass out of use or cease to be slang. One word that has passed from slang into the standard language is the verb *to chaff*; but for Mrs Todgers's apology, we should not recognize the word as slang when she says:

'There was a little chaffing going on – I hope that you don't consider that a low expression, Miss Pecksniff; it is always in our gentlemen's mouths.' (*MC*, ch. 31)

Slang is often facetious. The clerk Chuckster, in *The Old Curiosity Shop*, refers to a client as 'the ancient buffalo', but is forced by Abel Garland's obvious disapproval to translate the phrase by 'the old gentleman' (ch. 69).

Slang enters largely into the language of Miss Mowcher along with infantile language and terms of endearment. Some of her phrases belong to the language of children's games: 'That's telling, my blessed infant', 'Now, ducky, ducky, ducky, come to Mrs Bond and be killed'. Other slang expressions are:

D

'you're a downy fellow', 'man alive', 'What a world of gammon and spinnage it is', and 'you're a broth of a boy'. Sometimes her slang is more allusive. She chooses a very roundabout way of telling Steerforth that she will not answer questions:

> 'Do you know what my great grandfather's name was?'
> 'No,' said Steerforth.
> 'It was Walker, my sweet pet,' replied Miss Mowcher, 'and he came of a long line of Walkers, that I inherit all the Hookey estates from.' (*DC*, ch. 22)

Mr Mould, the undertaker in *Martin Chuzzlewit*, shows a rather unexpected fondness for slang. He was so impressed by Mr Nadgett that he 'openly said he was a long-headed man, a dry one, a salt fish, a deep file, a rasper; and made him the subject of many other flattering encomiums' (ch. 38).

Slang merges imperceptibly into colloquialism, and both are especially common in the speech of young men. The very self-assured language of young Martin Chuzzlewit when he comes to live with the Pecksniffs is a source of great embarrassment to Tom Pinch. His colloquialisms are quoted in reported speech: he 'troubled' Mr Pecksniff for the loaf, and, when Tom failed to follow his example in eating a hearty meal, he remarked 'that he didn't get on'. This last remark is said to be 'a speech of so tremendous a character, that Tom cast down his eyes involuntarily, and felt as if he himself had committed some horrible deed and heinous breach of Mr Pecksniff's confidence' (*MC*, ch. 6). Tom finds himself adopting some of the collo-quialisms of Mr Pecksniff's pupils, at least in his thoughts. One paragraph describing Tom's ruminations begins with the words: 'I'm a nice man, I don't think, as John used to say . . .' (ch. 6). When quoting John Westlock, Tom Pinch uses the phrase *cash up* and feels bound to apologize for it by saying 'he used strange expressions now and then, but that was his way'. Young Martin, who belongs to roughly the same age-group as John Westlock, sees no cause for apology:

> 'Cash-up's a very good expression,' observed Martin, 'when other people don't apply it to you.' (ch. 12)

In *Bleak House* Richard Carstone, having decided to become a lawyer, declares his intention to 'go at it'. Mr Kenge rather unctuously calls attention to Richard's slangy idiom: 'We shall soon be – shall I say in Mr Richard's own light-hearted manner, "going at it" – to our heart's content' (ch. 13).

There are dangers in the use of speeches in novels and short stories as evidence of the kind of colloquial language that was in use at the time when they were written. A novelist is not a philologist, and we are not entitled to assume either his ability or his intention to record the speech of his contemporaries. There is evidence, however, that Dickens, especially in his early novels and sketches, aimed at a high degree of realism. Forster says:

> What I had most indeed to notice in him, at the very outset of his career, was his indifference to any praise of his performance on the merely literary side, compared with the higher recognition of them as bits of actual life, with the meaning and purpose on their part, and the responsibility on his, of realities rather than creatures of fancy. (II, 1)

Forster elsewhere gives an example of the care with which Dickens, with the help of his friends, tried to make his characters use appropriate language. The Marchioness (*OCS*) recommends Dick Swiveller to try pieces of orange-peel in cold water as a substitute for wine. In the original version she had said 'If you make believe very much it's quite nice; but if you don't, you know, it hasn't much flavour'. In the revised version the last few words are replaced by 'it seems as if it would bear a little more seasoning, certainly'. Dickens says 'I think that's better', but he defends his original version by saying 'Flavour is a common word in cookery and among cooks, and so I used it' (Forster, II, 7).

When Doctor Marigold uses a cliché quite foreign to his usual style, 'Let me not anticipate', Dickens is conscious of the incongruity and, instead of deleting it, he turns it to account by making Doctor Marigold insert a parenthesis of explanation:

> I take that expression out of a lot of romances I bought for her (i.e. his adopted daughter Sophy). I never opened a single one of 'em – and I have opened many – but I found the romancer saying 'let me not anticipate'. Which being so, I wonder why he did anticipate, or who asked him to it. (*CS*, *Doctor Marigold*, ch. 1)

Because of the wide variety of the substandard speech of Dickensian characters, it is important to notice the names of the speakers. Mrs Gamp and Sam Weller both draw on a common stock of substandard language, but they each have their own distinctive way of speaking. It is, moreover, a point of literary interest to notice which characters use substandard speech. Squeers's constant use of vulgarisms helps to emphasize his unfitness to be a schoolmaster, while the failure of Oliver Twist and Lizzie Hexam to pick up even the smallest vulgarisms from the low-life characters with whom they come into contact reflects the author's belief that they are unsullied by their environment. On the other hand, Tom Gradgrind behaves like a lout and talks like one. His sister's refusal to marry Bounderby would 'put old Bounderby's pipe out', and her agreeing to marry him to please her brother is 'very game of her'. His reply to the question 'Do you smoke?' is 'I believe you' (*HT*, Bk II, ch. 3). In *Great Expectations* class dialect is used to emphasize the difference between Pip and Estella (Pip is the boy who doesn't know any better than to call knaves Jacks, ch. 8), and later to emphasize the difference between Joe and Pip (ch. 27). By noticing who uses particular features of substandard speech it is possible to throw light not only on the characters but also on the nature of substandard speech. When we find the prosperous farmer Wardle using vulgarisms, it suggests that substandard speech is not merely a question of income or social position, and when we find Sir Mulberry Hawk doing so, we are encouraged to look further into the way in which extremes meet in class dialect: upper and lower social classes often agree against the middle classes.

In *The Tuggses at Ramsgate* (*SB, Tales*, ch. 4) there is a good deal of light-hearted mockery of the class dialect of a lower-middle class London family. A legacy of £20,000 has immediate linguistic consequences: Simon and Charlotte become Cymon and Charlotta, while Cymon's father lags behind him in the attempt to acquire new speech-habits:

> 'Capital srimps!' said Mr Joseph Tuggs.
> Mr Cymon eyed his father with a rebellious scowl, as he emphatically said '*Shrimps*'.
> 'Well then, shrimps,' said Mr Joseph Tuggs. 'Srimps or shrimps, don't much matter.'

Mr Tuggs is equally ready to accept correction later, although he misses its point:

'How shall we go?' inquired the captain; 'It's too warm to walk.'
'A shay?' suggested Mr Joseph Tuggs.
'Chaise,' whispered Mr Cymon.
'I should think one would be enough,' said Mr Joseph Tuggs aloud, quite unconscious of the meaning of the correction. 'However, two shays if you like.'

Substandard speech is rich in catch-phrases, which have to be distinguished from the habitual phrases ascribed to particular characters, like Mr Micawber's 'waiting for something to turn up' and Wemmick's 'portable property'. Catch-phrases can be recognized by such characteristics as vividness of imagery and obscurity. They are features of class dialect and they are often used in repartee by Cockneys. They may occur only once in a particular novel, but they give the impression of being quotations from a large and constantly changing stock of vernacular idiom. Sometimes their meaning is clear enough, as when Jackson, the clerk from Dodson and Fogg, replies to a question by saying 'Not knowin', can't say' (*PP*, ch. 31). This is the low-life equivalent of the conventional reply 'No comment' addressed to an importunate journalist. Less conventional but equally clear is the turnkey's encouragement 'Lord set you up like a corner-pin' (*LD*, Bk I, ch. 6). The origin of some of these phrases is easy to see; others had their origin in some forgotten anecdote or piece of slang whose obscurity to the uninitiated was its chief attraction. To the first category belongs Tip Dorrit's 'I believe I am! About!' (*LD*, Bk I, ch. 8) and Wackford Squeers's reply to his father's suggestion that he should not let the waiter see him 'tuck into something fat': 'I'm awake!' (*NN*, ch. 39). To the second category belong Tony Weller's 'Walker' with the meaning 'Rubbish' (*PP*, ch. 27) and the catch-phrases, quite meaningless except to the initiated, which Mr Bonney describes as being in use among the muffin-sellers of London: *Snooks, Walker, Ferguson, Is Murphy right?* (*NN*, ch. 2).

A catch-phrase may become even more obscure when it is expressed in reported speech:

After staring vacantly about us for some minutes, we appealed, touching the cause of this assemblage, to a gentleman in a suit of tarpaulin, who was smoking his pipe on our right hand; but as the only answer we obtained was a playful inquiry whether our mother had disposed of her mangle, we determined to wait the issue in silence. (*SB, Scenes*, ch. 20)

When catch-phrases are quoted in reported speech it is not always easy to reconstruct the original phrase, as in the reference to a pawnbroker's clerk 'whose allusions to "that last bottle of soda-water last night", and "how regularly round my hat he felt himself when the young 'ooman gave 'em in charge", would appear to refer to the consequences of some stolen joviality on the preceding evening' (*SB, Scenes*, ch. 23).

A common catch-phrase, generally used in self-congratulation, is 'I know wot's o'clock'. It is with these words that Tony Weller expresses his resentment when one of his malapropisms is corrected (*PP*, ch. 43), and Bailey elaborates on it when he is left to watch the drunken Pecksniff, with instructions to summon help if necessary:

> To which Mr Bailey modestly replied that 'he hoped he knowed wot o'clock it wos in gineral, and didn't date his letters to his friends, from Todgers's, for nothing.' (*MC*, ch. 9)

A phrase of similar meaning is 'up to snuff'. Before Sam Weller is engaged by Mr Pickwick, he is clearly rather impressed by Jingle's smartness:

> 'Oh – you remember me, I suppose?' said Mr Pickwick.
> 'I should think so,' replied Sam, with a patronising wink. 'Queer start, that 'ere, but he was one too many for you, warn't he? Up to snuff and a pinch or two over – eh?' (*PP*, ch. 12)

Substandard speech has a number of idiomatic phrases, some of them very expressive, others rather obscure:

> he had had 'the sun very strong in his eyes', [i.e. he had been drunk.] (Swiveller, *OCS*, ch. 2)
>
> He imparted to her the mystery of going the odd man or plain Newmarket. (Swiveller, *OCS*, ch. 36)
>
> requesting him to cut and come again with all speed, [i.e. to go away.] (Chuckster, *OCS*, ch. 38)
>
> I'm afraid I must cut my stick, [i.e. go.] (Chuckster, *OCS*, ch. 40)

Catch-phrases are frequently used to express insult or derision. Sam Weller expresses affectionate contempt for Mr Pickwick's surprise at his anecdotes by asking 'Why where was you half baptized?' (*PP*, ch. 13). Light is thrown on the meaning of this catch-phrase by Mrs Nubbles, who replies to a query of the single gentleman that two of her children are 'only half baptized as yet' (*OCS*, ch. 47). The word *half-baptized* was used in the nineteenth century to describe a child who had been baptized privately or without full rites. The most common motive for such private baptism was fear that the child might die before arrangements could be made for full baptism. Mrs Nubbles's use of the words 'as yet' suggests that she had not obeyed the injunction in *The Book of Common Prayer* that

> if the child, which is after this sort baptized, do afterward live, it is expedient that it be brought into the Church, to the intent that . . . the Congregation may be certified of the true Form of Baptism.

Many of Dickens's low-life characters speak from time to time in a strain of poetical eloquence which, whether true to life or not, is a source of much amusement to the reader. Silas Wegg calls Mr Boffin 'the minion of fortune and the worm of the hour' (*OMF*, Bk II, ch. 7), and he seeks to flatter Mr Venus by describing a simple act in eloquent language:

> 'I have an opinion of you, sir, to which it is not easy to give mouth. Since I called upon you that evening when you were, as I may say, floating your powerful mind in tea, I have felt that you required to be roused with an object.' (Bk II, ch. 7)

Mr Venus himself can be poetical at times: 'the world that appeared so flowery has ceased to blow!' and 'Don't sauce me in the wicious pride of your youth' (Bk I, ch. 7). The eloquence of the last remark derives greater force from the contrast with the professional reflection with which Mr Venus consoles himself: 'You've no idea how small you'd come out if I had the articulating of you.' In *Sketches by Boz* visitors to tea-gardens who swagger about in a dignified manner are described by a satirical observer as 'cutting it uncommon fat' (*Scenes*, ch. 9). The hostler who overcomes Mr Pickwick's reluctance to drive a chaise begins, conventionally enough, by saying of the horse: 'Warrant him quiet, sir; a hinfant in arms might drive him', but he becomes much more expressive when he is asked if the horse will shy:

> 'Shy, sir? – He wouldn't shy if he was to meet a vaggin-load of monkeys with their tails burnt off.' (*PP*, ch. 5)

On the other hand substandard speech is occasionally capable of very emphatic conciseness. When Jo in *Bleak House* is asked if he is hungry, there is real emotion in his reply 'Jist!' (ch. 25). When asked if Captain Hawdon looked very ill and poor, he replies 'O jist!', and there is a certain melancholy pride in his reply to a further question:

'Did he look – not like *you*?' says the woman with abhorrence.
'O not so bad as me,' says Jo. 'I'm a reg'lar one, *I* am!' (ch. 16)

Again in *Bleak House*, in reply to Guppy's appeal whether he has not heard him remark that he can't make Krook out, Young Smallweed replies 'A few' (ch. 20). Sometimes ellipsis leads to ambiguity, as in Mrs Plornish's 'People think more of it than people think' (*LD*, Bk I, ch. 12).

Irony is so much a part of Cockney speech that it becomes almost unconscious. Bailey, in *Martin Chuzzlewit*, makes frequent use of a rather elementary kind:

'Don't their country set a valley on 'em, mind you! Not at all.' (ch. 11)
'An't she a-putting in the water? Oh! not at all, neither.' (ch. 9)

Sometimes irony verges on obscurity. After Bailey has complained to Pecksniff that it is not his fault if Mrs Todgers's lodgers 'consume the pervishuns', she tries to comfort him:

'Surely no one says it is,' said Mercy.
'Don't they though?' retorted the youth. 'No. Yes. Ah. Oh. . . . '
(*MC*, ch. 11)

Cockney wit is seen at its best when it is deflating insincerity and pretentiousness. Mr Mantalini's talk cries out for such deflation, and the scene where the broker's men Scaley and Tix confront the Mantalinis with a writ of execution is one of the most amusing in *Nicholas Nickleby*. Mr Mantalini is not taken by surprise:

'What's the demd total?' was the first question he asked.
'Fifteen hundred and twenty-seven pound, four and ninepence ha'penny,' replied Mr Scaley, without moving a limb.
'The halfpenny be demd,' said Mr Mantalini, impatiently.
'By all means if you vish it,' retorted Mr Scaley; 'and the ninepence.'
'It don't matter to us if the fifteen hundred and twenty-seven pound went along with it, that I know on,' observed Mr Tix. (ch. 21)

One gets the impression that, with a few exceptions such as Tom Pinch, the characters in the novels of Dickens are not great readers. This does not prevent them from being shrewd and quick-witted, and they have developed their own methods of rapid calculation. Mr Boffin's way of working out how much he ought to pay Silas Wegg is unconventional but effective:

'Twopence halfpenny an hour,' said Mr Boffin, taking a piece of chalk from his pocket and getting off the stool to work the sum on the top of it in his own way; 'two long'uns and a short'un – twopence halfpenny; two short'uns is a long'un, and two two long'uns is four long'uns – making five long'uns; six nights a week at five long'uns a night,' scoring them all down separately, 'and you mount up to thirty long'uns. A round'un! Half-a-crown!' (*OMF*, Bk I ch. 5)

One can imagine this calculation being made at great speed, and, this impression is even stronger when Bart Smallweed is asked to calculate the cost of a meal for three:

Mr Smallweed, compelling the attendance of the waitress with one hitch of his eyelash, instantly replies as follows: 'Four veals and hams is three, and four potatoes is three and four, and one summer cabbage is three and six, and three marrows is four and six, and six breads is five, and three Cheshires is five and three, and four pints of half-and-half is six and three, and four small rums is eight and three, and three Pollys is eight and six. Eight and six in half a sovereign, Polly, and eighteen-pence out!' (*BH*, ch. 20)

Failure to understand the meanings of words is a common source of humour in Dickens. Pecksniff provides an example:

'There is no mystery; all is free and open. Unlike the young man in the Eastern tale – who is described as a one-eyed almanack, if I am not mistaken, Mr Pinch?'
'A one-eyed calendar, I think, sir,' faltered Tom.
'They are pretty nearly the same thing, I believe,' said Mr Pecksniff, smiling compassionately; 'or they used to be in my time.' (*MC*, ch. 6)

Mr Pickwick seems to vary a good deal in his ability to understand the slang used by the other characters in the novel. When Bob Sawyer asks him 'Where do you hang out?' he replies that he is 'at present suspended at the George and Vulture' (*PP*, ch. 30). The reader is left to decide for himself whether 'suspended' is the word used by Mr Pickwick in a vain

attempt to imitate the slang of his juniors or whether it is the
author's playful translation of Bob Sawyer's slang into standard
English. It may be that by the time Mr Pickwick is imprisoned
in the Fleet, he has grown accustomed to Sam Weller and
his language, but he there takes in his stride an idiom that is
not without difficulty. He asks Sam Weller how one prisoner
came to be there:

> 'Wy he did wot many men as has been much better know'd has
> done in their time, sir,' replied Sam, 'he run a match agin the
> constable, and vun it.'
> 'In other words, I suppose,' said Mr Pickwick, 'he got into debt.'
> 'Just that, sir,' replied Sam. (*PP*, ch. 41)

When Captain Cuttle is giving instructions to Rob the
Grinder, he is impatient at Rob's failure to understand the
order to 'stand off and on'. He translates it for him:

> 'Here's a smart lad for you!' cried the Captain, eyeing him sternly,
> 'as don't know his own native alphabet! Go away a bit and come
> back alternate – d'ye understand that?' (*DS*, ch. 32)

Mrs Chick fails to understand the words she herself uses:

> 'Lucretia Tox, my eyes are opened to you all at once. The scales,'
> here Mrs Chick cast down an imaginary pair such as are commonly
> used in grocers' shops: 'have fallen from my sight.' (*DS*, ch. 29)

Mrs Nickleby is conscious of only one meaning of the word
'nightcap' and recommends Nicholas to wear one with strings
on the grounds that young men at college are uncommonly
particular about their nightcaps; she adds that the Oxford
nightcaps are quite celebrated for their strength and goodness
(*NN*, ch. 37). Mr Gregsbury pretends not to understand the
word 'gammon' when one of his constituents applies it to his
speech (*NN*, ch. 16). Some of the remarks of the low-life
characters cause delight by their sheer inconsequential nonsense, but the remarks that give most pleasure are those which
are superficially absurd but can be seen on examination to have
a logic of their own. For example, Mrs Blockson, the char-
woman, is resentful when Mortimer Knag addresses her as
'female': 'and with regard to being a female, sir, I should wish
to know what you considered yourself?' (*NN*, ch. 18). Mrs
Blockson has realized that the word 'female' is more than a

colourless word describing the sex of the person to whom it is
applied; it is also a word carrying pejorative implications. That
is the sense in which Mr Knag uses the word, and Mrs Blockson
shows a firm grasp of essentials in seizing upon that aspect of
the word as the basis of her reply. The word *female*, when applied
to a woman still causes resentment today, but in Dickens, and
perhaps to some extent today, the word 'woman' is also
regarded as offensive. When Benjamin Allen remonstrates with
Mrs Raddle, saying 'But you are such an unreasonable woman'
(*PP*, ch. 32), he causes offence. What offends Mrs Raddle is
not the charge of being unreasonable but the accusation that she
is a woman.

As a term of abuse the masculine of *woman* is *fellow*. Fanny
Squeers, resentful at the lack of respect shown to her father at
the Saracen's Head, says indignantly, 'As if he was a feller!'
(*NN*, ch. 39). It is clear that this is a word indicating intense
disapproval. Even the good-humoured Sam Weller takes
umbrage at it: 'a indiwidual in company has called me a feller'
(*PP*, ch. 48), and Sloppy, who is similarly good-humoured as
a rule, breaks off from successive peals of laughter to threaten
to throw Silas Wegg out of the window for applying the word
to him (*OMF*, Bk IV, ch. 14).

Since the characters in novels usually communicate with one
another in speech rather than in writing, there are as a rule few
opportunities for the introduction of substandard spellings into
novels. Two exceptions are the epistolary novel, like Smollett's
Humphry Clinker, and the novel, like many of Thackeray's
minor works, in which one of the low-life characters is the
narrator. A badly-spelt letter by a semi-literate character had
come to be almost a convention in comic novels, and Dickens
tried his hand at it in Fanny Squeers's letter to Ralph Nickleby
(*NN*, ch. 15). Substandard spelling is fairly common in the
novels of Dickens with a function which may seem hard to
justify, where it is simply a rather more phonetic way than the
standard English spelling of representing the normal pronunciation. Examples are innumerable and include *conker* (Mrs Gamp,
MC, ch. 29), *passinger* (Mrs Gamp, *MC*, ch. 40), *vittles*
(Squeers, *NN*, ch. 5), *minnit* (Scaley, *NN*, ch. 21), *bisness*
(Scaley, *NN*, ch. 21), *privilidge* (*PP*, ch. 33). The spelling
sometimes seems arbitrary or mechanical, as in *womin* (Sam

Weller, *PP*, ch. 34), where it is not easy to see why the spelling of the first vowel should be traditional while that of the second is phonetic, or in *vas* (Sam Weller, *PP*, ch. 10) or *vhite* (Sam Weller, *PP*, ch. 10), where the substitution of *v* for *w* leaves other non-phonetic spellings unchanged. Sometimes it is a matter for speculation what pronunciation is represented by an unusual spelling. What, for example, is the significance of the double *v* in Scaley's *govvernor* (*NN*, ch. 21)? Doubling a consonant is often a device to show that the preceding vowel is short, but the preceding vowel here is short in standard English. The double consonant may be simply a warning that the author is aiming at a phonetic spelling and the meaning may be that the *o* represents [ɔ] and not [ʌ]. Caddy Jellyby describes one kind of substandard spelling that Dickens had no doubt seen:

> Caddy told me that her lover's education had been so neglected that it was not always easy to read his notes. She said, if he were not so anxious about his spelling, and took less pains to make it clear, he would do better; but he put so many unnecessary letters into short words, that they sometimes quite lost their English appearance. (*BH*, ch. 14)

In general it may be said that the interest of spelling to the student of substandard speech is peripheral. Spelling presents problems only to the partly literate; the completely illiterate man would be inclined to reply with Mr Boffin:

> 'Why, as to the spelling of it, that's *your* look out.' (*OMF*, Bk I, ch. 8)

Both in his novels and in his letters Dickens occasionally indulged in very bold word-formation. The doctor who brings Little Dorrit into the world in the Marshalsea is described as 'hoarser, puffier, more red-faced, more all-fourey, tobaccoer, dirtier and brandier' than his companion (*LD*, Bk I, ch. 6). The only word here that needs a gloss is *all-fourey*, and this is provided by the context, since the doctor and his fellow-prisoner are playing at all-fours. Occasionally in the narrative part of a novel Dickens resorts to a coinage that involves a play on words. Mr Snagsby's meeting with Jo is described as 'his Joful and woful experience' (*BH*, ch. 19), and here the rhyme with *woful* no doubt prompted the coinage. In the same novel the opinion expressed by Little Swills that the inquest on Captain Hawdon is 'a rummy start' causes the author to say that the speaker's strength lies 'in a slangular direction' (ch. 11). In a letter Dickens writes 'Last night I was unutterably and impossible-to-form-an-idea-of-ably miserable' (Forster, II, 9).

The characters in the novels indulge in similar bold experiments. Silas Wegg, for example, coins the word *milk and water-erily* (*OMF*, Bk IV, ch. 3), and Joe Gargery gives a new look to the word *architectural* by changing it to *architectooralooral* (*GE*, ch. 27). This is an example of the practice of playing tricks with newly-discovered words in which children often indulge and which was a habit of H. G. Wells's Mr Polly.

New words are sometimes coined by the addition of new suffixes to common existing words without any significant change of meaning. Rogue Riderhood produces two examples: *bullyers* 'bullies' (*OMF*, Bk II, ch. 12) and *argueyfied* 'argued' (Bk III, ch. 8). Sometimes a word that looks like a new formation is one that has a long history although it happens to have passed out of use in standard English. An example is Betty Higden's *heighth* 'height' (*OMF*, Bk I, ch. 16).

The most common kind of verbal corruption is that known as malapropism, a name which does too much honour to Mrs Malaprop, who was merely one of a long line of characters in English drama and fiction who have indulged in this practice. Most people who use language beyond their strength are occasionally guilty of malapropisms, but it is not often in real life that we find malapropisms occurring as frequently as they do in the speech of characters like Mistress Quickly and Mrs Malaprop.

The way in which malapropisms come into existence is illustrated when Mr Boffin asks Silas Wegg if he knows the Annual Register:

> 'Know the Animal Register, sir?' returned the Imposter, who had caught the name imperfectly. 'For a trifling wager, I think I could find any Animal in him, blindfold, Mr Boffin.' (*OMF*, Bk III, ch. 6)

The simplest form of malapropism is confusion with a word of completely different meaning, where amusement is caused by the inappropriateness of the word in the context in which it is used. To this class belong Mrs Gamp's use of *mortar* for *motto* (*MC*, ch. 40), Plornish's *manufacturer* for *malefactor* (*LD*, ch. 12), Chollop's *spotted painter in the bush* (*MC*, ch. 33), John Willet's *patrole* for *parole* (*BR*, ch. 29), the coachman's *soap* for *scope* (*PP*, ch. 37), Jo's *consequential* for *consecrated* (*BH*, ch. 16), Kenwigs' *spear* for *sphere* (*NN*, ch. 52), and Tix's reference to a high room in which there was no danger of a man 'bringing his head into contract with the ceiling' (*NN*, ch. 21). Tony Weller makes frequent use of malapropisms. He says *probe* for *probate* (*PP*, ch. 55) and speaks of *a reg'lar prodigy son* (ch. 43) and each time resents correction; elsewhere he uses *referee* for *reverie*, *infernally* for *eternally*, *counsels* for *consols*, and *contract* for *contact* (chs. 51, 52). Mistakes of this kind are not always intended to be funny. When Mrs Boffin says *friendliest* for *most friendless* (*OMF*, Bk IV, ch. 13), she is simply revealing her imperfect command of language, and similarly when the spokesman of the warehousemen of the Cheeryble Brothers makes a speech, he thanks his employers 'for all their goodness as is so constancy a diffusing of itself over everywhere' (*NN*, ch. 37). Confusion between two words is often helped by phonetic resemblance, as in the use of *busk* for *bust* (*LD*, Bk II, ch. 13), which involves the replacement of one voiceless plosive by another. Such amusement as can be derived from mistakes soon palls unless it is reinforced by some double meaning, as when Mrs Gamp uses the language of her profession in saying *aperiently* for *apparently* (*MC*, ch. 49) or speaks of the *Inquisition* as the *Imposition* (*MC*, ch. 29). The most satisfying type of malapropism is one where the word wrongly used fits the context in a ludicrous sense not intended by the speaker, as when Mrs Rogers asks Mrs Raddle, 'Ah, what has decomposed you, ma'am?' (*PP*, ch. 46). There is sometimes unconscious irony, as when the Artful Dodger speaks of 'deformation of character' (*OT*, ch. 43) or when Bumble uses *fondling* for *foundling* (*OT*, ch. 2). This confusion tends to recur in Dickens. Mr Kenwigs, on hearing of the marriage of Mr Lillyvick, says: 'We want no babies here. Take 'em away, take 'em away to the Fondling' (*NN*, ch. 36). Mrs Squeers makes the same mistake when she suggests that Nicholas Nickleby may be a 'fondling'. The author calls attention to the confusion:

Mrs Squeers intended to say 'foundling', but, as she frequently remarked when she made any such mistake, it would be all the same a hundred years hence. (*NN*, ch. 9)

This is only one of several examples of Dickens's determination that his readers should not miss the point of a malapropism. When Mr Boffin speaks of 'a gorging Lord-Mayor's Show' (*OMF*, Bk I, ch. 5), the author adds 'probably meaning gorgeous, but misled by association of ideas'. Similarly when Mrs Todgers says 'She wanted but a pair of wings . . . to be a young syrup', the author explains that she means *sylph* or *seraph* (*MC*, ch. 9). When Mrs Gamp says 'Where's the pelisse?' he adds the gloss 'meaning the constabulary' (*MC*, ch. 40), and when she says 'Now that the marks is off that creetur's face', he interposes 'by which Mrs Gamp is supposed to have meant mask' (*MC*, ch. 49). At Mr Dombey's wedding breakfast a very tall young man is described as already smelling of sherry and as staring at objects without seeing them:

> The very tall young man is conscious of this failing in himself; and informs his comrade that it's his exciseman. The very tall young man would say excitement but his speech is hazy. (*DS*, ch. 31)

Polysyllabic words are the most likely to form the basis of malapropisms. Fanny Squeers has no feeling for John Browdie but 'one of unliquidated pity', where it may be assumed that *unmitigated* was the word aimed at (*NN*, ch. 42).

Since proper names are often unfamiliar to their users, they are especially liable to form the basis of malapropisms. Corruption may take the form of mispronunciation without making the name resemble anything else, as when Susan Nipper changes *Methuselah* to *Meethosalem* (*DS*, ch. 44) or when a sedan-chair man changes *Morpheus* to *Porpus* (*PP*, ch. 36). More often the name is completely or partially assimilated to another proper name. Mrs Snagsby's attitude towards names is a not uncommon one:

> 'My little woman hasn't a good ear for names,' proceeds Mr Snagsby, after consulting his cough of consideration behind his hand, 'and she considered Nemo equally the same as Nimrod.' (*BH*, ch. 11)

Sampson Brass, trying to flatter Quilp by praising his knowledge of natural history, speaks of him as 'quite a Buffoon' (*OCS*, ch. 52). Mr Boffin's interest in Roman history leads him to make many malapropisms out of proper names. He begins by describing the book he has bought as *Decline-and-Fall-Off-The-Rooshan-Empire*, and he goes on to remould the proper names into a more familiar form. *Belisarius* becomes *Bully Sawyers*, *Polybius* becomes *Polly Beeious*, and *Vitellius* becomes *Vittle-us* (and well named too) (*OMF*, Bk I, chs. 5, 15). Proper names can result from the malformation of words and phrases, especially those of learned origin, as in the boy at Mugby's *Wicer Warsaw* for *vice versa* (*CS*, *Mugby Junction*, ch. 3). Riderhood is not alone in transforming *affidavit* into *Alfred David* (*OMF*, Bk I, ch. 12), and an intermediate stage is reached by Squeers with *afferdavid* (*NN*, ch. 56). John Browdie tells the coachman to drive to the Sarah's Head and accepts the correction to Saracen's Head by saying 'Surely. I know'd it was something aboot Sarah's Son's Head' (*NN*, ch. 39). Mrs Gamp speaks of being led 'a Martha to the Stakes' (*MC*, ch. 26), and Mrs Joe Gargery is anxious that Pip shall not be *Pompeyed*, which he understands to mean 'pampered' (*GE*, ch. 7).

The distortion of part of a word may take the form of the substitution of a different prefix or suffix. Examples are: *companionation* for *companionship* (Joe, *GE*, ch. 27), *dispensary* for *dispensation* (Tony Weller, *PP*, ch. 52), *except* for *accept* (Sam Weller, *PP*, ch. 10), *incred'lous* for *incredible* (Sam Weller, *PP*, ch. 33), *indepency* for *independence* (Mrs Gamp, *MC*, ch. 40), *permiscuous* for *promiscuous* (*PP*, ch. 34), *perportion* (Sam Weller, *PP*, ch. 39), *persecution* for *prosecution* (Mrs Gamp, *MC*, ch. 40), *per-vishuns* (Bailey, *MC*, ch. 11), *perwailed* for *prevailed* (Sam Weller, *PP*, ch. 43), *perwent* for *prevent* (Sam Weller, *PP*, ch. 56), *plaintive* for *plaintiff* (*BH*, ch. 11), *proticipate* for *anticipate* (Mrs Gamp, *MC*, ch. 40), *purfession* (*SB*, *Tales*, ch. 10), *purvided* (Kenwigs, *NN*, ch. 52), *purwide* (Sam Weller, *PP*, ch. 12), *relude* for *allude* (Miggs, *BR*, ch. 41), *repeal* for *appeal* (Miggs, *BR*, ch. 19), *repeatually* for *repeatedly* (*BH*, ch. 11), *unpossible* (Sam Weller, *PP*, ch. 38), *unreg'lar* (Mrs Gamp, *MC*, ch. 29). The substitution may be combined with further distortion of the rest of the word, as in Mrs Gamp's *perwisin'* for *providing* (*MC*, ch. 25), or it may produce a different word, like Bumble's *prosecution* for *persecution* (*OT*, ch. 17). When Sam Weller speaks of *a priory 'tachment*

(*PP*, ch. 39), he is confusing *prior* with *priory* and using an aphetic form of *attachment*.

Sometimes unnecessary prefixes and suffixes are added, as in *disrespectable* (Susan Nipper, *DS*, ch. 56), *One-er* (Marchioness, (*OCS*, ch. 58), *disregardless* (Mrs Gamp, *MC*, ch. 40), *abear* (*MC*, ch. 40), *Uncommon Counsellors* (Mrs Gamp, *MC*, ch. 29), *respections* (Pumblechook, *GE*, ch. 12), *summonsizzing* (*BH*, ch. 19). The piling up of suffixes in *Methodistical* (Tony Weller, *PP*, ch. 22) is no doubt intended pejoratively. The burlesque Report of the Second Meeting of the Mudfog Association includes an account of the section devoted to *Umbugology and Ditchwateristics* (*SB*, *Mudfog Papers*).

Malapropisms in Dickens are fairly well distributed among a number of characters. There is no major character who stands out, like Sheridan's Mrs Malaprop, as an unfailing source of supply. A few of the minor characters, however, do have more than their share. Mrs Bloss, who appears in only half a chapter of *Sketches by Boz* (*Tales*, ch. 12) manages to produce *obtrusion* for *seclusion*, *unitarian* for *valetudinarian*, *incited* for *excited*, *pervades* for *provides*, and *creditable* for *credible*.

Malapropisms have something in common with popular etymology; the difference lies in the extent to which the speaker believes that his malformation provides the etymology of the word. Those who indulge in malapropisms are not as a rule very much interested in etymology, but Sam Weller's *have-his-carcase* for *habeas corpus* (*PP*, ch. 43) provides an etymology whose inaccuracy one must regret, whereas Silas Wegg's *atomspear* for *atmosphere* (*OMF*, Bk IV, ch. 3), Joe Gargery's *coddleshell* for *codicil* (*GE*, ch. 57), Jo's *Inkwhich* for *Inquest* (*BH*, ch. 16), Riderhood's *stifficate* for *certificate* (*OMF*, Bk III, ch. 11) and Grummer's *your wash-up* (*PP*, ch. 24), can hardly be regarded as etymologies. The malformation of a word may be due, not to a confusion with other words, but to unfamiliarity with its spelling, thus we get *hottergruff* for *autograph* (*SB*, *Mr Robert Bolton*). When Silas Wegg says 'I only put it ha'porthetically', Mr Venus accepts his etymology but not his argument by replying testily 'Then I'd rather, Mr Wegg, you put it another time penn'orthetically' (*OMF*, Bk II, ch. 7). The false etymology may be revealed only by the spelling. When Mr Boffin tells Silas Wegg that he and his wife 'live on a compittance, under the will of a diseased governor' (*OMF*, Bk I, ch. 5), the first of his two malapropisms suggests an etymology, but there is little difference in pronunciation between *competence* and *compittance*.

The point of a malapropism may be lost to a modern reader if it is based on a topical allusion. Tony Weller says 'If I wos locked up in a fire-proof chest with a patent Brahmin' (*PP*, ch. 52). The allusion is to a Bramah lock, familiar to nineteenth-century readers but not to those of today. Even so, it is a rather erudite malapropism for Tony Weller, who was likely to know more about Bramah locks than about Brahmins.

Malapropisms may be found combined with other features of word-formation, such as back-formation. When Tony Weller uses *leg-at-ease* for *legatee* (*PP*, ch. 55), he is guilty of the same confusion between singular and plural as were those who added the word *pea* to the English language by wrongly assuming that *pease* was plural. Similarly Mrs Raddle's use of *sect* for *sex* (*PP*, ch. 46) may have been helped by the similarity in pronunciation of *sects* and *sex*.[1] When Squeers calls Peg Sliderskew 'this here blessed old dowager petty larcenerer' (*NN*, ch. 57), he is coining a new formation from *larceny*.

Some similarity in pronunciation between the two words confused is necessary to make a malapropism plausible, but the similarity may at one time have been greater than it is today. When Grummer uses *sufferin* for *sovereign* (*PP*, ch. 24), the two words resemble each other enough to make the malapropism credible, but the resemblance may have been even closer, as is evidenced by the spelling *suverins* (*SB, Our Parish*, ch. 5).

Sometimes only part of a word is distorted to produce a blend-word, as in *purple leptic* for *apoplectic* (Joe, *GE*, ch. 7), or *prodigygality* (Pumblechook, *GE*, ch. 58). The result may be a blend-word like *owldacious* (Mrs Gamp, *MC*, ch. 25) beside *outdacious* (Joe, *GE*, ch. 9) or *appleplexy* (Tony Weller, *PP*, ch. 45), *cabrioily* (ch. 46), *reconsize* for *reconcile* (Mrs Gamp, *MC*, ch. 25), *pennywinkles* (Sam Weller, *PP*, ch. 38). Sometimes the blend-word is not a mistake but a deliberate coinage, as when Mr Jarndyce produces the word *Wiglomeration*

---

[1] See Stanley Gerson, 'Dickens's Use of Malapropisms', *The Dickensian*, lxi (1965), 41, and Dobson, § 407.

to describe the processes of the law (*BH*, ch. 8). The best blend-words are those in which both form and meaning of two words are blended, as when Durdles complains of the *tombatism* that he gets from working among the tombs before day-break on winter mornings (*ED*, ch. 4), and Durdles quite rightly contradicts Mr Sapsea, who tells him that he means rheumatism. Micawber's servant, who describes herself as 'a Orfling' (*DC*, ch. 11) is no doubt combining *ophan* with the suffix -*ling* found in such words as *fledgling*. The reconciliation of Mr Lillyvick with the Kenwigs family produces two blend-words. Such a feeling of vengeance comes over Mr Kenwigs 'as no language can depicter' (*depict* and *picture*), while Mrs Kenwigs declares that her 'feelings have been lancerated' (*lance* and *lacerated*) (*NN*, ch. 52). When Squeers says *substracted* (*NN*, ch. 57) he is maltreating the word *subtract* as others have done, possibly by confusing it with words like *distract*. Other examples are *terrimengious* (Silas Wegg, *OMF*, Bk IV, ch. 3), *squench* (Marchioness, *OCS*, ch. 58), *carrywan* for *caravan* (Sam Weller, *PP*, ch. 24), *gashliness*, Mrs Wickam's term to describe the dullness of her life (*DS*, ch. 8), and *feariocious* (*BH*, ch. 11). Sam Weller's *prewailance* (*PP*, ch. 42) can be regarded as a blend of *prevail* and *prevalence*. Mr Carker does not normally use substandard speech, but he produces a blend-word of *beldam* and *Bedlamite* when he addresses a fortune-teller as *Beldamite* (*DS*, ch. 27). One common type of blend-word is produced by selecting certain sounds from one or more words and re-arranging them with additions to produce a new word. It is by some such process that the common word *blizzard* was introduced into American English in comparatively recent times, and by a similar process Lamps in *Mugby Junction* (*CS*) creates *skirmishun* for an excursion train. Such distortion of words was in the time of Dickens, as it is today, a common type of substandard pleasantry. When Doctor Marigold uses the word *melancholy*, he adds a note: 'N.B. In the Cheap Jack patter, we generally sound it lemonjolly, and it gets a laugh' (*CS*, *Doctor Marigold*, ch. 1). Deputy's *Kinfreederal* for *Cathedral* (*ED*, ch. 18) contains enough material to keep a philologist happy for a long time. The insertion of *n* may have something in common with the process by which *passager* became *passenger* and *nihtegale* became *nightingale*. The *e* that has developed as a glide between *d* and *r* has its parallel in the frequently-heard pronunciations *umberella* and *Henery*. The use of *f* for *th* results from the similarity in sound of the two voiceless fricatives, just as the similarity between the corresponding voiced fricatives causes many speakers, especially Cockneys, to use [v] for [ð] in words like *the* and *with*. All these phonetic considerations combine with the influence of quite unrelated words like *kin* and *free* and no one can say exactly how much of the resultant word is due to phonetic changes and how much to blending.

The curtailment of words by the loss of lightly-stressed syllables has for long been common in English, especially in substandard English, and Swift railed against the practice. Some of the curtailments that he deplored, such as *poz* for *positive*, have passed out of use; others, like *mob* for *mobile vulgus*, have come to be accepted as normal. There are many examples in Dickens. *'Tiser* and *'Tizer* are used for *Advertiser* (*SB, Scenes*, ch. 2; Sam Weller, *PP*, ch. 44), and the Marchioness puzzles Dick Swiveller by telling him: 'they've been a tizing of me' (*OCS*, ch. 64).[1] Other examples are: *'pike* for *turnpike* (Tony Weller, *PP*, ch. 56), *'pend* for *depend* (Tony Weller, *PP*, ch. 45), *on spec* (Sam Weller, *PP*, ch. 34), *'cause* (Sam Weller, *PP*, ch. 43), *gents* for *gentlemen* (Tigg, *MC*, ch. 7), *'ticing* (*SB, Scenes*, ch. 5).

Many English adverbs, such as *always*, *besides* and *sometimes*, end in -*s*. On the analogy of such adverbs, substandard speech has formed several other adverbs ending in -*s*: *anywheres* Lillyvick, *NN*, ch. 14), *leastways* (John Chivery, *LD*, Bk II, ch. 27), *likeways* (Mrs Gamp, *MC*, ch. 25), *otherways* (Mrs Gamp, *MC*, ch. 25), *otherways than* 'unless' (Miggs, *BR*, ch. 7), *everyways* (Jo, *BH*, ch. 19), *anyways* (Snagsby, *BH*, ch. 42), *somewheres* (Jo, *BH*, ch. 31), *nohows* (Cuttle, *DS*, ch. 56), *anyveres* (Tony and Sam Weller, *PP*, ch. 52), *noweres* (Sam Weller, *PP*, ch. 47). The genitive ending in -*s*, which was the origin of the adverbial -*s*, is found in many surnames, such as *Brooks* and *Wills*, and Mrs Gamp extends the ending to *Sweedlepipes* (*MC*, ch. 49).

[1] Gerson (§ 9.4) takes *a tizing* to mean 'teasing', but it suits both context and phonology better to regard it as an apheptic form of *advertizing* (cf. Gerson § 47.1).

4

REGIONAL DIALECTS

There is a marked contrast between Dickens's thorough knowledge of substandard London English and his much more superficial acquaintance with English regional dialects. One result of this difference, as will be seen from the examples quoted later in this chapter, is that when he sets out to represent a regional dialect, rural characteristics are outnumbered by substandard non-regional features.

Dickens's rather sketchy use of regional features does not arise from lack of interest; it is the natural result of his way of life. He spent much more of his life in London than in any country district. It is clear that he took a keen interest in the variations of dialect that came his way. When he went to America he was very sensitive to the differences between British and American English and he introduced many Americanisms into *American Notes* and *Martin Chuzzlewit*. In his travels in the British Isles he was quick to notice regional differences and in his letters to Forster he quoted specimens of the dialect of Wigton and parts of Ireland (Forster, VIII, 1, 4).

There are three English regions whose dialects are represented in some detail in the novels of Dickens: East Anglia in *David Copperfield*, Yorkshire in *Nicholas Nickleby* and Lancashire in *Hard Times*. To these may be added the dialects of the United States used in *American Notes* and in the American chapters of *Martin Chuzzlewit*. Brief specimens of local dialect occur from time to time in the other novels. The Scottish doctor in *Bleak House* uses expressions like *nae gude*, *tak' my depairture* and *Air you in the maydickle prayfession?* (ch. 11). In *Great Expectations* Mrs Joe speaks of *meshes*, and Pip, as narrator, adds 'We always used that name for marshes in our country' (ch. 2).

East Anglia

The Yarmouth chapters of *David Copperfield* are rich in dialect. Mr Peggotty is the chief dialect speaker, but his nephew Ham, Mrs Gummidge and Barkis all make a contribution. The dialect forms occur in chapters 3, 5, 7, 30 to 32, 40, 46, 51 and 63.

Vocabulary. Distinctive vocabulary is fairly common in these chapters and Dickens is faced with the problem of making sure that readers with no knowledge of the dialect understand the meaning of the dialect words. The context usually makes the meaning clear but, when any doubt is left, Dickens does not hesitate to introduce a gloss into the text, putting it into the mouth of David, the supposed narrator. Mr Peggotty describes David and Em'ly as 'like two young mavishes', and his description is followed by the comment 'I knew this meant, in our local dialect, like two young thrushes, and received it as a compliment' (ch. 3). In the same chapter Mr Peggotty addresses Mrs Gummidge as 'old Mawther', and this is followed by the comment '(Mr Peggotty meant old girl)'. When Mr Peggotty visits David at Salem House, he says 'I'm a reg'lar Dodman, I am'. David then does his duty as glossator by adding 'by which he meant snail, and this was an allusion to his being slow to go' (ch. 7).

Some of the dialect words used in *David Copperfield* are peculiar to East Anglia; others are found in many parts of England. Sometimes they are printed with an initial capital to call attention to their dialectal status. Some of these words are common standard English words used in dialects with a difference of form, function or meaning; others are words that do not occur in standard English. Examples are:

afeerd 'afraid'
afore 'before'
arrize oneself 'to make up one's mind'
bacheldore 'bachelor'
bahd's neezing 'bird's nesting'
Bein', *Beein'* 'home'
bor, term of endearment to a child
clicketten 'chattering'
dame, term of endearment to an elderly woman

fisherate 'to provide'

gorm 'damn' ('I'm Gormed – and I can't say no fairer than that', Mr Peggotty, ch. 63)

inquiration 'enquiry'

kiender 'kind of'

lass, term of endearment to a girl

lorn 'forlorn'

lugs 'boats'

Mawther, term of endearment to a woman

merry-go-rounder 'figure expressive of a complete circle of intelligence' (Mr Peggotty, ch. 7). This may perhaps be regarded as a feature of Mr Peggotty's idiolect.

mort 'large amount'

muck 'dirt'

nowt 'nothing'

oncommon 'very well'

pound 'to wager'

sermuchser 'so much so'

what-all 'everything'

wheer all 'everywhere'

wimicking 'crying'

Pronunciation. Mr Peggotty's *wured* and *wureld* suggest a strongly-rolled *r* in words where the *r*, followed by a consonant, is silent in standard English. Intervocalic fricative [ð] has become a plosive in Ham Peggotty's *furder* and Mr Peggotty's *furdest* as it has done in standard English *burden* (OE *byrðen*). Mr Peggotty's *fur* for *for* is probably to be explained as a lightly-stressed form. The guard of the stage-coach which takes David from Yarmouth to London on his way to Salem House uses a rounded variety of *u* in *yoongster, Bloonderstone, Sooffolk*. Barkis speaks of *stage-cutch* and *apple-paisties*. Corresponding to the [ɔ:] of standard English *thought* and *naught* there is probably a diphthong in Peggotty's *thowt* and Mrs Gummidge's *nowt*. The *ow* in Mr Peggotty's *wownd* and *fower* probably represents [au].

Syntax. Redundant personal pronouns are a feature of many regional dialects, and Mr Peggotty provides us with a particularly good example. After producing 'two prodigious lobsters, and an enormous crab, and a large canvas bag of shrimps', which he modestly describes as 'a little relish with your wittles', he makes it clear that they have been boiled:

'The old Mawther biled 'em, she did. Mrs Gummidge biled 'em. Yes,' said Mr Peggotty, slowly, who I thought appeared to stick to the subject on account of having no other subject ready, 'Mrs Gummidge, I do assure you, she biled 'em.' (ch. 7)

An idiomatic use of *fare* occurs more than once: Mr Peggotty asks David 'How do you fare to feel about it?' and again 'I wouldn't fare to feel comfortable to try and get his mind upon't' (ch. 46). Ham says 'I fare to feel sure on't' (ch. 51).

The following features of phonology, accidence and syntax are paralleled in the speech of low-life London characters. Paragraph references are to the Appendix.

1. Change of final [ŋ] to [ŋk] (§ 2): *anythink, nothink, thinks* 'things'.

2. Change of final [ŋ] to [n] (§ 3): *Barkis is willin', writin', goin', waitin'*. All these examples are used by Barkis.

3. Loss of initial *h* (§ 17): *art* 'heart', *Am* 'Ham'.

4. Loss of *f* in *arter* (§ 20): *arter she's married and gone*.

5. Loss of *w* before vowels in lightly-stressed syllables (§ 21): *allus* 'always', *summat* 'somewhat'.

6. Loss of medial *l* (§ 22): *on'y*.

7. Loss of final consonant (§ 24): *kep*.

8. Use of indefinite article *a* before initial vowel (§ 25): *a Angel, a answer, a inn*.

9. Assimilation of *nd* to *nn* (§ 26): *unnerstan', unnerneath* beside *drownded*.

10. Use of [iː], spelt *ee*, in *obleege* (§ 33): *I'm much obleeged to her*.

11. Variation between *er* and *ar* (§ 40): *arnest, book-larning* beside *fur* 'far'.

12. Raising of the first element of the diphthong [ɛə] (§ 41): *theer*.

13. Change of [ɔi] to [ai] (§ 42): *pinted*.

14. Change of [juː] to [uː] (§ 43): *dooty, dootiful*.

15. Lengthening and shortening of vowels (§ 44): *leetle, babby, dorgs, hosses*.

16. Change of lightly-stressed [juː] to [i] or [ə] (§ 51): *porkypine, Thankee*.

17. Variation of stress from that current today (§ 55): *contrairy*.

18. Loss of medial vowel (§ 57): *nat'ral, Em'ly, fam'ly*.

19. Change of lightly-stressed [ou] to [ə] (§ 58): *winder, widder*.

20. Analogical comparison of adjectives (§ 66): *littlest*.

21. Personal pronouns with final *-n* (§ 69): *I'm a friend of your'n, it ain't no fault of yourn*.

22. Strong past participle without *-en* (§ 72): *fear of not being forgiv*.

23. Use of preterite for past participle (§ 73): *I think theer is something I could wish said or wrote*.

24. Survival of vowel of strong preterite plural (§ 74): *I doen't know . . . when her 'art begun to fail her, I writ a letter*.

25. Use of past participle for preterite (§ 75): *That done my Em'ly good*.

26. Apparent use of present for preterite (§ 76): *you was but the heighth of the littlest of these, when I first see you; she always giv Em'ly flowers; She come to London; Ever so fur she run*.

27. Use of weak forms of strong verbs (§ 77): *know'd pret., know'd pp., growed pp.*

28. Confusion between strong verbs and their weak causatives (§ 78): *If her uncle was turned out of house and home, and forced to lay down in a dyke, He'll set and talk to her*.

29. False concord (§ 82): *afore we parts, I takes, I touches of 'em*.

30. Double negatives (§ 83): *Money's of no use to me no more*.

31. Use of adjective as adverb (§ 85): *I thank Him hearty for having guided of me, I touches of 'em as delicate as if they was our Em'ly*.

32. Use of *that there* (§ 87): *that there blue water, that theer spotted snake*.

33. Use of indefinite article with *many* (§ 88): *It was a dark night with a many stars a shining*.

34. Use of objective pronoun as subject (§ 89): *Them belonging to the house would have stopped her*.

35. Use of the preposition *on* for *of* (§ 91): *all on us*.

36. Use of *for to* with the infinitive (§ 93): *my house ain't much for to see*.

37. Use of *as* for *that* (§ 97): *I have felt so sure as she was living*.

38. Construction of verbs with *of* (§ 104): *I'm expecting of her; the vine leaves as she see at the winder . . . contradicted of her.*

39. Use of verbal noun with *a* (§ 103): *She's a looking at it, Em'ly's a coming, what little needs a doing of.*

40. Use of *as* for *which* (§ 96): *everything in her life as ever had been, or as ever could be.*

Yorkshire

One of the most sustained attempts to portray a regional dialect in the novels of Dickens is in the speech of the Yorkshireman John Browdie in *Nicholas Nickleby*. Most of the examples which follow are from his speech and are to be found in chapters 9, 13, 39, 42, 45 and 64. A few are from the speech of the guard on the stage-coach which takes Nicholas and Squeers to Yorkshire (ch. 6).

1. Several words are used which are especially common in Northern dialects, such as *lass, gang* 'go', *nowt* 'nothing', *reckon* 'think', *gin* 'if', *na' but* 'only', *yon* adj. and pron. 'that', *afeared, daft, till* 'to'.

2. *t* is sometimes replaced by *th* and *tt* by *tth*. These spellings probably represent the replacement of an alveolar [t] by a dental consonant approaching [θ] in its place of formation. Examples are: *matther, schoolmeasther, monsther, thried, betther, threat* 'treat', *efther, pasthry, garthers, misther, wather* (cf. Gerson § 40.5).

3. A *v* is sometimes inserted to avoid hiatus between a word ending with a vowel and a following word beginning with a vowel.[1] Examples are: *intiv'em, tiv'ee, tiv'un.* The form with *v* occurs, possibly by analogy, before a consonant in *divn't.*

4. ME [iː] is diphthongized to [ɔi] by an independent change, as in *loike, soizable, foind, broide, troifling, noice* (cf. Gerson § 13.5).

5. When ME [iː] was followed by [çt], spelt *ght*, three developments are found:

(a) The most common development is identical with the

---

[1] See Harold Orton, *The Phonology of a South Durham Dialect* (Kegan Paul, 1933), § 120.

independent development of [iː]: *loight an' toight, soight, loight* sb.

(b) [iː] remains, spelt *ee*, as in *reeght, neeght*. This is the usual Northern development.

(c) The long vowel becomes a diphthong with a front half-open first element, as in *neight*. This is the usual Midland development (cf. Gerson § 13.3.2).

6. ME ([uː] remains, spelt *oo*, instead of being diphthongized to [au], as in RP. Examples are *aboot, noo, hoo, ootside, proodest, doon, toon, pooder* (cf. Gerson § 14.3).

7. In RP there are two sounds represented by the spelling *u* (sometimes replaced by *o*): a close rounded vowel [u], as in *pull*, and a more centralized vowel [ʌ], as in *run*. In Browdie's speech, as in many north-country dialects, both sounds seem to have fallen together as a back close rounded vowel. The usual spelling is *oo*, which does not necessarily imply lengthening, but rather the vowel-sound of RP *book*. Examples are: *anoother, bootuns, coom* (beside *cums*), *dooble-latthers, doozen, droonk, hoongry, loonching, moonths, moothers, oop, room* adj., *snoog, soomat* (beside *summat*), *soop, t'oother, yoong, yoongster*.

8. In Middle English, short vowels were lengthened in open syllables of words which were then disyllabic. In many regional dialects, and occasionally in standard English, short vowels have been restored by analogy with monosyllabic or trisyllabic forms in which no lengthening took place. Forms with short vowels are common in Browdie's speech; examples are *brokken, shak, tak, takken, wakken* (cf. Gerson § 19.21). On the other hand, short *a* is sometimes lengthened in monosyllables, as in *wa'at, ba'ad*, and long *a*, instead of being shortened, has been diphthongized in *feyther* and *godfeyther*.

9. ME [oː] has a twofold development. It is represented by *ea* in *deane, dean't, eneaf, wean't*, but by *oa* in *doant*. The front vowel which has given *ea* has been shortened to *i* in *dinnot*. The Scots development to a front close rounded vowel is found in *bluid* (cf. Gerson § 5.4).

10. ME [ɔː] is represented by *oa* in *boan, noa*, but the Northern form, in which OE *ā* has not been rounded, is found in *gane*, and *ea* is found in *neane*. The *w* that develops before initial [ɔː] (or its development) in many North Midland dialects is found in *whoam*, where it is probable that initial [h] had disappeared in pronunciation, and the more northerly development of a front semivowel is found in *yan*.

11. ME [a:] (in open syllables and French loan-words) appears as *ea*, as in *feace, schoolmeasther, sheame-feaced* (cf. Gerson 15.8.1).

12. ME [e] is lowered in *dooble-latthers, prasant, vary*.

13. A number of common English words have Northern variants, developed as the result of a variety of sound-changes. Examples are *wur* 'was', *theer* 'there', *sike* 'such', *'ooman* 'woman', *warking* 'working'.

14. The definite article is often reduced to *t'*, and when this occurs before a word beginning with *t* or *d*, it may disappear or be replaced by a pause, which is often imperceptible to south-country ears, as in *I heerd door shut*.

15. Various dialectal forms of pronouns are used. *'ee* is used for *you* in both the subjective and objective cases, as in *did 'ee though?* and *tellee* 'I tell you'. *Thee* is used as the second person singular subjective pronoun, as in *thee'lt pay me*. The same form with a different origin, is used for the possessive pronoun, as in *Give us thee hond* beside *at thy loodgin'*. *A* is used as a lightly-stressed form of *I*, as in *a've heerd*.

Many features are primarily substandard, though sometimes they are found also in regional dialects:

1. Change of final [ŋ], usually spelt *ng*, to [n] (§ 3): *coaxin', deein', puttin', squeedgin', weddin', wheedlin'*.

2. Loss of *f* in *arter* (§ 20).

3. Loss of medial *l* (§ 22): *on'y, a'most*.

4. Loss of final consonants (§ 24): *wi', ha' done*. The loss of final *l* in *a'* and *ca'* may be either substandard or regional (cf. Lancashire Regional Features *l* below).

5. Disappearance of *d* after *n* (§ 26): *stan', un'erstan', Lunnon*.

6. Rounding of [a] to [ɔ] (§ 37): *dom'd, glod, hond, thot*, This feature is so common in Browdie's speech that it may perhaps be regarded as a feature of regional dialect.

7. The lengthening of [i] has parallels in substandard speech (§ 44), but is so common in Browdie's speech that it may perhaps be regarded as regional: *feeckle, leetle, skeen, deedn't*.

8. Aphesis (§ 47): *'stead, 'joy* 'enjoy', *drat* 'God rot'.

Lancashire

Stephen Blackpool and Rachael, in *Hard Times*, speak with a strongly-marked regional dialect. Many of the features of this dialect can be paralleled in north-country speech today, but some of them seem to be of doubtful authenticity. The dialectal forms occur in Book I, chapters 10, 11, 13, Book II, chapters 4, 5, 6, and Book III, chapters 4, 6.

Vocabulary. The dialect vocabulary in *Hard Times* is strongly marked, and some of the dialect words, like *haply, mun* and *sin,* cj., occur many times. The following are the chief north-country words used in the novel.

afore 'before'
ahind, ahint 'behind'
along of 'on account of'
dree 'dreary, painful'
ere 'before'
fewtrils 'furniture'
fratch 'quarrel'
fro 'from'
haply 'perhaps'
har-stone 'hearth'
hetter 'violent'. Slackbridge is twice described as 'over hetter'.
hey-go-mad 'enthusiastic'
hottering 'raving'
humanly 'human'
Hummobee 'humming bee'
lad is not confined to young people. It is the term by which Rachael affectionately greets Stephen.
lass is used by Stephen to greet Rachael and to describe his wife when a girl.
leetsome 'glad'
missus (as term of address, not followed by a proper name)
moydert 'confused'
mun 'must'
na' 'not'
nowt 'nothing'
sin cj. 'since', adv. 'ago'
sure 'certainly'

Dialect vocabulary often includes in everyday use words which in standard English are regarded as poetical. Thus, Stephen describes his wife, with the understatement of which dialect speakers are fond, as having been 'pretty enow', and when remonstrating with Bounderby's mother, he bids her 'hearken'. There are compound words, some of which occur also in standard English, such as *overmuch*. When Stephen says that his wife was 'twenty nighbut' he uses *nighbut* in the sense 'almost'; he also uses the much more common north-country word *nobbut* 'only'. Some compound words are formed by joining together words which are not joined in standard English: *nommore, sommuch, dunnot, dunno, donno* 'don't know', *Gonnows* 'God knows'.

In word-formation we find the substitution of one prefix for another, as in *unpossibility*. The addition of adverbial -*s* to a word that has no -*s* in standard English is seen in *somehows*. Both these features are found in substandard speech. The form *heighth*, on the other hand, has parallels in literary English. It shows the retention of the consonant found in OE *hīehðu*, which in standard English has become *t*.

Features of Stephen's speech which seem to be intended as regional include the following:

1. The disappearance of final -*l*, as in *aw* 'all', *fearfo'*, *dreadfo'*, *wishfo'*, *wa'*, *faithfo'*. The loss of *l* in *faw'in* 'falling' and *sma'est* may be analogical.

2. The loss of *l* before a consonant. When the preceding vowel is [a], the *l*, before disappearing, causes it to become [ɔ:], as in standard English; examples are *awmost, fawt*. When the preceding vowel is [ɔ], the *l* is vocalized to [u], spelt *w*, which combines with the preceding vowel to form a diphthong, as in *owd, gowd, towd, howd*.

3. The use of a voiced plosive [g] in words which in standard English have the affricate [dʒ]. The plosive in such words is common in northern dialects as a result of Scandinavian influence. Stephen has *brigg* 'bridge'.

4. The replacement of an alveolar [t] by a dental consonant, suggested by the spelling *matther* (cf. Gerson 40.5).

5. The vocalization of medial [v] to [w] in *ower*.

6. The insertion of the semi-vowel [j] before a vowel

which became initial as a result of loss of *h*-, in *year* 'hear'.

7. The change of [sk] to [ʃ], spelt *sh*, in *ashes* 'asks', used by the chairman of the meeting which condemns Stephen.

8. The unvoicing of final [d] in the group [ld] found in *chilt*.

9. The loss of medial [ð] in *wi'out*.

10. The use of a close rounded vowel [u] (usually spelt *oo*) instead of the vowel [ʌ] found in standard English *come*. Examples are *coom* pp., *discoosed*, *doon*, *amoong*, *anoother*, *soom*, *coop*, *coompany*, *tooches*.

11. The change of *o* to *u* in *awiung* 'along', used by Stephen and the chairman of the meeting of workers. This pronunciation is found in RP *among*, where it is generally thought to have been introduced from a regional dialect (cf. Wright *EHNEG* § 139, Gerson § 4.5).

12. The use of a diphthong in *nowt* 'naught' and *thowt* 'thought' in place of RP [ɔ:] (cf. Gerson § 10.5).

13. The use of *o* in *monny* and *onny*. RP *any* and *many* are anomalous in that their spellings are not derived from the forms that have given their pronunciations. Stephen's *monny* is regularly developed from OE *monig* while his *onny*, also a common northern form, probably owes its stem-vowel to the analogy of *monny*.

14. The use of the spelling *e*, which may represent [ə], in place of *i* in lightly-stressed syllables: *promess* 'promise', *hard-worken* 'hard-working', *likens* 'likings'.

15. The use of the diphthong [iə] in place of [ɛə]: *theer*, *wheer*, *wheerever*.

16. The reduction of the definite article to *th'*. In some northern dialects it is reduced to *th'* before vowels and to *t'* before consonants, but Stephen says *nowt o' th' kind* and his wife says *Come awa' from th' bed*. Other examples are *th' papers*, *th' side*, *th' time*, *th' chance*, *th' question*, *th' kind*, *th' mischeevous strangers*. Reduction to *t* is less common, and the *t* in *t'oother* is probably from the final consonant of *that*.

17. The frequent use of the strong past participle ending in *-en*. This has been preserved in some strong verbs in standard English, especially when they are used as adjectives, such as *frozen*, *bounden*, and in the past participles of some verbs originally weak, such as *hidden*, but the number of examples in

Hard Times is very large and they do not all seem very convincing. Some of these past participles, like *ett'n, droonken, growen, gotten*, are from strong verbs; others, like *enden, ridden* (beside *ridded*) 'rid', *heern* 'heard', *overlooken, toil'n, pray'n, suspect'n, lov'n, expecten, looken, outcasten*, are from weak verbs. Several participles have strong endings added to forms which are already preterites or past participles: *had'n, took'n, lef'n, broughten, cud'n*. Even when *-ed* is not the participial ending, it is liable to be replaced by *-(e)n*. Stephen uses a comparative form *lighter heart'n*, derived from *light-hearted*, where *-ed* is from OE *-ede*, a suffix used to form adjectives from nouns. Similarly the adjective *fit* 'well adapted', is treated as a past participle to give *fitten*. The ending *-n* is used in other verbal forms, such as the present participle: *He were ett'n and drinking*. It is not certain whether *setten* and *seet'n* are present participles 'sitting' or participial adjectives 'seated' when Stephen says: *Let me see thee setten by the bed*, and *thou didst work for her seet'n all day long in her little chair*, but *seet'n* must be a past participle when he says: *I, that ha' ett'n an' droonken wi' 'em, an' seet'n wi' 'em*. The ending *-n* is used to form preterites: *When I got thy letter, I easily believe that what the yoong ledy sen and done to me, was one*. Final *-n* is sometimes found, with more historical justification, in the infinitive: *I ha' nowt to sen*.

18. The preservation of *-(e)n* as a plural ending in nouns which in standard English have analogical plurals in *-s: een* 'eyes', *eern* 'ears'.

19. The use of *-seln* in reflexive pronouns, which in standard English have *-self* or *-selves* as their second element: *myseln, herseln, himseln, ourseln, themseln*.

20. Unusual forms in the comparison of adjectives. *Liefer* 'rather' is an archaic form preserved in many regional dialects. *Worsen* is used as a superlative: *from bad to worse, from worse to worsen*.

21. The use of the second person singular of the personal pronoun especially among intimates: *thou mak'st, thou knowest, thou art not the man*.

22. The use of *for that* with the meaning 'because': *when they dunnot agree, for that their tempers is ill-sorted; for that she worked with me when we were girls both; I coom fer that I were*

sent for. This construction is found in standard English but is thought of as rather archaic or literary.

23. The use of *right* as an adverb with the meaning 'very': *I . . . am right sure and certain.*

Many of the features of Stephen's speech are primarily substandard:

1. The change of the velar nasal [ŋ], spelt *ng*, to the alveolar nasal [n] finally in lightly-stressed syllables (§ 3): *wakin', dreamin', shinin', bein', reg'latin', draggin', reproachin', dealins, openin'.*

2. The change of the affricate [tʃ], from earlier [tj], to [t] (§ 9): *fortnet* 'fortunate', *misfortnet, unnat'rally.*

3. The loss of pre-vocalic [w] in lightly-stressed syllables (§ 21): *awlus, forrard.*

4. The loss of medial [t] when preceded by another consonant (§ 23): *genelman, Eas'r, Chrisen* 'Christian'.

5. The loss of final consonants, especially in lightly-stressed words (§ 24): *fro', o', fra', ha'* 'have', *kep', wi'* 'with'.

6. The loss of the final -*n* of the indefinite article, even when the next word begins with a vowel (§ 25): *A unkind husband.*

7. Variation between [nd] and [n] (§ 26): *unnerstan'in, stan'* 'stand', *an'* 'and'.

8. The use of *i* for *u* (§ 30): *sitch-like.*

9. Variations in vowel-length, sometimes accompanied by a difference in the quality of the vowel (§ 44): *yo* 'you', *spok'n, lickly, fok* 'folk', *spit* 'spite', *yor* 'your', *hed* 'heard', *nobbody.* Some of these variations are features of regional dialect, as, for example, *mak, tak, weel.* On *weel* (also frequently used by Browdie in *Nicholas Nickleby*) see Gerson § 2.5.

10. Aphesis, the loss of a lightly-stressed initial syllable (§ 47): *'Sizes* 'Assizes', *'deed* 'indeed', *times* 'sometimes', *'stead* 'instead', *fectionate* 'affectionate', *ceptin* 'except', *'bout* 'about'. A group of words belonging to the same breath-group is treated as a single word, and so we find the vowel of *it* disappearing in *'t happens, 'twill, 'ta'nt, 't might.*

11. The change of the prefix *un-* to *on-* (§ 48): *onquiet, onmade.*

12. Reduction of [ou] to [ə] in lightly-stressed syllables (§ 58): *widder.*

E

13. Uninflected plurals of nouns, especially after numerals (§ 63): *twenty time, these five year, a dozen year.*

14. The use of preterites for past participles (§ 73): *I ha' fell, I should'n ha' been . . . so mistook.*

15. Apparent use of present for preterite of strong verbs (§ 76): *coom* 'came' (OE *cōm*); standard English *came* is analogical.

16. Addition of weak endings to stems of strong verbs (§ 77): *If Mr Bounderby had ever know'd me right.*

17. Confusion between strong verbs and their weak causatives (§ 78): *laying down and dying.*

18. Lack of concord between subject and verb (§ 82): *I wishes, they has, their tempers is ill-sorted, they taks, the mills is awlus a-goin, the people's leaders is bad, There have been a meeting to-night where he have been spoken of in the same shameful way.*

19. Double and triple negatives (§ 83): *they never works us no nigher to ony dis'ant object, I hope I never had nowt to say, not fitten for a born lady to year.*

20. The use of *for to* with the infinitive (§ 93): *I . . . should fail fur to stan by 'em; fur to weave; agreeing fur to mak one side unnat'rally awlus and for ever right.*

21. The use of *as* as a relative referring to both persons and things (§ 96): *'Tis them as is put ower me; They taks such as offers; What were it, sir, as yo were pleased to want wi' me?*

22. Construction of verbs with *of* (§ 104): *Look how you considers of us, I were never good at showin o't, though I ha had'n my share in feeling o't.*

America

When Dickens went to America he did not at first think that the differences between British and American English were very great. He wrote to Forster:

> but for an odd phrase now and then – such as *Snap of cold weather;* a *tongue-y man* for a talkative fellow; *Possible?* as a solitary interrogation; and *Yes?* for indeed – I should have marked, so far, no difference whatever between the parties here and those I have left behind. (Forster, III, 2)

He soon noticed other American words and phrases and amused himself by incorporating many of them in a letter to Forster describing the steamer that brought him to America.

> The daily difference in her rolling, as she burns the coals out, is something absolutely fearful. Add to all this, that by day and night she is full of fire and people, that she has no boats, and that the struggling of that enormous machinery in a heavy sea seems as though it would rend her into fragments – and you may have a pretty considerable damned good sort of a feeble notion that it don't fit nohow; and that it a'nt calculated to make you smart, overmuch; and that you don't feel 'special bright; and by no means first rate; and not at all tonguey (or disposed for conversation); and that however rowdy you may be by natur', it does you up com-plete, and that's a fact; and makes you quake considerable, and disposed toe damn the engine! – All of which phrases, I beg to add, are pure Americanisms of the first water. (Forster, III, 3)

His comments on American English become increasingly unfriendly. After failing to receive in the spirit in which it was intended the compliment that his wife's manner of speaking was such that she might have been taken for an American anywhere, he goes on to mention the things that had struck him most forcibly about the American variety of English:

> I need not tell you that out of Boston and New York a nasal drawl is universal, but I may as well hint that the prevailing grammar is also more than doubtful; that the oddest vulgarisms are received idioms; that all the women who have been bred in slave-states speak more or less like negroes, from having been constantly in their childhood with black nurses; and that the most fashionable and aristocratic (these are two words in great use), instead of asking you in what place you were born, enquire where you 'hail from!!' (Forster, III, 6)

Many of the Americanisms which Dickens mentions in his letters are later incorporated in the American chapters of *Martin Chuzzlewit*, but he is able to spread himself more in his letters. His comments on the word *fix* show that he had the instincts of a lexicographer:

> I told you of the many uses of the word 'fix'. I ask Mr Q on board a steamboat if breakfast be nearly ready, and he tells me yes he should think so, for when he was last below the steward was 'fixing the tables' – in other words, laying the cloth. When we have been writing, and I beg him (do you remember anything of my love of order, at this distance of time?) to collect our papers, he

answers that he'll 'fix 'em presently'. So when a man's dressing he's 'fixing' himself, and when you put yourself under a doctor he 'fixes' you in no time. T'other night, before we came on board here, when I had ordered a bottle of mulled claret and waited some time for it, it was put on table with an apology from the landlord (a lieutenant-colonel) that 'he fear'd it wasn't fixed properly'. And here, on Saturday morning, a Western man, handing the potatoes to Mr Q at breakfast, enquired if he wouldn't take some of 'these fixings' with his meat. (Forster, III, 5)

When Dickens describes variations of pronunciation, it is not always easy to decide exactly what pronunciation his spellings are intended to represent. For example, he says that the word *prairie* is variously pronounced 'P*a*rer; par*e*rer; and par*o*rer' (Forster, III, 6). The choice of letters to be italicized seems rather arbitrary.

Dickens wrote the American chapters of *Martin Chuzzlewit* when the experiences of his first American visit were still fresh in his mind, and the Americanisms which he introduced very freely into those chapters are similar to those which he recorded in *American Notes* and his letters to Forster. In these chapters he portrays both regional and class dialects. The Americans whose speech he records are for the most part a seedy lot, and it is clear that Dickens intended them to be; their imposing array of titles, General, Colonel, and The Honourable, are all part of the satirical picture. Dickens was therefore portraying substandard American speech, and many of the linguistic features in these American chapters have their parallels in the substandard speech of British characters in *Martin Chuzzlewit* and other novels. Side by side with these vulgarisms there are genuinely regional characteristics. However kindly disposed Dickens may have been towards his British characters with substandard speech, his attitude to American dialects, whether regional or class, is generally hostile. Americans of whom he approves, like Mr Bevan, speak in rather formal standard English. When Mr Bevan does use an Americanism in saying 'I was "raised" in the State of Massachusetts', the word is placed in quotation marks, as if by way of apology.

The American chapters of *Martin Chuzzlewit* are chapters 16, 17, 21, 22, 23, 33 and 34, and all the Americanisms here quoted from the novel are from those chapters.

Vocabulary. A few words must have been completely new to most British readers of the novel. The newsboy in New York offers details of 'the patriotic *loco-foco* movement'; Mark Tapley discovers the reviving effect of a *cobbler*, which becomes less obscure when called by its full name *sherry cobbler; catawam-pous* is a term of abuse applied to insects 'as graze upon a human pretty strong'; Scadder complains that when he does his duty, it raises the *dander* of his friends and they *rile* up rough; and Mrs Hominy complains that 'the jolting in the cars is pretty nigh as bad as if the rail was full of *snags* and *sawyers*.'

A large group of Americanisms consists of words commonly used in British English in different senses. Examples are:

admire 'to be surprised or gratified'
bright 'well'
clear 'to go away'
compensation 'rent'
concluded 'decided'
diggings 'place'
Fall 'Autumn'
locate himself 'to stay'
location 'apartments, accommodation'
locomotive 'mobile'
muniment 'written notice'
realize 'to understand'
rout 'journey'
spanking 'good, excellent'. The corresponding noun is *spanker*.
whipped 'surpassed'

At the time when Dickens wrote, and even more today, there was so much contact between England and the United States that it is always dangerous to speak of any word or usage as distinctively American. Anyone writing about American English has to beware of behaving like Mrs Hominy's escort in his conversation with Martin Chuzzlewit:

'. . . Start is not a word you use in your country, sir.'
'Oh yes, it is,' said Martin.
'You air mistaken, sir,' returned the gentleman, with great decision, 'but we will not pursue the subject, lest it should awake your prejŭ-dīce.' (ch. 22)

Phrases, as well as single words, can be regarded as Americanisms, and they too are sometimes adopted in other parts of the English-speaking world with the result that their origin is lost sight of. When Mrs Hominy asks Martin 'Where do you hail from?' he cannot understand her. A reader of today has no difficulty in understanding the phrase, and is likely to feel that it is more idiomatic than Mrs Hominy's translation 'Where was you rose?' (ch. 22). The phrase is not often used in British English today, not because it is an Americanism but because it seems rather literary and old-fashioned. Another of Mrs Hominy's phrases, 'a'most used-up' is expressive enough and the meaning is clear, but it has not passed into general use in British English. A third possibility is illustrated in Major Pawkins's description of a bar-room as 'only in the next block' and General Choke's 'ride me on a rail'. These phrases are understood by most British readers, but they are still regarded as Americanisms. Other phrases that are apparently regarded as American are 'Only think!' and 'Possible!' (by ellipsis for 'Can that be possible?') used by the Norris family to express their surprise that General Fladdock has crossed the Atlantic in the same boat as Martin without meeting him.

Another class of Americanisms consists of words coined in America from elements that are familiar separately in British English. Both Colonel Diver and Scadder use *eventuate* in the sense 'turn out' and General Choke uses *opinionate* in the sense 'think'. A less pretentious formation is Scadder's *tongue-y* 'talkative', and Kettle's *slantindicularly* is a blend-word.

Pronunciation and Grammar. Apart from the information provided about the pronunciation of particular words, there are several passages in *Martin Chuzzlewit* which describe the general impression which American speech made on Dickens. He had clearly noticed distinctive features in New England intonation. The captain of the packet-boat that brought Martin to America describes the journey:

'Well now! It was a pretty spanking run, sir,' said, or rather sung, the captain, who was a genuine New Englander. (ch. 16)

The greater care with which lightly-stressed words are pronounced in American speech is the subject of an amused comment of the kind that linguistic differences are apt to arouse. A remark of Colonel Diver is received by Martin with a smile, partly occasioned by what the gentleman said, and partly by his manner of saying it, which was odd enough, for he emphasised all the small words and syllables in his discourse, and left the others to take care of themselves; as if he thought the larger parts of speech could be trusted alone, but the little ones required to be constantly looked after. (ch. 16)

The American manner of speaking is described:

Major Pawkins then reserved his fire, and looking upward, said, with a peculiar air of quiet weariness, like a man who had been up all night: an air which Martin had already observed both in the colonel and Mr Jefferson Brick:
'Well, colonel!' (ch. 16)

Mark Tapley describes another American as speaking 'not exactly through his nose, but as if he'd got a stoppage in it, very high up' (ch. 21).

One general characteristic of pronunciation is indicated by the insertion of a hyphen in the spelling of many words of more than one syllable. The hyphen may indicate a pause, but it is more likely that it is a way of showing that the lightly-stressed syllables of the word receive more stress than they usually do in British English. Examples are: *a-dopted*, *a-larming*, *con-clude*, *con-siderin*, *do-minion*, *en-tirely*, *e-tarnal*, *Eu-rope*, *in-doors*, *po-session*, *Pro-fessor*. The frequency with which examples occur shows that this is a feature of American speech that had made a strong impression on Dickens. Louise Pound thinks that the purpose of the hyphen is to indicate the protraction of the initial syllable and suggests that the characters who use these pronunciations are in general those who are impressed with their own importance.[1] This may well be true, but so many of the Americans in *Martin Chuzzlewit* are self-important that the description has little defining value: the hyphenated forms are attributed to so many different characters that it seems better to suppose that Dickens regarded the characteristic as one belonging to American speech generally. He did not think of it as confined to American speakers; it is, for example, a marked feature of the pronunciation of Sam Weller (cf. Appendix § 56). The American tendency to give greater stress to syllables

---

[1] Louise Pound, 'The American Dialect of Charles Dickens', *American Speech* xxii (1947), p. 128.

which in British English bear little stress is illustrated by occasional spellings, such as *territoary*.

Dickens occasionally uses diacritic marks to indicate American pronunciations, and, when he does so, it may be that he is trying to indicate stress as well as vowel-length. For example, Mrs Hominy's escort uses the word *prejudice*, which is spelt 'prĕjŭdīce'. The first two vowels are short in standard English, and the only reason for marking them as short would seem to be the desire to emphasize the comparative length, or more probably diphthongal quality, of the vowel of the final syllable. Similarly Kettle's pronunciation of *engine* is indicated by the spelling 'ĕn-gīne', and his pronunciation of the noun *produce* is indicated by 'prŏdūce'.

Distinctively American pronunciations are no doubt indicated by spellings like *chawed* and *chawers* and by a Negro servant's *sa* for *sir*, but in general in Dickens's portrayal of American English, as in his portrayal of British regional dialects, regional features are heavily outnumbered by substandard features, and there are close parallels between the substandard speech of American and British characters. The following are some of the chief categories:

1. Change of the medial affricate [tʃ] to [t] (§ 9), suggested by spellings like *fortun*, *natur*. Kettle and Scadder use the form *critter*, which shows this change as well as the shortening of the stem-vowel (cf. § 44).

2. The loss of *r* in spelling before consonants (§ 19): *bust*.

3. The loss of [f] before a consonant in *arter* (§ 20).

4. The loss of [w] in a lightly-stressed syllable (§ 21): *back'ards*.

5. The use of the indefinite article without final *n*, even when the following word begins with a vowel (§ 25): *a eatin room, a ĕn-gīne*.

6. The raising of [e] to [i] (§ 30): *gin'ral*.

7. The spelling *toe* for the preposition *to* (§ 34): *I go back Toe my home*. The initial capital suggests that the preposition is strongly stressed, and the pronunciation is no doubt due to the stress.

8. The use of [ai] for [ɔi] (§ 42): *biler*.

9. The loss of [j] before [u:] (§ 43): *dooel*. Dickens may

well have heard this pronunciation in America as it is today thought of as distinctively American.

10. The disappearance of a lightly-stressed medial vowel (§ 57): *partick'ler, calc'lated*.

11. The reduction of lightly-stressed [ou] to [ə], spelt *er* (§ 58): *feller*.

12. The use of *air* as a variant of *are* (§ 80).

13. The use of adjectives as adverbs (§ 85): *most uncommon bright, one moderate big 'un, That's dreadful true, used up considerable, frightful wholesome, awful lovely*.

14. The use of *as* for *who, whom* or *which* (§ 96): *I raise the dander of my feller critters, as I wish to serve; It is a lot as should be rose in price*.

15. The use of the verbal noun in *-ing* preceded by the preposition *a* (§ 103): *still a-printing off*.

16. The construction of verbs with *of* (§ 104): *Feel of my hands*.

The use of one part of speech for another is perhaps especially common in American English (cf. § 101): *You might loan me a corkscrew, There is considerable of truth, I find, in that remark*. Confusion between strong verbs and their cognate causatives (cf. § 78) and the creation of analogical forms of past participles (cf. § 73) are both illustrated in the forms of the past participle of the verb meaning 'raise'. Scadder uses *rose* and *ris* as past participles where standard English would have *raised*. The first of these forms is from the old preterite singular of the strong verb *rise* (OE *-rās*) while the second is from the old past participle of the strong verb (OE *-risen*). What is unusual here is that the forms of the strong verb are used instead of the weak; in substandard British speech the confusion is usually the other way round, with the result that we get *lay* for *lie* and *set* for *sit*. Since *ought* is historically the past tense of the verb *owe*, there are objections to its use as an infinitive, which even hatred of the prescriptive grammarian has not completely overcome. Scadder, like many an English schoolboy, says *you didn't ought*.

5

IDIOLECTS

One of the problems that every novelist must face is that he has to use the written language to represent the very much wider ranges of expression that are available to a speaker. Some novelists simply give up the attempt to portray spoken language realistically, and the result is that their characters 'talk like a book'. What makes it worse is that when a character talks like a book, he usually talks like a bad book. In the novels of Dickens Nicholas Nickleby is the chief offender. Some of his speeches are the sort of thing that would have gone over well with Vincent Crummles and his patrons. Three examples must suffice:

> its hardest, coarsest toil were happiness to this (ch. 13)
> Exhausted as I am, and standing in no common need of rest . . . (ch. 15)
> For God's sake, consider my deplorable condition. (ch. 13)

Fortunately for the author's reputation, such speeches are not typical of those used by Dickensian characters. Dickens took a lot of trouble to individualize the speech of his characters, and for many of them he devised what have been called 'special languages'. Each of these special languages may well be described as an idiolect, the term used to describe the speech-habits of an individual, in contrast with a dialect, which describes the speech-habits of a group.

Dickens realized the difficulty of representing in writing the wide range of effects that can be achieved in speech. When Doctor Marigold decides to write a book for his adopted daughter, he realizes this difficulty:

> I was aware that I couldn't do myself justice. A man can't write his eye (at least *I* don't know how to), nor yet can a man write his voice, nor the rate of his talk, not the quickness of his action, nor his general spicy way. But he can write his turns of speech, when he

is a public speaker, – and indeed I have heard that he very often does, before he speaks 'em. (*CS, Doctor Marigold*, ch. 1)

The practice of reading aloud was common in the nineteenth century. Betty Higden speaks admiringly of Sloppy's skill:

You mightn't think it, but Sloppy is a beautiful reader of a newspaper. He do the Police in different voices. (*OMF*, Bk I, ch. 16)

Mr Wopsle, in *Great Expectations*, goes further:

A highly popular murder had been committed, and Mr Wopsle was imbrued in blood to the eyebrows. He gloated over every abhorrent adjective in the description, and identified himself with every witness at the Inquest. He faintly moaned, 'I am done for,' as the victim, and he barbarously bellowed, 'I'll serve you out,' as the murderer. He gave the medical testimony, in pointed imitation of our local practitioner; and he piped and shook, as the aged turnpike-keeper who had heard blows, to an extent so very paralytic as to suggest a doubt regarding the mental competency of that witness. The coroner, in Mr Wopsle's hands, became Timon of Athens; the beadle, Coriolanus. (ch. 18)

Elsewhere the variations of expression that a speaker can use are the subject of light-hearted satire. When Silas Wegg is trying to flatter Venus after the disclosure of his attempt to conceal from him the will that he has discovered, he begins by saying 'Comrade, what a speaking countenance is yours!' Venus continues to be grim and Wegg becomes increasingly loquacious:

'The question,' returned Wegg, with a sort of joyful affability, 'why I didn't mention sooner that I had found something. Says your speaking countenance to me: "Why didn't you communicate that when I first come in this evening? Why did you keep it back till you thought Mr Boffin had come to look for the article?" Your speaking countenance,' said Wegg, 'puts it plainer than language. Now you can't read in my face what answer I give?'
'No, I can't,' said Venus. (*OMF*, Bk III, ch. 7)

Recent investigation of speech, assisted by the tape-recording machine, has shown how great are the differences between speech and writing. We have come to realize that we speak much less grammatically than we think we do, or perhaps it would be better to say that speech has a grammar of its own. Dickens realized how great was the difference. As a rule he makes no attempt at a completely realistic representation of spoken language, but occasionally, for his own and his readers' amusement, he records the sort of thing that people actually say rather than what they think they say. The waiter at the coffee-house in *Little Dorrit* provides an example:

> 'Beg pardon, sir,' said a brisk waiter, rubbing the table. 'Wish see bedroom?'
> 'Yes. I have just made up my mind to do it.'
> 'Chaymaid!' cried the waiter. 'Gelen box num seven wish see room!'
> 'Stay!' said Clennam, rousing himself. 'I was not thinking of what I said; I answered mechanically. I am not going to sleep here. I am going home.'
> 'Deed, sir? Chaymaid! Gelen box num seven not go sleep here, gome.' (Bk I, ch. 3)

The character in Dickens who makes most frequent use of disjointed phrases is Alfred Jingle, but he is not alone. The languid Mortimer Lightwood does the same when talking to Mr Boffin, partly because such detached phrases are in keeping with his pose of gentlemanly fatigue and partly to conceal from Mr Boffin the fact that he is making fun of him. Mr Boffin describes how old Harmon had snatched off Mrs Boffin's bonnet 'in a manner that amounted to personal' and how she afterwards intercepted a blow, intended for her husband, which 'dropped her'. Lightwood's murmured comment is 'Equal honour – Mrs Boffin's head and heart'. On being told that Mrs Boffin had called her employer a flinty-hearted rascal, Lightwood's comment is: 'Vigorous Saxon spirit – Mrs Boffin's ancestors – bowmen – Agincourt and Cressy' (*OMF*, Bk I, ch. 8). In a passage in *Dombey and Son* we can see Walter Gay's rather formal speech disintegrating into detached phrases in a very life-like way when he realizes that he has an unsympathetic listener:

> 'but if you would allow them – accumulate – payment – advance – uncle – frugal, honourable, old man.' (ch. 10)

The characters who use idiolects are not only major characters. They are especially the comic characters, and Dickens's fondness for repetition soon makes the reader familiar with the idiolects of the characters who have distinctive speech-habits.[1]

[1] On Dickens's habit of giving 'a fantastic private language' to some of his characters see Dorothy Van Ghent, *The English Novel: Form and Function* (Harper Torchbooks, 1961), pp. 125 ff.

Sometimes the author tries to make things easier for the reader by describing an idiolect as well as by illustrating it, but his description does not always call attention to the most obvious characteristic. He gives two specimens of the conversation of Mrs Chivery, and after each he adds a comment calling attention to its linguistic eccentricities:

> 'Sir,' said Mrs Chivery, 'sure and certain as in this house I am. I see my son go out with my own eyes when in this house I was, and I see my son come in with my own eyes when in this house I was, and I know he done it.' Mrs Chivery derived a surprising force of emphasis from the foregoing circumstantiality and repetition.
> 'That,' said Mrs Chivery, 'took place on the same day when to this house I see that John with these eyes return. Never been himself in this house since. Never was like what he has been since, not from the hour when to this house seven years ago me and his father, as tenants by the quarter came.' An effect in the nature of an affidavit was gained for this speech, by Mrs Chivery's peculiar power of construction. (*LD*, Bk I, ch. 22)

Here the most obvious characteristic is one which the author does not specifically mention: the inversion of the normal word-order of an English sentence in order to put the verb at the end. Mrs Chivery's son does it too, and this imitation of an idiolect involves no loss of realism. It would have been surprizing if a man of John Chivery's gentle disposition had not acquired some of his mother's tricks of speech for use when he was deeply moved:

> 'I shouldn't have given my mind to it again, I hope if to this prison you had not been brought, and in an hour unfortunate for me this day!' (In his agitation Young John adopted his mother's powerful construction of sentences.) . . . 'now, after all, you dodge me when I ever so gently hint at it, and throw me back upon myself. For do not, sir,' said Young John, 'do not be so base as to deny that dodge you do, and thrown me back upon myself you have!' (Bk II, ch. 27)

John is usually very self-effacing, but we must admire the delicacy with which he calls attention to his sufferings, in reply to Mr Dorrit's enquiry about his mother's health:

> 'Thank you, sir, she's not quite as well as we could wish – in fact, we none of us are, except father – but she's pretty well, sir.' (Bk I, ch. 31)

John has linguistic habits of his own, notably that of composing epitaphs for himself:

And Mr Chivery, junior, went his way, having spontaneously composed on the spot an entirely new epitaph for himself, to the effect that Here lay the body of John Chivery, Who, Having at such a date, Beheld the idol of his life, In grief and tears, And feeling unable to bear the harrowing spectacle, Immediately repaired to the abode of his inconsolable parents, And terminated his existence by his own rash act. (Bk I, ch. 31)

Dickens obtains some of his best effects by contrasting two idiolects. In *Little Dorrit* Clennam's interview with Tite Barnacle presents a contrast between the direct and straightforward, though rather literary, style of Clennam and the stately and evasive style of the civil servant:

'I have found a debtor in the Marshalsea prison of the name of Dorrit, who has been there many years. I wish to investigate his confused affairs, so far as to ascertain whether it may not be possible, after this lapse of time, to ameliorate his unhappy condition. The name of Mr Tite Barnacle has been mentioned to me as representing some highly influential interest among his creditors. Am I correctly informed?'

It being one of the principles of the Circumlocution Office never, on any account whatever, to give a straightforward answer, Mr Barnacle said, 'Possibly'.

'On behalf of the Crown, may I ask, or as a private individual?'

'The Circumlocution Department, sir,' Mr Barnacle replied, 'may have possibly recommended – possibly – I cannot say – that some public claim against the insolvent estate of a firm or copartnership to which this person may have belonged, should be enforced. The question may have been, in the course of official business, referred to the Circumlocution Department for its consideration. The Department may have either originated, or confirmed, a Minute making that recommendation.'

'I assume this to be the case, then.'

'The Circumlocution Department,' said Mr Barnacle, 'is not responsible for any gentleman's assumptions.' (Bk I, ch. 10)

This conversation takes place in the private house of a civil servant absent from work because of an attack of gout. It is therefore possible to feel more sympathy for Tite Barnacle than the author intended that we should.

The members of the Barnacle clan do not all talk alike. There is a strong contrast between the dignified aloofness of Tite Barnacle and the slangy style of his young relative who describes the Circumlocution Office as a 'hocus-pocus piece of machinery for the assistance of the nobs in keeping off the snobs' (Bk I,

ch. 10). In the course of less than a page this member of the
Barnacle family is described by a number of different adjectives
all set in the same framework, a device which critics of the
popular ballads call incremental repetition. He is 'this airy
young Barnacle', 'this dashing young Barnacle', 'this engaging
young Barnacle', and 'this sparkling young Barnacle'. Nothing
could be more colloquial and simple than his advice: 'You had
better take a lot of forms away with you. Give him a lot of
forms.' (Bk I, ch. 10).

The linguistic feature that goes to make up an idiolect may
be an eccentric pronunciation, like Dennis's 'Muster Gashford'
for 'Mr Gashford', which occurs many times in *Barnaby Rudge*.
It may be a feature of accidence or syntax, like Miggs's plurals
of abstract nouns, which come in bursts in moments of excite-
ment. On one page of *Barnaby Rudge* (ch. 41) she has *satisfac-
tions, dispositions, in the rights, to go that lengths, separations,
endings*. She then goes on all right for some time but has another
attack near the end of the novel:

> 'My sentiments is of little consequences, I know,' cried Miggs, with
> additional shrillness, 'for my positions is but a servant, and as sich,
> of humilities, still I gives expressions to my feelings, and places
> my reliances on them which entertains my own opinions!' (ch. 63)

One of the simplest linguistic devices that can be used as an
aid to characterization is the habitual phrase, and it is a device
of which Dickens is very fond. When we think of Mr Dick, we
at once think of King Charles's head. Similarly we remember
that Barkis is willing, that Mrs Micawber never will desert
Mr Micawber, that Dennis likes to see people worked off and
that Wemmick is fond of portable property. We have become
very familiar with the trick of habitual phrases in the mouths of
innumerable music-hall and variety artists. It is possible to take
an unsympathetic view of these phrases and to say that their
use rests on the assumption that a commonplace idea becomes
funny if it is repeated often enough. It may be, however, that
part of the secret of Dickens's success is that he makes things
easy for his readers by his constant repetitions, and his habitual
phrases are remembered by readers who are not used to reading
with close attention. Such repetition gives pleasure to un-
sophisticated readers and audiences because it reminds them of

other amusing contexts in which the phrase has been used. This is no doubt the reason why the mere mention of certain place-names, such as Wigan or Aberdeen, is enough to bring broad smiles to the faces of an audience. There is an element of self-congratulation in the satisfaction with which a reader recognizes an habitual phrase.

Habitual phrases may occur in the speech of particular characters, like Jenny Wren's 'Person of the house' and 'My back's bad and my legs are queer', Mrs Wilfer's 'It is as you think, RW, not as I do', Mr Snagsby's 'Not to put too fine a point on it', Matthew Bagnet's 'Discipline must be maintained', or Mrs Chick's 'make an effort', or they may be phrases habitually used by the author about one of his characters, like the Peruvian mines, whose failure had soured Mrs Pipchin's temper. Sometimes it is an action, rather than a phrase that is habitual, like the Fat Boy falling asleep or Mrs Micawber suckling her baby.

An habitual phrase becomes the 'signature tune' by which a character may be recognized. When the Deputy Lock refers twice to the sweat of his brow (*OMF*, Bk III, ch. 8), it is enough to make it clear to the reader that he is Rogue Riderhood. An habitual phrase acquires a special meaning for the character who uses it. When John Jarndyce says 'The wind's in the east', it is his way of saying that he is distressed about something. The obtuse Richard Carstone, unconscious of the symbolism, corrects him by saying that the wind is in the north. Mr Jarndyce rightly brushes this objection aside:

> 'My dear Rick,' said Mr Jarndyce, poking the fire; 'I'll take an oath it's either in the east, or going to be. I am always conscious of an uncomfortable sensation now and then when the wind is blowing in the east.'
> 'Rheumatism, sir?' said Richard.
> 'I dare say it is, Rick.' (*BH*, ch. 6)

It is usually clear quite soon after the introduction of a new character what his habitual phrase, if he has one, is to be, but in introducing Edmund Sparkler, Dickens goes out of his way to make things easy for the reader. He tells us at once, instead of leaving us to deduce the fact from his conversation, what is his outstanding characteristic and what is to be his habitual phrase. He says that Sparkler was monomaniacal in offering marriage to all manner of undesirable young ladies, and in remarking of every successive young lady to whom he tendered a matrimonial proposal that she was 'a doosed fine gal – well educated too – with no biggodd nonsense about her'. (*LD*, Bk I, ch. 21)

Some characters have distinctive linguistic characteristics which are more subtle than habitual phrases but which serve the same purpose of individualizing the character in a way that is easy to recognize. In *Dombey and Son* Susan Nipper makes frequent use of a sentence-pattern in two parts, introduced by 'may' and 'but' respectively. Examples are:

I may wish, you see, to take a voyage to Chaney, Mrs Richards, but I mayn't know how to leave the London Docks. (ch. 3)

A person may tell a person to dive off a bridge head foremost into five-and-forty feet of water, Mrs Richards, but a person may be very far from diving. (ch. 5)

I may not have my objections to a young man's keeping company with me, and when he puts the question, may say 'yes', but that's not saying 'would you be so kind as like me'. (ch. 12)

Dowler, in *Pickwick Papers*, is very fond of a type of sentence in keeping with his peremptory disposition. It consists of two monosyllabic words, the first of them a verb in the imperative and the second usually a pronoun. This pattern is appropriate enough when he is first introduced as an irascible bully: 'Know me', 'Drink it', but he adheres to it when he is trying to be conciliatory after being exposed as a coward: 'Sit down', 'Hear me', 'Grasp it', 'Tell me', 'Join me' (ch. 35, 38).

Dickens was fond of imitating particular styles of writing, and the short stories collected together in *Christmas Stories* contain many examples. *Doctor Marigold* (1865) is written throughout in the style of a cheap-jack auctioneer:

Bid for the working model of the old Cheap Jack, who has drunk more gunpowder-tea with the ladies in his time than would blow the lid off a washer-woman's copper, and carry it as many thousands of miles higher than the moon as naught nix naught, divided by the national debt, carry nothing to the poor-rates, three under, and two over. Now, my hearts of oak and men of straw, what do you say for the lot? Two shillings, a shilling, tenpence, eightpence, sixpence, fourpence. Twopence? Who said twopence? The gentleman in the scarecrow's hat? I am ashamed of him for his want of public spirit. (ch. 1)

With this patter we may compare the croupier at the gambling-booth in *Nicholas Nickleby* of whom the author says that he poured out unconnected phrases all day long, with the same monotonous emphasis and almost in the same order:

> 'Rooge-a-nore from Paris! Gentlemen, make your game and back your own opinions – any time while the ball rolls – rooge-a-nore from Paris, gentlemen, it's a French game, gentlemen, I brought it over myself, I did indeed! – Rooge-a-nore from Paris – black wins – black – stop a minute, sir, and I'll pay you directly – two there, half a pound there, three there – and one there – gentlemen, the ball's a rolling – any time, sir, while the ball rolls! – The beauty of this game is, that you can double your stakes or put down your money, gentlemen, any time while the ball rolls – black again – black wins – I never saw such a thing – I never did, in all my life, upon my word I never did; if any gentleman had been backing the black in the last five minutes he must have won five and forty pound in four rolls of the ball, he must indeed.' (ch. 50)

The Schoolboy's Story (1853) uses many schoolboyish turns of phrase that have changed little during the century that has passed since the story was written:

> Being rather young at present – I am getting on in years, but still I am rather young – I have no particular adventures of my own to fall back upon. It wouldn't much interest anybody here, I suppose, to know what a screw the Reverend is, or what a griffin *she* is, or how they do stick it into parents – particularly hair-cutting, and medical attendance. One of our fellows was charged in his half's account twelve and sixpence for two pills – tolerably profitable at six and threepence a-piece, I should think – and he never took them either, but put them up the sleeve of his jacket.

The third chapter of *Mugby Junction* (1866), which differs completely in style from the two earlier chapters, uses the more worldly-wise style of the boy who has left school to work in a railway refreshment room:

> What a lark it is! We are the Model Establishment, we are, at Mugby. Other Refreshment Rooms send their imperfect young ladies up to be finished off by Our Missis. For some of the young ladies, when they're new to the business, come into it mild! Ah! Our Missis, she soon takes that out of 'em. Why, I originally come into the business meek myself. But Our Missis, she soon took that out of *me*.

Sometimes Dickens's idiolects seem to be introduced for their own sake rather than to give individuality to a character.

His love of light-hearted and exuberant parody is illustrated in one of the American chapters of *Martin Chuzzlewit* (ch. 34). There are two women characters called Toppit and Codger, but it is doubtful whether many readers of the novel remember their names; they are thought of as the two Literary Ladies who seek to persuade the Mother of the Modern Gracchi to introduce them to Elijah Pogram on the grounds that they are 'Transcendental'. They make no contribution whatever to the plot and are clearly introduced because Dickens wanted to parody a particular way of writing. Each of them makes a short speech and they are then heard of no more:

'To be presented to a Pogram,' said Miss Codger, 'by a Hominy, indeed, a thrilling moment is it in its impressiveness on what we call our feelings. But why we call them so, or why impressed they are, or if impressed they are at all, or if at all we are, or if there really is, oh gasping one! a Pogram or a Hominy, or any active principle to which we give those titles, is a topic, Spirit searching, light abandoned, much too vast to enter on, at this unlooked-for crisis.'

'Mind and matter,' said the lady in the wig, 'glide swift into the vortex of immensity. Howls the sublime, and softly sleeps the calm Ideal, in the whispering chambers of Imagination. To hear it, sweet it is. But then, outlaughs the stern philosopher, and saith to the Grotesque, "What ho! arrest for me that Agency. Go, bring it here!" And so the vision fadeth.' (ch. 34)

Dickens is no doubt here taking his revenge for the boredom he had suffered during his visit to America. In a letter to Forster, dated 3 April, 1842, he mentions a general who had called on him in Washington with two literary ladies. He describes the general as 'perhaps *the* most horrible bore in this country' and declares: 'The LL's have carried away all my cheerfulness' (Forster, III, 5, 6). It is probable that the very distinctive manner of speech of the Literary Ladies also had a literary source. At the time of Dickens's visit to America Transcendentalism was a popular theme for parodists, and the official periodical of the movement, *The Dial*, contains many passages, intended quite seriously, which illustrate the kind of writing which Dickens was no doubt trying to burlesque. The following is a typical example:

The soul lies buried in a ruined city, struggling to be free, and calling for aid. The worldly trafficker in life's caravan hears its

cries, and says, it is a prisoned maniac. But one true man stops, and
with painful toil lifts aside the crumbling fragments; till at last, he
finds beneath the choking mass a mangled form of exceeding
beauty. Dazzling is the light to eyes long blind; weak are the limbs
long prisoned; faint is the breath long pent. But oh! that mantling
blush, that liquid eye, that elastic spring of renovated strength.
The deliverer is folded to the breast of an angel.[1]

Another idiolect which Dickens seems to introduce just for
the fun of it is that of the oracular Jack Bunsby in *Dombey and
Son*. Amusement is caused by the contrast between Captain
Cuttle's admiration of his profundity and the nonsensical
obscurity of his remarks when he gives utterance:

'For why?' growled Bunsby, looking at his friend for the first time.
'Which way?' 'If so, why not? Therefore.' With these oracular
words – they seemed almost to make the Captain giddy; they
launched him upon such a sea of speculation and conjecture – the
sage submitted to be helped off with his pilot-coat . . . (ch. 39)

The idiolects of Dickensian characters contain some surprises.
Rogue Riderhood is the sort of man who might be expected to
be inarticulate, but he is anything but that. Sometimes he seems
to be intoxicated with words, and makes long speeches. He
shows inventiveness in his use of oaths to emphasize the truth
of what he says: 'by George and the Draggin I'm a-coming to
it now!' (*OMF*, Bk I, ch. 12), and 'this here world-without-
end-everlasting-chair'. He shows similar inventiveness in
nomenclature. To address Lightwood as Lawyer Lightwood is
natural enough, and Wrayburn then becomes 'the T'other
Governor'. He soon finds a way of addressing Bradley
Headstone, the third well-dressed man to enter his life:

'Hooroar T'other T'other Governor. Hooroar T'otherest Governor!
I am of your way of thinkin.' (*OMF*, Bk III, ch. 11)

The variety of styles of speech used by Riderhood does not
always carry conviction. In speaking to Bradley Headstone he
makes use of such dissimilar remarks as 'You'll be for another
forty on 'em, governor, as I judges, afore you turns your mind

[1] *The Dial*, Vol. ii, No. 1 (July 1841), p. 49. I am indebted to
Professor Dennis Welland for this quotation and to him and Professor
Marcus Cunliffe for much valuable information about Transcendent-
alism.

to breakfast' beside 'I myself should recommend it' and 'Prove your opinion' (Bk III, ch. 11; Bk IV, ch. 7).

Riderhood is not alone in using language of a rather literary turn. His former partner Hexam rises to heights of eloquence in defending his occupation of taking away the possessions of men found drowned:

> 'No. Has a dead man any use for money? Is it possible for a dead man to have money? What world does a dead man belong to? T'other world. What world does money belong to? This world. How can money be a corpse's? Can a corpse own it, want it, spend it, claim it, miss it? Don't try to go confounding the rights and wrongs of things in that way. But it's worthy of the sneaking spirit that robs a live man.' (Bk I, ch. 1)

The highly individual language of Mrs Gamp includes many features of substandard speech that are shared by other characters in the novels together with others that are her own. To the first class belong such features of pronunciation as *sech*, beside *sich*, *obserwation*, *widder*, *chimley-piece*, *nater*, *nothink*, *ansome*, *ast* 'ask', *creetur*, *wunst*, *arterwards*, *raly* 'really', such features of accidence as *you earns*, *you know'd*, *draw'd mild*, and *to have wrote*, and such features of syntax as *for them as has their feelings tried*, *a many places*, and *in course*. She shows an almost Elizabethan readiness to use one part of speech for another, as when she says 'whether I sicks or monthlies' (*MC*, chs. 19, 25).

Mr A. O. J. Cockshut[1] has called attention to the strongly-marked religious element in Mrs Gamp's language. She is unmoved by the report of young Bailey's death, but responds with conventional resignation:

> 'He was born into a wale,' said Mrs Gamp with philosophical coolness; 'and he lived in a wale; and he must take the consequences of sech a sitiwation.' (ch. 49)

She has a respect for biblical English, for when Jonas Chuzzlewit expresses horror at her quoting Chuffey's question 'Who's lying dead upstairs?' she assures him, 'Such was his Bible language' (ch. 46). Her references to her late husband include a mixture of biblical and colloquial language:

---

[1] A. O. J. Cockshut, *The Imagination of Charles Dickens* (Collins, 1961), pp. 19 f.

'Ah dear! When Gamp was summoned to his long home, and I see him a-lying in Guy's Hospital with a penny-piece on each eye, and his wooden leg under his left arm, I thought I should have fainted away. But I bore up.' (ch. 19)

'And as to husbands, there's a wooden leg gone likeways home to its account, which in its constancy of walkin' into wine vaults, and never comin' out again 'till fetched by force, was quite as weak as flesh, if not weaker.' (ch. 40)

We have to remember that Mrs Gamp spends most of her time in a half-drunken haze, which effects striking transformations of familiar biblical passages:

'Rich folks may ride on camels, but it ain't so easy for 'em to see out of a needle's eye. That is my comfort and I hope I knows it.' (ch. 25)

She is equally vague about the Old Testament, and Dickens calls special attention to one of her more startling adaptations:

'That is the Antwerp packet in the middle,' said Ruth.

'And I wish it was in Jonadge's belly, I do,' cried Mrs Gamp, appearing to confound the prophet with the whale in this miraculous aspiration. (ch. 40)

Biblical images of lambs and worms become merged in 'But the words she spoke of Mrs Harris, lambs could not forgive . . . nor worms forget' (ch. 49).

Mrs Gamp realizes the value of an accumulation of apparently irrelevant detail to give verisimilitude to her anecdotes:

I have heerd of one young man, a guard upon a railway, only three years opened – well does Mrs Harris know him, which indeed he is her own relation by her sister's marriage with a master sawyer – as is godfather at this present time to six-and-twenty blessed little strangers, equally unexpected, and all on 'um named after the Ingeins as was the cause. (ch. 40)

Now, ain't we rich in beauty this here joyful arternoon, I'm sure. I knows a lady, which her name, I'll not deceive you, Mrs Chuzzlewit, is Harris, her husband's brother bein' six foot three, and marked with a mad bull in Wellington boots upon his left arm, on account of his precious mother havin' been worrited by one into a shoe-maker's shop, when in a sitiwation which blessed is the man as has his quiver full of sech, . . . (ch. 46)

I never see a poor dear creetur took so strange in all my life, except a patient much about the same age, as I once nussed, which his calling was the custom-'us, and his name was Mrs Harris's own father, as pleasant a singer, Mr Chuzzlewit, as ever you heerd, with a voice like Jew's harp in the bass notes, that it took six men to hold at sech times, foaming frightful. (ch. 46)

Her sentences are sometimes inordinately long, and the syntax is involved and sometimes obscure. She is particularly fond of using *which* as a conjunction (cf. Appendix, § 94) and of inverting the usual word-order of subject and verb. All these characteristics are to be noticed in her last long speech in the novel:

'Which, Mr Chuzzlewit,' she said, 'is well beknown to Mrs Harris as has one sweet infant (though she do not wish it known) in her own family by the mother's side, kep in spirits in a bottle; and that sweet babe she see at Greenwich Fair, a-travelling in company with the pink-eyed lady, Prooshan dwarf, and livin' skelinton, which judge her feelins when the barrel organ played, and she was showed her own dear sister's child, the same not bein' expected from the outside picter, where it was painted quite contrairy in a livin' state, a many sizes larger, and performing beautiful upon the Arp, which never did that dear child know or do: since breathe it never did, to speak on, in this wale! And Mrs Harris, Mr Chuzzlewit, has knowed me many year, and can give you information that the lady which is widdered can't do better and may do worse than let me wait upon her, which I hope to do.' (ch. 52)

She is occasionally capable of bold word-formation. One has to consider for some time before deciding what is the meaning of *disregardlessness*; she uses it in the sense *disregard* (ch. 40). In syntax she achieves new constructions by welding two different constructions into a single idiom. 'Directly' and 'this minute' are two different idioms indicating promptness; Mrs Gamp combines them: 'She'll be here directly minnit' (ch. 51). She uses clichés that have become virtually meaningless: 'Gamp is my name and Gamp my nater' (ch. 26), and she is fond of self-exculpatory phrases like *I will not deceive you* and *I will not deny* (ch. 25).

A feature of Mrs Gamp's idiolect is the tendency of many consonants to become [dʒ], usually spelt *g*, less often *dg* or *j*. The consonant most often affected is [z]; there are several examples of other consonants. Even words ending in vowels sometimes add a final *ge*, as in *denige* (ch. 40); the *dg* in *Jonadge's belly* (ch. 40) may have this origin or, more probably, Mrs Gamp thought that the prophet's name was *Jonas*. In

indiwidgle (ch. 40) and *perfeejus* (ch. 49) Mrs Gamp's pronunciation could be paralleled among many speakers of old-
fashioned or substandard English; for example, Rob the
Grinder says *individgle* (*DS*, ch. 46). The [dʒ] in these words
is a development of [dj] and was at one time regarded as an
aristocratic pronunciation. Examples of Mrs Gamp's fondness
for the [dʒ] sound are:

[z] *abuged* (ch. 49), *Bragian* for *brazen* (ch. 29), *compoging*
(ch. 46), *dispoged* (ch. 19), *dispogician* (ch. 46), *excuge* (ch.
52), *half-a-dudgeon* (ch. 49), *impoged* (ch. 40), *impogician*
(ch. 40), *nige* for *noise* (ch. 52), *noge* (ch. 52), *propojals* (ch.
49), *rager* (ch. 52), *reagion* for *reason* (ch. 40), *repoge* (ch. 49),
roge (ch. 46), *rouge* (ch 46), *Saint Polge's fontin* ch. (29),
suppoging (ch. 25), *surprige* (ch. 46)

[s]: *bage* (ch. 49), *debage* (ch. 49), *expredge* (ch. 51),
experienge (ch. 29), *furnage* (ch. 49), *notige* (ch. 46), *poultige*
(ch. 46), *releage* (ch. 46), *sacrifige* (ch. 40), *satigefaction* (ch.
46)

[ʃ]: *wexagious* (ch. 46)

[ʒ]: *confugion* (ch. 40), *occagion* (ch. 49)

[tʃ]: *impeaged* (ch. 49)

[t]: *brickbadge* (ch. 25), *package* (ch. 40), *parapidge* (ch. 25)

[d]: *inwalieges* (ch. 29)

[gr]: *Piljian's Projiss* (ch. 25)

[v]: *turjey* (ch. 52); no doubt influenced by the preceding
topjy.

Mrs Gamp occasionally indulges in strikingly figurative
language:

'which fiddle-strings is weakness to expredge my nerves this
night.' (ch. 51)

When she is waiting to welcome the newly-married Jonas
Chuzzlewit and his wife, her allusion to the Wings of Love is
conventional enough, and Bailey's real or pretended belief that
the Wings of Love is a racehorse is an adequate comment on
the image, but Mrs Gamp is provoked by Bailey into using a
much more homely and expressive metaphor:

'There's nothin' he don't know; that's my opinion,' observed Mrs
Gamp. 'All the wickedness of the world is Print to him.' (ch. 26)

The general intention of Mrs Gamp's imagery is usually
clear, though the images do not always stand up to detailed
scrutiny, as, for example:

> if I may make so bold as speak so plain of what is plain enough to
> them as needn't look through mill-stones, Mrs Todgers, to find out
> what is wrote upon the wall behind. (ch. 46)

> Some people . . . may be Rooshans, and others may be Prooshans;
> they are born so, and will please themselves. Them which is of
> other naturs thinks different. (ch. 19)

She takes liberties with both the form and the meaning of
English words, as when she says 'in this promiscous place' (ch.
46), where *promiscous* is used with the meaning 'very' and with
a simplified suffix.

It is clear that Dickens enjoyed using the language of Mrs
Gamp. It may be that his delight in her language helps to
explain the frequency of her appearances in the novel. Her
reason for being present to watch the sailing of 'the Ankworks
package', for example, seems inadequate (ch. 40). How much
the style appealed to Dickens is clear from the long passage
from which the following is an extract:

> Which Mrs Harris's own words to me, was these: 'Sairey Gamp,'
> she says, 'Why not go to Margate? Srimps,' says that dear creetur,
> 'is to your liking, Sairey; why not go to Margate for a week, bring
> your constitootion up with srimps, and come back to them loving
> arts as knows and wallies of you, blooming? Sairey,' Mrs Harris
> says, 'you are but poorly. Don't denige it, Mrs Gamp, for books is
> in your looks. You must have rest, Your mind,' she says, 'is too
> strong for you; it gets you down and treads upon you, Sairey. It is
> useless to disguise the fact – the blade is a wearing out the sheets.'

Even those who know their *Martin Chuzzlewit* very well may
have difficulty in placing this passage, though they will feel
that the style is familiar. It is not from *Martin Chuzzlewit*; it
is the opening of a long pastiche of the style of Mrs Gamp
written by Dickens and printed by Forster (VI, 1).

Mr Pickwick describes Sam Weller's way of speaking as
'somewhat homely and occasionally incomprehensible' (*PP*,
ch. 16). The most characteristic type of Wellerism begins with
a familiar phrase and then suggests some imaginary occasion

when that phrase might have been used. The occasion is generally gruesome or humorous:

> No, no; reg'lar rotation, as Jack Ketch said, wen he tied the men up. (ch. 10)

> He wants you particklar; and no one else'll do, as the Devil's private secretary said ven he fetched avay Doctor Faustus. (ch. 15)

> Werry sorry to 'casion any personal inconwenience, ma'am, as the house-breaker said to the old lady when he put her on the fire. (ch. 26)

> the wery best intentions, as the gen'lm'n said ven he run away from his wife 'cos she seemed unhappy with him. (ch. 27)

> out with it, as the father said to the child, wen he swallowed a farden. (ch. 12)

> That's what I call a self-evident proposition, as the dog's meat man said, when the house-maid told him he warn't a gentleman. (ch. 22)

> Werry glad to see you indeed, and hope our acquaintance may be a long 'un, as the gen'lm'n said to the fi'pun'note. (ch. 25)

> Fine time for them as is well wropped up, as the Polar Bear said to himself, ven he was practising his skating. (ch. 30)

Sam Weller is so fond of this type of remark that it is reasonable to associate it with his name, but he has no exclusive rights. It is Tony Weller who says of marriage:

> but vether it's worth while goin' through so much to learn so little, as the charity-boy said ven he got to the end of the alphabet, is a matter of taste. (ch. 27)

Sam is very fond of using nicknames. His father is 'old Nobs' (ch. 27), 'the old 'un' (ch. 20), 'my ancient' (ch. 20), 'old codger' (ch. 20), 'old feller' (ch. 22) and 'my Prooshan blue' (ch. 33). Master Bardell is 'young townskip' (ch. 26), and 'my hinfant fernomenon' (ch. 26), and the Fat Boy is 'young twenty stun' (ch. 28) and 'young dropsy' (ch. 28). Grummer is 'old Strike-a-light' (ch. 25). Boys are 'young leathers' (ch. 19), 'young touch-and-go' (ch. 19) and 'young brockeley sprout' (ch. 33).

In the scenes where Sam Weller is together with Job Trotter, the linguistic qualities of each are heightened by contrast. Sam is cheerfully disrespectful to everybody and his speech is substandard and colloquial; Job shows extreme courtesy towards strangers and his speech is almost painfully correct. When Sam first speaks to him he addresses him familiarly as 'governor', but Job replies by addressing Sam twice as 'sir', and, as soon as he learns Sam's assumed name, he addresses him frequently as 'Mr Walker' in the best middle-class tradition. If 'sir' is a suitable greeting to a fellow-servant, Job's respect for Mr Pickwick can be expressed only by excessive repetition:

> 'I know it is my duty, sir,' replied Job, with great emotion. 'We should all try to discharge our duty, sir, and I humbly endeavour to discharge mine, sir; but it is a hard trial to betray a master, sir, whose clothes you wear and whose bread you eat, even though he is a scoundrel, sir.' (ch. 16)

Job Trotter emphasizes the qualities of Sam Weller's speech by contrast; Tony Weller emphasizes them by similarity. When they are together, Sam and his father egg each other on to linguistic extravagance.

> 'He's a cabbin' it, I suppose,' said the father.
> 'Yes, he's a havin' two mile o' danger at eightpence,' responded the son. (ch. 22)

In spite of the resemblances, the two do not talk alike; Tony is more ambitious and more ready to take offence if corrected. Tony's description of Jingle, though it puzzles Mr Pickwick, reveals a good gift of phrase: 'slim and tall, with long hair, and the gift o' the gab wery gallopin' ' (ch. 20). A feature of his language is the incongruous effect produced by the inclusion of slightly learned or literary words in sentences otherwise highly colloquial. Thus he congratulates his son on his prowess as a drinker by saying 'Werry good power o' suction, Sammy' (ch. 23). If the literary word or phrase is not quite the right one, so much the better, as in the last three words of the further praise: 'You'd ha made an uncommon fine oyster, Sammy, if you'd been born in that station o' life.'

Tony Weller shares his son's interest in language, and the scene in which Tony helps Sam to write a letter to Mary gives them both scope. After arguing about the relative merits of the words 'circumscribed' and 'circumwented', they are at last able to reach agreement:

'Go on, Sammy.'

' "Feel myself ashamed and completely circumscribed in a dressin' of you, for you are a nice gal and nothin' but it".'

'That's a werry pretty sentiment,' said the elder Mr Weller, removing his pipe to make way for the remark.

'Yes, I think it is rayther good,' observed Sam, highly flattered. (ch. 33)

There is a contrast between the fluency with which Sam Weller expresses himself in speech and the difficulty that he has in writing a letter. His epistolary style has its own charm, but it is the charm of the unidiomatic, whereas Sam's colloquial style is extremely natural and idiomatic, though the idiom is not that of the present day.

In pronunciation, accidence, and syntax Sam Weller speaks the substandard language used by many Dickensian characters. He has one characteristic, shared by several very diverse characters, of frequently pausing in the middle of a word of two or more syllables, if that is the significance of the hyphen in words such as *gen-teel* (ch. 10), *hot-el* (ch. 10), *col-lecting* (ch. 13), *hex-traordinary* (ch. 13).

The chief feature of Dick Swiveller's idiolect is his poetic eloquence, which fights a losing battle with slangy colloquialism:

'But what,' said Mr Swiveller with a sigh, 'what is the odds so long as the fire of soul is kindled at the taper of conwiviality, and the wing of friendship never moults a feather! . . . Say not another syllable. I know my cue; smart is the word. Only one little whisper, Fred – *is* the old min friendly?' (*OCS*, ch. 2)

'Fred,' said Mr Swiveller, 'remember the once popular melody of "Begone dull care"; fan the sinking flame of hilarity with the wing of friendship; and pass the rosy wine!' (ch. 7)

'Immolating herself upon the shrine of Cheggs—' (ch. 21)

'Go, deceiver, go, some day, sir, p'r'aps you'll waken, from pleasure's dream to know, the grief of orphans forsaken.' (ch. 23)

Some of his poetic eloquence is the result of quotation of half-remembered fragments of verse or popular song.

'It's rather sudden,' said Dick, shaking his head with a look of infinite wisdom, and running on (as he was accustomed to do) with scraps of verse as if they were only prose in a hurry; 'when the

heart of a man is depressed with fears, the mist is dispelled when
Miss Wackles appears: she's a very nice girl: she's like the red,
red rose that's newly sprung in June – there's no denying that –
she's also like a melody that's sweetly played in tune.' (ch. 8)

When he abandons his poetic style, he shows a rather attractive
diffidence, as when reporting the failure of his visit to the single
gentleman:

'he . . . didn't hint at our taking anything to drink; and – and in
short rather turned us out of the room than otherwise.' (ch. 50)

Another of his characteristics is a love of logic, which endears
him to the single gentleman when Dick, 'yielding to his destiny
and saying whatever came uppermost', claims that anyone who
sleeps as much as the single gentleman ought to be prepared to
pay for a double-bedded room (ch. 35). The same logic enables
him to say that a party of twenty will make 'two hundred light
fantastic toes in all, supposing every lady and gentleman to have
the proper complement' (ch. 7).

Squeers has many different styles of language, suitable for
many different occasions. When he is alone with his boys, he
uses the direct and unambiguous language of the bully: 'Put
your handkerchief in your pocket, you little scoundrel, or I'll
murder you when the gentleman goes' (*NN*, ch. 4). On the
entrance of a parent whom he wishes to impress, he switches
over to a style of benevolent admonition:

My dear child, all people have their trials. This early trial of yours
that is fit to make your little heart burst, and your very eyes come
out of your head with crying, what is it? Nothing; less than
nothing. You are leaving your friends, but you will have a father
in me, my dear, and a mother in Mrs Squeers. At the delightful
village of Dotheboys, near Greta Bridge in Yorkshire . . .

The last sentence, a quotation from his advertisement, appeals
so strongly to Squeers that it tends to recur like a refrain when
he is trying to make a good impression. When he departs from
his carefully prepared script, he uses a more distinctive style
which involves the expression of unexceptionable sentiments in
a highly colloquial idiom with a free use of slang. He tells
Snawley that his stepsons 'have come to the right shop for
morals' (ch. 4). When he is in this vein there is not much

difference between Squeers drunk and Squeers sober. He tipsily addresses Peg Sliderskew in praise of philosophy:

> 'The heavenly bodies is philosophy, and the earthly bodies is philosophy. If there's a screw loose in a heavenly body, that's philosophy . . . Philosophy's the chap for me.' (ch. 57)

Remonstrating with Ralph Nickleby, he speaks in the same strain:

> I am the man as is guaranteed, by unimpeachable references, to be a out-and-outer in morals and uprightness of principle. (ch. 60)

In the course of the same interview he combines poetry with vulgarisms and slang:

> 'My family!' hiccupped Mr Squeers, raising his eye to the ceiling; 'my daughter, as is at that age when all the sensibilities is a coming out strong in blow – my son as is the young Norval of private life, and the pride and ornament of a doting willage – here's a shock for my family! The coat of arms of the Squeerses is tore, and their sun is gone down into the ocean wave!'

Pecksniff's language has many special characteristics, some of which reflect his character while some of them seem accidental, making him to some extent a figure of fun. He and Jonas Chuzzlewit can be regarded as the most villainous characters in *Martin Chuzzlewit*; the difference between them is that the villainy of Jonas is unrelieved, while Pecksniff, for all his unpleasantness, is one of Dickens's great comic characters. The author's dislike of Pecksniff soon becomes apparent, but in the earlier part of the novel it is thinly disguised by irony. Pecksniff stands by old Martin's bedside 'in all the dignity of Goodness' (ch. 3); when he puts his ear to the keyhole he does so 'in the fervour of his affectionate zeal' (ch. 4); he is 'the best of architects and land-surveyors' (ch. 5). When he shows young Martin round his house, the pride that apes humility is revealed in almost every sentence: 'my works (slight things at best)', 'I have scribbled myself, but have not yet published', 'a poor first-floor to us, but a bower to them' (ch. 5). When he is praising his daughter Mercy to old Martin, the element of burlesque becomes more marked:

> 'We sometimes venture to consider her rather a fine figure, sir. Speaking as an artist, I may perhaps be permitted to suggest that

its outline is graceful and correct. I am naturally,' said Mr Pecksniff, drying his hands upon his handkerchief, and looking anxiously in his cousin's face at almost every word, 'proud, if I may use the expression, to have a daughter who is constructed on the best models.' (ch. 10)

Like Squeers, Pecksniff, with an author's pride in his work, quotes his own advertisement once when sober (ch. 2) and again when drunk (ch. 9). The first quotation is full of what has since come to be called uplift:

He will avail himself of the eligible opportunity which now offers, for uniting the advantages of the best practical architectural education with the comforts of a home, and the constant association with some who (however humble their sphere, and limited their capacity) are not unmindful of their moral responsibilities. (ch. 2)

Mercy's arch recognition of the quotation leads Pecksniff to call her a 'playful warbler', and the author's comment suggests that Pecksniff was at first intended to have a linguistic habit which is not particularly marked in the course of the novel:

It may be observed in connexion with his calling his daughter a 'warbler' that she was not at all vocal, but that Mr Pecksniff was in the frequent habit of using any word that occurred to him as having a good sound, and rounding a sentence well, without much care for its meaning.

It is true that he confuses the word *metaphysically* with *metaphorically* ('I believe that our dear friend Mr Chuffey is, metaphysically speaking, a – shall I say a dummy?' ch. 18) but this is a word that is frequently misused. It may seem that the explanation 'When I say olive-branches, . . . I mean our unpretending luggage' (ch. 6) points to another misuse of words, but the context shows that this is a far-fetched simile rather than an example of the use of words at random. When Dickens wants to illustrate a characteristic, he generally hammers his point home more than this.

A habit which Pecksniff shares with Carker, in *Dombey and Son*, is that of immediately repeating remarks that have been made to him. With Carker this is probably merely a way of withholding comment, but Pecksniff's friends apparently find the habit soothing rather than infuriating:

'A gentleman taken ill upon the road, has been so very bad up-stairs, sir,' said the tearful hostess.

'A gentleman taken ill upon the road, has been so very bad up-stairs, has he?' repeated Mr Pecksniff. 'Well, well!'

Now there was nothing that one may call decidedly original in this remark, nor can it be exactly said to have contained any wise precept theretofore unknown to mankind, or to have opened any hidden source of consolation: but Mr Pecksniff's manner was so bland, and he nodded his head so soothingly, and showed in every-thing such an affable sense of his own excellence, that anybody would have been, as Mrs Lupin was, comforted by the mere voice and presence of such a man; and, though he had merely said 'a verb must agree with its nominative case in number and person, my good friend,' or 'eight times eight are sixty-four, my worthy soul', must have felt deeply grateful to him for his humanity and wisdom. (ch. 3)

The special language of Mr Micawber is marked chiefly by its smoothly flowing circumlocutions.[1] This characteristic is most noticeable in his letters, but the style of his letters sometimes seems to overflow into his conversation. Long sentences are more at home in the written than in the spoken language, and Mr Micawber's spoken sentences often get out of hand, with the result that aposiopesis is frequent in his conversation. The usual indication that a sentence is proving too much for him is the phrase 'in short'. This phrase is sometimes as misleading as the 'I will be brief' of Polonius, but usually it marks the transition from a circumlocutory style to one that is extremely direct and colloquial. The prolixity and Latinized vocabulary of the earlier part of the sentence are emphasized by the brevity and directness of its conclusion. The two styles are illustrated on Mr Micawber's first appearance in the book:

'My address,' said Mr Micawber, 'is Windsor Terrace, City Road. I – in short,' said Mr Micawber, with the same genteel air, and in another burst of confidence – 'I live there.'

I made him a bow.

'Under the impression,' said Mr Micawber, 'that your peregrina-tions in this metropolis have not as yet been extensive, and that you might have some difficulty in penetrating the arcana of the Modern Babylon in the direction of the City Road – in short,' said Mr Micawber in another burst of confidence, 'that you might lose

[1] On the special language of Mr Micawber see J. Hillis Miller, *op. cit.*, p. 151.

yourself – I shall be happy to call this evening, and install you in the knowledge of the nearest way.' (*DC*, ch. 11)

Other examples are:

'The twins no longer derive their sustenance from Nature's founts – in short . . . they are weaned!'
'a widow lady, and one who is apparently her offspring – in short . . . her son.'
'in short . . . it is an intellect capable of getting up the classics to any extent.'
'Sometimes my difficulties have – in short, have floored me.' (all from ch. 17)

Even without the warning 'in short', Mr Micawber is capable of sudden and surprising colloquialism: 'My advice is, never do tomorrow what you can do today. Procrastination is the thief of time. Collar him!' (ch. 12).

Mrs Micawber shares some of her husband's linguistic characteristics, including a tendency to talk like a book, or rather like the leading article of a provincial newspaper. A comic effect is achieved by the use of genteel clichés in a context that is not genteel: 'My papa lived to bail Mr Micawber several times, and then expired, regretted by a numerous circle' (ch. 12). The same fondness for the genteel makes her quote Latin, after a fashion: 'experientia does it – as papa used to say' (ch. 11). Mrs Micawber's mistake would be more readily appreciated by Dickens's contemporaries, familiar with the 'unreformed' pronunciation of *docet*, than it is by the reader of today.

It is not only major characters who have distinctive idiolects. Plornish, in *Little Dorrit*, has his own language. His usual manner is described as 'a little obscure, but conscientiously emphatic'. The remark which prompts this comment is:

'and if Mr Casby an't well off, none better, it an't through any fault of Pancks. For, as to Pancks, he does, he really does, he does indeed!' (Bk I, ch. 24)

Here, as elsewhere, Plornish's obscurity is the result of diffidence. He is deeply moved, but he feels that it would be unbecoming for one in his humble station to be more specific about what it is that Pancks actually does. When he does complain of Mr F's Aunt, he cannot bring himself to use the first personal pronoun: 'The way she snapped a person's head

F

off, dear me!' (Bk I, ch. 24). The same preference for an impersonal approach causes him to describe Mr F's Aunt as a 'party': 'she is, I do assure you, the winegariest party'. He is capable of an occasional expressive idiom, as when he praises his father-in-law's singing: 'I never heard you come the warbles as I have heard you come the warbles this night' (Bk II, ch. 13). He is fond of making speeches addressed to his father-in-law, who replies in the same style:

> 'John Edward Nandy,' said Mr Plornish, addressing the old gentleman. 'Sir. It's not too often that you see unpretending actions without a spark of pride, and therefore when you see them give grateful honour unto the same, being that if you don't and live to want 'em it follows serve you right.'
> To which Mr Nandy replied:
> 'I am heartily of your opinion, Thomas, and which your opinion is the same as mine, and therefore no more words, and not being backwards with that opinion, which opinion giving it as yeas, Thomas, yes, is the opinion in which yourself and me must ever be unanimously jined by all, and where there is not difference of opinion there can be none but one opinion, which fully no, Thomas, Thomas, no!' (Bk II, ch. 13)

These speeches are obscure, but here the obscurity does not spring from diffidence. It is the result of the two speakers attempting a task beyond their strength. They are anxious to express warm feelings ceremoniously but they do so in sentences which are too long and which consequently get out of hand.

Sometimes two characters, in different novels, talk in a rather similar way. Mrs Nickleby and Flora Finching both run on a good deal, but they run on in different ways. When Forster read *Nicholas Nickleby*, he felt sure that Mrs Nickleby's long speeches were based on those of Miss Bates in *Emma*, whom Jane Austen describes as 'a great talker upon little matters' (ch. 3), but Dickens assured him that when he wrote *Nicholas Nickleby* he had not read *Emma* (Forster, II, 4). The resemblance is undoubtedly close, but it is not to be attributed to literary imitation; it is more probable that both are based on life and that both Jane Austen and Dickens had recognised the comic possibilities of undisciplined loquacity. Miss Bates, Mrs Nickleby and Flora Finching all use long sentences made up of a large number of clauses, each of them mentioning some

unimportant detail or qualifying unimportant statements. The
sentences acquire added complications from the speaker's habit
of correcting herself and from her failure to ensure that
adjectival clauses occur reasonably near to the nouns which
they qualify. Mrs Nickleby gives an example of what she can
achieve in a conversation with Kate and Ralph Nickleby:

> 'I remember when your poor papa and I came to town after we
> were married, that a young lady brought me home a chip cottage-
> bonnet, with white and green trimming, and green persian lining,
> in her own carriage, which drove up to the door full gallop; – at
> least, I am not quite certain whether it was her own carriage or a
> hackney chariot, but I remember very well that the horse dropped
> down dead as he was turning round, and that your poor papa said
> he hadn't had any corn for a fortnight.' (*NN*, ch. 10)

The things that Mrs Nickleby forgets are usually the important
ones, but even here she is unreliable, and she is liable to forget
unimportant things too. To her a fact is a fact, and she has no
power of discrimination to tell her which facts are significant.
She will go to endless trouble to remember irrelevant details
and then brush aside a distinction that makes all the difference
between sense and nonsense. When Madeline Bray is suffering
from loss of appetite, Mrs Nickleby suggests a remedy:

> 'I am sure I don't know, but I have heard that two or three dozen
> native lobsters give an appetite, though that comes to the same
> thing after all, for I suppose you must have an appetite before you
> can take 'em. If I said lobsters, I meant oysters, it's all the same.'
> (ch. 55)

The impression which Flora Finching's speech makes on
Arthur Clennam after his long absence is one of 'disjointed
volubility' (*LD*, Bk I, ch. 13). Her style is admirably suited to
the monopolizing of conversation. Random recollections from
the past mingle with small talk about the present to fill the
rag-bag of her conversation. When memory and invention run
dry, she falls back on a refrain, which has the advantage of
preventing Clennam from saying anything while it does not
make heavy demands on the speaker: 'One remark I wish to
make, one explanation I wish to offer' (Bk I, ch. 13). She
passes abruptly from the commonplace to the poetical:

> 'Romance, however,' Flora went on, busily arranging Mr F's
> Aunt's toast, 'as I openly said to Mr F when he proposed to me and

you will be surprised to hear that he proposed seven times once in a hackney-coach once in a boat once in a pew once on a donkey at Tunbridge Wells and the rest on his knees, Romance was fled with the early days of Arthur Clennam, our parents tore us asunder we became marble and stern reality usurped the throne, Mr F said very much to his credit that he was perfectly aware of it and even preferred that state of things accordingly the word was spoken the fiat went forth and such is life you see my dear and yet we do not break but bend, pray make a good breakfast while I go in with the tray.' (Bk I, ch. 24)

Flora's word-order does not make things any easier for the reader, as in her explanation of the reason why she takes brandy in her tea:

'I am obliged to be careful to follow the directions of my medical man though the flavour is anything but agreeable being a poor creature . . . ' (Bk I, ch. 24)

Another cause of difficulty is that the use of a word is liable to start a new train of thought, with the result that one of Flora's sentences will contain parentheses within parentheses like a Chinese box:

'Really so sorry that I should happen to be late on this morning of all mornings because my intention and my wish was to be ready to meet you when you came in and to say that any one that interested Arthur Clennam half so much must interest me and that I gave you the heartiest welcome and was so glad, instead of which they never called me and there I still am snoring I dare say if the truth was known and if you don't like either cold fowl or hot boiled ham which many people don't I dare say besides Jews and theirs are scruples of conscience which we must all respect though I must say I wish they had them equally strong when they sell us false articles for real that certainly ain't worth the money I shall be quite vexed,' said Flora. (Bk I, ch. 24)

She says whatever is uppermost in her mind. It is natural that she should be conscious of the steps that she has had to climb to reach Arthur Clennam's workshop after his return from China, and this consciousness prompts an unexpected comparison:

A great deal superior to China not to be denied and much nearer though higher up. (Bk I, ch. 23)

Flora's good-humoured volubility is emphasized by its contrast with the grim and hostile taciturnity of Mr F's Aunt, and the two nearly always appear together.

Dickens is often accused of over-simplification, and it is true that his best-known characters are well known, not because of the variety of their linguistic characteristics but because of the frequency with which those characteristics are brought to the reader's notice. When he wished to do so, however, Dickens could portray extremely complicated idiolects. These are less well remembered than those of Micawber or Mrs Gamp, but they are more interesting and they show greater artistry. Two of the minor characters in *Bleak House* repay examination for this reason.

The chief characteristic of William Guppy's idiolect is the mixture of levels that arises from the speaker's pre-occupation with class distinctions joined with uncertainty about the kind of language that is appropriate to a particular occasion. The substandard nature of his speech is made clear quite early in the novel when he says cheerfully to Mrs Rouncewell, 'Us London lawyers don't often get an out' (*BH*, ch. 7), and there are many later examples. In a single chapter (ch. 29) we find substandard syntax ('the money for the stamp, which comes heavy'), slang ('it completely knocked me over'), tautology ('and which law-writer was an anonymous character, his name being unknown'), and lack of linguistic tact ('females'). His proposal of marriage to Esther Summerson (ch. 9) illustrates his mixture of styles. He uses stilted legal language combined with colloquial abbreviation in assuring her that, although his salary had stood at the same figure for 'a lengthened period', 'a rise of five has since taken place, and a further rise of five is guaranteed at the expiration of a term not exceeding twelve months from the present date'. After receiving an assurance that what he says will be treated as 'in total confidence', he is still reluctant to begin his proposal.

> All this time Mr Guppy was either planing his forehead with his handkerchief, or tightly rubbing the palm of his left hand with the palm of his right. 'If you would excuse my taking another glass of wine, miss, I think it might assist me in getting on, without a continual choke that cannot fail to be mutually unpleasant.'

Apart from the gestures, this opening shows a mixture of the genteel (the address *miss*), the literary (*assist, cannot fail to be, mutually*), and the colloquial (*getting on, a continual choke*). When the proposal is not well received, literary influences become more strongly marked: 'Cruel miss, hear but another word!' and 'Thy image has ever since been fixed in my breast' are straight out of circulating library novels. He concludes by referring to himself as 'Mr William Guppy', with the social climber's insistence on the use of titles. A similar jumble of many different levels of speech is to be found in Guppy's interviews with Lady Dedlock (ch. 29). There is no loss of realism in such a mixture of styles: it is an accurate reflexion of the speech-habits of a social climber anxious to make a good impression, with the variations heightened, no doubt, in order to give a comic effect.

It is obvious that Dickens approves of Inspector Bucket, but he is willing to make fun of him. The attitude of many readers towards him is no doubt similar to that of Matthew Bagnet. There is admiration mixed with the indignation with which Bagnet recalls Bucket's plausibility and audacity in arresting Mr George 'With a second-hand wiolinceller. Of a good tone. For a friend. That money was no object to' (*BH*, ch. 52). Bucket has a uniform technique in getting on good terms with those he wants to question. Flattery without restraint is his chief weapon, and this is followed up by an attempt to establish a common interest, however indirect, with the person he is addressing. Mrs Bagnet has children and therefore Bucket tells her that a friend of his has nineteen of them; one of the children plays the fife, whereupon Bucket declares that when he was a boy he played the fife himself (ch. 49); when interviewing Sir Leicester Dedlock's footman he is not content with saying that his own father had been a footman, but, for good measure, adds that his brother and brother-in-law are also in service (ch. 53). When Bucket is in pursuit of a criminal, he is not upon oath, and we learn to recognize his departures from truth by the vigour with which he piles up corroborative detail. Lady Dedlock's footman is easily trapped into admitting that he had let her into the garden on the night of Tulkinhorn's murder. Bucket makes use of the old trick of pretending that he already knew this:

> 'And left her there. Certainly you did. I saw you doing it.'
> 'I didn't see *you*,' says Mercury.
> 'I was rather in a hurry,' returns Mr Bucket, 'for I was going to

visit a aunt of mine that lives at Chelsea – next door but two to the old original Bun House – ninety year old the old Lady is, a single woman, and got a little property. Yes, I chanced to be passing at the time. Let's see. What time might it be? It wasn't ten.'

'Half past nine.'

'You're right. So it was.' (ch. 53)

Bucket uses slang very freely: 'Supposing I was to be picked off now', 'the nobbiest way of keeping it quiet', 'a toothful of your fine old brown East Inder sherry' (chs. 53, 54). Sometimes the slang is that of his profession: 'the deceased Mr Tulkinghorn employed me to reckon up her Ladyship – if you'll excuse my making use of the term we commonly employ' (ch. 54). He is loquacious, and in the effort to keep talking he can resort to a string of sententious proverbs:

'So it is, and such is life. The cat's away, and the mice they play; the frost breaks up, and the water runs.' (ch. 54)

Bucket's speech is full of vulgarisms. His habit of addressing Sir Leicester Dedlock as 'Sir Leicester Dedlock, Baronet' cannot be completely explained as an attempt to conciliate one who was very conscious of his rank. He has pronunciations like *for'ard* (ch. 53; see Appendix § 21) and analogical forms like *littlest* (ch. 56, see Appendix § 66).

6

LANGUAGE TO SUIT
THE OCCASION

When ways of speaking can be associated with groups of people, they constitute a dialect; when they can be associated with an individual, they form an idiolect. There remain linguistic characteristics which can be associated with neither an individual nor a group but with an occasion. A good example occurs in the burlesque passage in which Mr Sapsea describes his wooing of Miss Brobity:

> When I made my proposal, she did me the honour to be so over-shadowed with a species of Awe, as to be able to articulate only the two words, 'O Thou!' meaning myself. (*ED*, ch. 4)

The use of the pronoun 'thou' in religious contexts had given the word such associations for Miss Brobity that she could use it as a way of expressing ecstatic veneration for her future husband.

It is clear that Dickens paid a good deal of attention to the choice of appropriate language for his characters. When Jingle proposes to Rachael Wardle, he completely abandons his usual jerky manner of speaking and instead uses the sentimental style of a circulating library novel, a style much more likely to appeal to Miss Wardle. The author calls attention to the change of style by saying that this address was the most consecutive that Jingle was ever known to utter. When Jingle goes on, the author's comment is no doubt intended to remind the reader that Jingle is a strolling actor and that it is therefore quite natural that he should use such language:

> 'Never!' exclaimed Jingle, with a professional (i.e. theatrical) air. (*PP*, ch. 8)

But a Dickensian character does not have to be an actor to use the language of the stage. Mr Moddle sometimes talks like a member of Vincent Crummles's company. When Charity Pecksniff urges him to agree to the inclusion of Jinkins among the wedding guests, he replies:

> Let him come! He has ever been my rock ahead through life. 'Tis meet he should be there. Ha, ha! Oh, yes! let Jinkins come! (*MC*, ch. 54)

It is natural that a keen social observer like Dickens should provide examples of such varieties of language as parliamentary oratory. His experience as a reporter of debates in parliament gave him a familiarity with that type of oratory and a distaste for it that find frequent expression in the novels. Such passages are natural enough in the early novels, when his reporting experiences were still fresh in his memory. The first chapter of *Pickwick Papers* contains a parody of the minutes, prolix and full of clichés, of a small debating society, and Mr Pickwick's speech to the members of the Pickwick Club is a parody of the sort of speech that such societies encourage, with its mixture of acrimony and conventional courtesy: 'The hon. gent. was a humbug'. The chapter has given one useful phrase to the English language: many a difficult situation has been eased when one of the parties to a quarrel, feeling that he has gone too far but unwilling to withdraw what he has said, claims that the words that he has used are to be understood in a Pickwickian sense.

Dickens returns to the attack on prolix and self-important public speakers in his account of Mr Staple's speech in the Blue Lion Inn at Muggleton after the cricket match with the team from Dingley Dell (*PP*, ch. 7). There are the same debating society clichés, the apologetic use of slang phrases, and the inappropriate anecdote.

Another object of satire is the man who addresses his friends and acquaintances as though they were a public meeting. Pott, the editor of the Eatanswill Gazette, is first introduced as an orator of this type and, what is worse, an inefficient one:

> 'The press is a mighty engine, sir,' said Pott.
> Mr Pickwick yielded his fullest assent to the proposition.
> 'But I trust, sir,' said Pott, 'that I have never abused the enormous power I wield. I trust, sir, that I have never pointed the noble instrument which is placed in my hands, against the sacred bosom of private life, or the tender breast of individual reputation; – I

trust, sir, that I have devoted my energies to – to endeavours – humble they may be, humble I know they are – to instill those principles of – which – are—'

Here the editor of the Eatanswill Gazette, appearing to ramble, Mr Pickwick came to his relief, and said – 'Certainly.' (*PP*, ch. 13)

There is a parody of turgid oratory in *Nicholas Nickleby*. Mr Gregsbury, M.P., is described as a man with 'a loud voice, a pompous manner, a tolerable command of sentences with no meaning in them, and, in short, every requisite for a very good member indeed' (ch. 16). We are then given a specimen of his oratorical style:

'My conduct, Pugstyles,' said Mr Gregsbury, looking round upon the deputation with gracious magnanimity – 'My conduct has been, and ever will be, regulated by a sincere regard for the true and real interests of this great and happy country. Whether I look at home, or abroad; whether I behold the peaceful industrious communities of our island home: her rivers covered with steam-boats, her roads with locomotives, her streets with cabs, her skies with balloons of a power and magnitude hitherto unknown in the history of aeronautics in this or any other nation – I say, whether I look merely at home, or, stretching my eyes farther, contemplate the boundless prospect of conquest and possession – achieved by British perseverance and British valour – which is outspread before me, I clasp my hands, and turning my eyes to the broad expanse above my head, exclaim, "Thank Heaven, I am a Briton!".'

It may be that in these parodies Dickens is taking his revenge for the boredom that had been induced in him by the necessity of transcribing large numbers of bad speeches. Sometimes the reports are in the indirect speech that would be used in a newspaper report, and they are of a length more appropriate to the spacious days of the novel than to the present day. Such a passage is the report in the second chapter of *Nicholas Nickleby* of the public meeting held to promote the formation of the United Metropolitan Improved Hot Muffin and Crumpet Baking and Punctual Delivery Company. The report contributes nothing to the plot and very little to the characterization of the novel; it is there because Dickens enjoyed writing such passages, and the fashion of the time allowed the introduction of such matter into a novel. The habit persists even in the later novels. Slackbridge, in *Hard Times*, is a good example of the wordy orator familiar with all the mechanical tricks such as 'elegant variation' and alliteration: 'this degrading and disgusting document, this blighting bill, this pernicious placard, this abominable advertisement' (Bk III, ch. 4). Veneering's election speech in *Our Mutual Friend* (Bk II, ch. 3) is in the same tradition, as is his speech at the breakfast to celebrate the first anniversary of the wedding of the Lammles (Bk II, ch. 16).

Inappropriateness of the style of speech to the occasion can be a source of humour, as when Mrs Wilfer, with stately and polysyllabic ill-humour, consents to give Bella instructions on how to prepare the dinner:

> 'First,' returned Mrs Wilfer solemnly, 'if you persist in what I cannot but regard as conduct utterly incompatible with the equipage in which you arrived—'
> ('Which I do, Ma.')
> 'First, then, you put the fowls down to the fire.'
> 'To – be – sure!' cried Bella; 'and flour them, and twirl them round, and there they go!' sending them spinning at a great rate. 'What's next, Ma?'
> 'Next,' said Mrs Wilfer with a wave of her gloves, expressive of abdication under protest from the culinary throne, 'I would recommend examination of the bacon in the sauce-pan on the fire, and also of the potatoes by the application of a fork. Preparation of the greens will further become necessary, if you persist in this unseemly demeanour.'
> 'As of course I do, Ma.' (*OMF*, Bk III, ch. 4)

Whenever Dickensian characters are deeply moved, they are liable to make speeches, and this habit is not confined to those who have mastered the principles of English grammar. There are many speeches in which poetic eloquence shines through substandard syntax. Mr Plornish, in *Little Dorrit*, finds relief for his feelings in speeches beginning 'John Edward Nandy, Sir'. Mr Kenwigs speaks with real eloquence after his reconciliation with Mr Lillyvick:

> When I see that man a mingling, once again, in the spear which he adorns, and see his affections deweloping themselves in legitimate sitiwations, I feel that his nature is as elewated and expanded, as his standing afore society as a public character is unimpeached, and the woices of my infant children purvided for in life, seem to whisper to me softly, 'This is an ewent at which Evins itself looks down!' (*NN*, ch. 52)

Flora Finching describes the death of her husband in a poetic vein which is all the more striking in that it occurs in a context which is not poetic:

I will draw a veil over that dreamy life, Mr F was in good spirits his appetite was good he liked the cookery he considered the wine weak but palatable and all was well, we returned to the immediate neighbourhood of Number Thirty Little Gosling Street London Docks and settled down, ere we had yet fully detected the house-maid in selling the feathers out of the spare bed Gout flying upwards soared with Mr F to another sphere. (*LD*, Bk I, ch. 24)

By all accounts Dickens was himself a ready talker, not unduly shy in company, but he was very conscious of the plight of the shy young man without much conversation, and many of his best comic scenes deal with the sufferings of such a man. Toots is one of the most engaging of these unskilful conversationalists. It is characteristic of his inoffensive modesty that his habitual phrase is 'It's of no consequence'. Fascination Fledgeby acquires his nickname as a piece of facetious homage to the smallness of his talk (*OMF*, Bk II, ch. 4). He has something in common with Marlow in *She Stoops to Conquer* in that he is most at a loss for words in talking to young women of his own social class; when he is talking to Lammle, Riah or Jenny Wren, his shyness disappears, to be replaced by aggressiveness (Bk II, ch. 5). It is clear that Dickens loathes him, but many readers will think that Fledgeby's commonplaces, which are held up to ridicule, compare favourably with the forced pleasantries of the Lammles (Bk II, ch. 4).

Georgiana Podsnap's shortcomings as a conversationalist are amusingly but sympathetically represented. Mrs Lammle tries to draw her out by engaging her in 'a little quiet talk':

It promised to be a very quiet talk, for Miss Podsnap replied in a flutter, 'Oh! Indeed, it's very kind of you, but I am afraid I *don't* talk. . . . But Ma talks! . . .'
'Fond of reading, perhaps?'
'Yes. At least I – don't mind that so much,' returned Miss Podsnap. (*OMF*, Bk I, ch. 11)

There is some justification for Fledgeby's comment 'that Georgiana don't seem to be of the pitching-in order' (Bk II, ch. 5).

Edmund Sparkler is another man of few words, and his mother has an uphill task in getting him to report what he has heard. When he does speak, he shows the same tendency to omit lightly-stressed words as Sir Leicester Dedlock's languid cousin in *Bleak House* (ch. 40). Mrs Merdle calls on him to report what people say about his stepfather:

'I couldn't,' said Mr Sparkler, after feeling his pulse as before, 'couldn't undertake to say what led to it – 'cause memory desperate loose. But being in company with the brother of a doosed fine gal – well educated too – with no biggodd nonsense about her – at the period alluded to—'

'There! Never mind the sister,' remarked Mrs Merdle, a little impatiently. 'What did the brother say?'

'Didn't say a word, ma'am,' answered Mr Sparkler. 'As silent a feller as myself. Equally hard up for a remark,'

'Somebody said something,' returned Mrs Merdle. 'Never mind who it was.'

('Assure you I don't in the least,' said Mr Sparkler.)

'But tell us what it was.'

Mr Sparkler referred to his pulse again, and put himself through some severe mental discipline before he replied:

'Fellers referring to my Governor – expression not my own – occasionally compliment my Governor in a very handsome way on being immensely rich and knowing – perfect phenomenon of Buyer and Banker and that – but say the Shop sits heavily on him. Say he carries the Shop about, on his back rather – like Jew clothesmen with too much business.' (*LD*, Bk I, ch. 33)

Fascination Fledgeby and Edmund Sparkler are examples of men who are bores because they talk too little; Dickens was also familiar with the bore who talks too much. Lord Decimus Tite Barnacle is an example, and the reader has cause to be grateful that his anecdote about a pear tree (*LD*, Bk II, ch. 12) is summarized instead of being quoted in full. Lord Decimus is the pompous type of bore who spares the hearer no detail because he is so convinced of the importance of every detail that concerns himself. Mrs Nickleby is another character with a firm grasp of the irrelevant, but her love of irrelevant detail is due not so much to self-importance as to muddle-headedness.

The absurdities of conversation, as practised by people who talk more than they think, sometimes calls for annotation by the author. Mrs Skewton entertains Mr Dombey:

' . . . Cows are my passion. What I have ever sighed for, has been to retreat to a Swiss farm, and live entirely surrounded by cows – and china.'

This curious association of objects, suggesting a remembrance of the celebrated bull who got by mistake into a crockery shop, was received with perfect gravity by Mr Dombey, who intimated his opinion that Nature was no doubt, a very respectable institution. (*DS*, ch. 21)

The difficulty of keeping up a conversation is matched by the difficulty of bringing one to a close. Mr Snagsby, in *Bleak House*, is the most inoffensive of men but on the night of Krook's death he drives Jobling to distraction by dwelling on painful subjects simply because he does not know how to get away. Many readers will sympathize with him as he 'coughs a cough expressive of not exactly seeing his way out of this conversation' (ch. 32).

It is well known that speech serves many purposes beside the conveying of ideas, and Dickens realized this. When Bailey is showing off to Poll Sweedlepipe, he says 'Well! How are you?' and receives a reply to which he pays no attention. After a few more exchanges, he repeats the question:

> 'Oh! I'm pretty well,' said Poll.
> He answered the question again because Mr Bailey asked it again; Mr Bailey asked it again, because – accompanied with a straddling action of the white cords, a bend of the knees, and a striking forth of the top-boots – it was an easy, horse-fleshy, turfy thing to do. (*MC*, ch. 25)

Toots overdoes this type of conversation in seeking to ingratiate himself with Mrs Pipchin:

> he smiled on her with so much urbanity, and asked her how she did, so often, in the course of her visits to little Paul, that at last she one night told him plainly she wasn't used to it, whatever he might think; and she could not, and she would not bear it, either from himself or any other puppy then existing: at which unexpected acknowledgment of his civilities, Mr Toots was so alarmed that he secreted himself in a retired spot until she had gone. (*DS*, ch. 14)

Toots, anxious to be friendly with Walter Gay, makes use of all the small change of everyday conversation, but all the clichés come out at once:

> 'How-de-do? I hope you didn't take any cold. I – I shall be very glad if you'll give me the pleasure of your acquaintance. I wish you many happy returns of the day. Upon my word and honour,' said Mr Toots, warming as he became better acquainted with Walter's face and figure, 'I'm very glad to see you.'

'Thank you heartily,' said Walter. 'I couldn't desire a more genuine and genial welcome.'

'Couldn't you, though?' said Mr Toots, still shaking his hand. 'It's very kind of you. I'm much obliged to you. How-de-do? I hope you left everybody quite well over the – that is, upon the – I mean wherever you came from last, you know.' (ch. 50)

Completing other people's sentences is a common practice in the first few chapters of *Dombey and Son*. Miss Tox has the task of completing sentences for Mr Dombey and his sister:

'My dear Paul,' said Mrs Chick, after a moment's silence, 'it is of no use inquiring. I do not think, I will tell you candidly, that Wickam is a person of very cheerful spirit, or what one would call a—'

'A daughter of Momus,' Miss Tox softly suggested.

'Exactly so,' said Mrs Chick.

Again, Mrs Chick is anxious to mention the possibility that Paul might lose the use of his legs:

Mrs Chick was afraid to say limbs, after Mr Dombey's recent objection to bones, and therefore waited for a suggestion from Miss Tox, who, true to her office, hazarded 'members'. (ch. 8)

Doctor Parker Peps leaves sentences unfinished from sheer self-importance, and relies on the family doctor to finish his sentences for him:

'I should say, in your amiable lady. There there is a certain degree of languor, and a general absence of elasticity, which we would rather – not—'

'See,' interposed the family practitioner with another inclination of the head.

'Quite so,' said Doctor Parker Peps, 'which we would rather not see.' (*DS*, ch. 1)

It is one of the unattractive qualities of Fledgeby in *Our Mutual Friend* that he never accepts a suggestion of this kind, even when it has been made necessary by his own lack of conversational gifts.

Some of Dickens's less attractive characters make use of the debater's trick of asserting uncontestable truths with an implication that some adversary, real or imaginary, is, to his discredit, likely to deny them. Pumblechook reproaches Pip:

'This is him,' said Pumblechook, 'as I have rode in my shay-cart. This is him as I have seen brought up by hand. This is him untoe

the sister of which I was uncle by marriage, as her name was
Georgiana M'ria from her own mother, let him deny it if he can!'
    The waiter seemed convinced that I could not deny it, and that
it gave the case a black look. (*GE*, ch. 58)

Rogue Riderhood, using a not uncommon form of words, says
of the inn outside which he claims that Hexam confessed
himself guilty of murder, 'The Six Jolly Fellowships won't run
away'. When he leads Lightwood and Wrayburn to the inn, he
triumphantly calls attention to the inn as evidence of his
veracity:

> 'Look round here, Lawyer Lightwood, at them red curtains. It's
> the Fellowships, the 'ouse as I told you wouldn't run away. And
> has it run away?' (*OMF*, Bk I, ch. 12)

As used by Riderhood, the trick is so transparent as to be
farcical, but similar methods are used every day by more
sophisticated controversialists, who produce evidence in support
of some unimportant though incontestable detail, and then slip
in their main point unsupported by evidence.
    Dickensian characters are fond of criticizing one another's
linguistic habits. They are very much concerned about whether
what they say is 'English' or not. Mr Bucket is impatient when
his orders are queried: 'Up, I tell you! Up! Ain't it English?'
(*BH*, ch. 57). Mr Bounderby uses the word 'English' in the
sense 'outright, straightforward language' when expressing his
opinion of Jupe: 'He is a runaway rogue and a vagabond, that's
what he is, in English' (*HT*, Bk I, ch. 6).
    Criticism of one character by another is a useful way of
forestalling possible criticism by the reader. In the scene in
Barnaby Rudge where Edward Chester remonstrates with his
father, Edward makes long speeches whose syntax is that of
the written, not the spoken, language, and most readers will
find themselves agreeing with his father when he says:

> 'There is great earnestness, vast candour, a manifest sincerity in
> all that you say, but I fear I observe the faintest indications of a
> tendency to prose.' (ch. 15)

The most persevering critic of speech in the novels of
Dickens is Mrs General. It is natural that she should be a critic
of language, since she is employed to teach her pupils the
correct class-indicators, and these are often linguistic. When

Fanny Dorrit speaks of her uncle having tumbled over a
subject, Mrs General is quick to correct such a vulgar idiom:

> 'My dear, what a curious phrase,' said Mrs General. 'Would
> not inadvertently lighted upon, or accidentally referred to, be
> better?' (*LD*, Bk II, ch. 5)

She reproves Little Dorrit for using the word 'father':

> 'Papa is a preferable mode of address,' observed Mrs General.
> 'Father is rather vulgar, my dear. The word Papa, besides, gives
> a pretty form to the lips. Papa, potatoes, poultry, prunes and prism,
> are all very good words for the lips: especially prunes and prism.
> You will find it serviceable, in the formation of a demeanour, if you
> sometimes say to yourself in company – on entering a room, for
> instance – Papa, potatoes, poultry, prunes and prism, prunes and
> prism.'
>
> 'Pray, my child,' said Mr Dorrit, 'attend to the – hum – precepts
> of Mrs General.' (Bk II, ch. 5)

It is an interesting example of the way in which extremes meet
in matters of class dialect that, while *papa* is so genteel as to
earn the approbation of Mrs General, *pa* is distinctly substandard. It is Fanny Squeers who refers to her father as 'My
pa' (*NN*, ch. 39).

Eugene Wrayburn speaks of Mortimer Lightwood's 'reading'
of his weaknesses, and then criticizes his own use of the word
as though it had been used by somebody else:

> (By-the-bye, that very word, Reading, in its critical use, always
> charms me. An actress's Reading of a chambermaid, a dancer's
> Reading of a hornpipe, a singer's Reading of a song, a marine
> painter's Reading of the sea, the kettledrum's Reading of an
> instrumental passage, are phrases ever youthful and delightful.)
> (*OMF*, Bk III, ch. 10)

The most unexpected characters are upon occasion critics of
language. Sam Weller is one of the chief. He is particularly
fond of sardonically calling attention to hypocrisy or pretentiousness in the use of words. He invites Stiggins to have a drink:

> 'Wot's your usual tap, sir?' replied Sam.
> 'Oh, my dear young friend,' replied Mr Stiggins, 'all taps is
> vanities . . .'
> 'Well,' said Sam, 'I des-say they may be, sir; but which is your
> partickler wanity? Vich wanity do you like the flavour on best, sir?'
> (*PP*, ch. 45)

When the footmen of Bath invite Sam Weller to a convivial evening, they are clearly badly-informed about both spelling and meaning of the word 'swarry'. When Smauker's invitation refers to 'a friendly swarry, consisting of a boiled leg of mutton with the usual trimmings,' Sam Weller's comment is a reasonable one:

> 'Vell,' said Sam, 'this is coming it rayther powerful, this is. I never heerd a biled leg o' mutton called a swarry afore. I wonder wot they'd call a roast one.' (ch. 37)

Mrs Wilfer and her daughter Lavinia are stern critics of language. Mrs Wilfer considers *brisk* to be 'a low expression' (*OMF*, Bk III, ch. 4), and Lavinia describes George Sampson's *Go it* as an 'omnibus-driving expression' (Bk IV, ch. 16).

Mr Venus becomes a very exacting critic when his forth-coming marriage to Pleasant Riderhood is mentioned. His resentment at the use of the term 'the old party' to describe his future wife is understandable, but Silas Wegg's correction proves equally unacceptable:

> 'When is it to come off?' asked Silas.
> 'Mr Wegg,' said Venus, with another flush. 'I cannot permit it to be put in the form of a Fight. I must temperately but firmly call upon you, sir, to amend that question.'

There is a touch of satire in Wegg's further correction in which he takes refuge in the clichés of the novelette:

> 'When is the lady a-going to give her 'and where she has already given her 'art?' (*OMF*, Bk IV, ch. 14)

Mr Boffin can, on occasion, become a critic of language. When Mr Venus says 'I shall have to ask you for your word and honour that we are in confidence', he replies 'Let's wait a bit and understand what the expression means'. After demanding closer definition of the phrase 'in confidence', he takes exception to 'word and honour':

> 'My good fellow,' retorted Mr Boffin, 'you have my word; and how you can have that without my honour too, I don't know.' (*OMF*, Bk III, ch. 14)

This is the Mr Boffin who, not long before, had needed an explanation of the meaning of the word 'secretary' (Bk I, ch. 15).

A criticism is often all the more amusing for being expressed in substandard English. When Lewsome is taken ill at the Bull Inn at Holborn, John Westlock has to admit that he has no idea what friends or relatives he has or where they live, except that it is certainly not in London. This prompts a reasonable comment from the chambermaid (and the adverb lends emphasis to the criticism):

> . . . the chambermaid remarked, hysterically, 'that of all the many wague directions she had ever seen or heerd of (and they wasn't few in an hotel), that was the waguest.' (*MC*, ch. 25)

Sometimes criticism of an idiom is implicit in the reply made by another character to a remark in which the idiom occurs. When Bob Sawyer asks Mr Pickwick where he hangs out, Mr Pickwick replies that he is at present suspended at the George and Vulture (*PP*, ch. 30). Mr Pickwick is not given to satire, and we may therefore assume that the reply is an elderly man's unsuccessful attempt to adopt the slang idiom of his juniors. When Bella Wilfer promises to break it to her father gently that she is engaged, he playfully takes up the word 'break' and says that he is 'equal to a good large breakage' (*OMF*, Bk III, ch. 16).

One of the social uses of language is to introduce visitors, and Dickens took a delight in describing the way in which badly trained servants carried out the task. Mrs Jellyby's servant introduces Ada Clare and Esther Summerson with the words 'Them two young ladies, Missis Jellyby!' (*BH*, ch. 4). Mrs Snagsby's maid Guster, admonished not to omit the ceremony of announcing the Chadbands, achieves an even more startling effect before retiring in a panic:

> 'Mr and Mrs Cheeseming, least which, Imeantersay, whatsername!' (*BH*, ch. 19)

Clichés abound in the speech of all classes of society, and the choice of clichés often throws light on the habits of thought of the speaker. A member of the privileged classes does not find it necessary to protest that he is speaking the truth, but the under-privileged become accustomed to having their word doubted and so make use of clichés refuting an accusation of falsehood before it is made. When giving evidence in the case of Bardell v. Pickwick, Mrs Cluppins begins a reply to a question with the words 'My Lord and Jury, I will not deceive you', and this provokes the judge to the retort 'You had better not' (*PP*, ch. 34). Just how meaningless such a cliché can become is illustrated by Rogue Riderhood, who says 'and I don't deceive you' when accepting a glass of wine (*OMF*, Bk I, ch. 12). This cliché is one of which the inoffensive Mrs Plornish is very fond, and her use of it is the subject of a comment by the author:

> Not to deceive you, was a method of speech with Mrs Plornish. She would deceive you, under any circumstances, as little as might be; but she had a trick of replying in this provisional form. (*LD*, Bk I, ch. 12)

One field in which clichés abound is that of drinking, and imitation can lead to the use of clichés in very inappropriate circumstances. Jeremiah Flintwinch's disreputable brother drinks a glass of wine with the words 'And all friends round St Paul's', which the author describes as an 'ancient civic toast' (*LD*, Bk I, ch. 4). Mr Sapsea uses the equally inappropriate greeting:

> When the French come over,
> May we meet them at Dover! (*ED*, ch. 4)

Greetings when drinking could become very complicated. The sergeant who leads the hunt for Magwitch in *Great Expectations* is particularly exuberant. His reply to Pumblechook's invitation to have another glass is:

> 'With you. Hob and nob. The top of mine to the foot of yours – the foot of yours to the top of mine – Ring once, ring twice – the best tune on the Musical Glasses! Your health. May you live a thousand years, and never be a worse judge of the right sort than you are at the present moment of your life.' (ch. 5)

Invitations to drink did not demand quite so much elaboration. The stranger at the Three Jolly Bargemen asks Joe Gargery what he will have to drink 'to top up with'. Joe is reluctant to accept, but Mr Wopsle shows no such hesitation:

> 'And will the other gentleman originate a sentiment?'
> 'Rum,' said Mr Wopsle. (*GE*, ch. 10)

When the invitation is slow in coming, some prompting is needed, and David Copperfield's landlady, Mrs Crupp, shows impressive ingenuity:

> She came up to me one evening, when I was very low, to ask (she being then afflicted with the disorder I have mentioned) if I could oblige her with a little tincture of cardamums mixed with rhubarb, and flavoured with seven drops of the essence of cloves, which was the best remedy for her complaint; – or, if I had not such a thing by me, with a little brandy, which was the next best. It was not, she remarked, so palatable to her, but it was the next best. (ch. 26)

The Game Chicken, in *Dombey and Son*, makes the appeal 'There an't no drain of nothing short handy, is there?' and accepts a glass of rum, drinking 'after proposing the brief sentiment, "Towards us!".' Bart Smallweed is equally concise when, with two companions, he acknowledges a reference to himself by drinking and observing 'Gentlemen both!' (*BH*, ch. 20). Rob the Grinder proposes a toast to Mrs Brown with characteristic awkwardness: 'Here's your health. And long may you – et ceterer' (*DS*, ch. 52).

Imitation of the speech of a drunken man is a common literary convention. Jenny Wren's father provides an example. In his speech lightly-stressed words and syllables tend to disappear:

> 'I am ill-used vidual,' said Mr Dolls. 'Blown up morning t'night. Called names. She makes Mint money, sir, and never stands Threepenn'orth Rum.' (*OMF*, Bk III, ch. 10)

The loss of lightly-stressed words is at times so marked that his conversation reminds one of a telegram written by an economically minded sender:

> 'Shouldn't like it. Poor shattered invalid. Trouble nobody long.' (Bk II, ch. 2)

Direction becomes *d'rection*. Plosive consonants cause difficulty, with the result that *letters* becomes *lerrers* and *to* becomes *er*.

There are some resemblances between this kind of drunken speech and the speech of Mrs Skewton after she has had a stroke. After her first attack, she cuts down some polysyllabic words by the omission of initial, medial, or final syllables, and omits some short words altogether. She thus says *posively*, *prom* (for *promise*), *sterious* (for *mysterious*), *trordinry*, *quire* (for *require*), *proach* (for *approach*). There is also confusion in proper names, with the result that *Dombey* becomes *Domber* and *Granger* becomes *Grangeby* (*DS*, ch. 40). Examples of the effect on speech of extreme old age are the maunderings of Chuffey in *Martin Chuzzlewit* and of Mrs Smallweed in *Bleak House*. The mention of a single word is enough to start Mrs Smallweed off on the repetition of half-forgotten sentences containing the word. Her granddaughter mentions the name of their maid Charley:

> This touches a spring in Grandmother Smallweed, who, chuckling, as usual, at the trivets, cries – 'Over the water! Charley over the water, Charley over the water over the water to Charley, Charley over the water, over the water to Charley!' and becomes quite energetic about it. (ch. 21)

The mention of any number is particularly liable to impress one whose thoughts have been much concerned with money. When her husband says that their son has been dead for fifteen years, her response is:

> 'Fifteen hundred pound. Fifteen hundred pound in a black box, fifteen hundred pound locked up, fifteen hundred pound put away and hid.' (ch. 21)

Some of Dickens's characters make very free use of gesture language. Bailey, in *Martin Chuzzlewit*, has a wide range at his command. His delight at the beginning of a quarrel between Charity and Mercy Pecksniff finds expression in a series of gestures:

> This artless inquiry might have led to turbulent results, but for the strong emotions of delight evinced by Bailey junior, whose relish in the turn the conversation had lately taken was so acute, that it impelled and forced him to the instantaneous performance of a dancing step, extremely difficult in its nature, and only to be achieved in a moment of ecstasy, which is commonly called The Frog's Hornpipe. A manifestation so lively, brought to their immediate recollection the great virtuous precept, 'Keep up appearances whatever you do', in which they had been educated. They forbore at once, and jointly signified to Mr Bailey that if he should presume to practise that figure any more in their presence, they would instantly acquaint Mrs Todgers with the fact, and would demand his condign punishment at the hands of that lady. The young gentleman having expressed the bitterness of his

contrition by affecting to wipe away scalding tears with his apron, and afterwards feigning to wring a vast amount of water from that garment, held the door open while Miss Charity passed out: and so that damsel went in state up-stairs to receive her mysterious adorer. (ch. 11)

Job Trotter shows great fondness for gesture language. When Sam Weller's questions become too insistent, Job is unco-operative:

> He emptied his glass, looked mysteriously at his companion, winked both of his small eyes, one after the other, and finally made a motion with his arm, as if he were working an imaginary pump-handle, thereby intimating that he (Mr Trotter) considered himself as undergoing the process of being pumped by Mr Samuel Weller. (*PP*, ch. 16)

The pumping gesture is immediately followed by another: 'he turned his glass upside down, as a means of reminding his companion that he had nothing left wherewith to slake his thirst.' The gesture proves effective and Sam, having ordered more liquor, asks whether Job's master is rich. The response is another gesture:

> Mr Trotter smiled, and holding his glass in his left hand, gave four distinct slaps on the pocket of his mulberry indescribables with his right, as if to intimate that his master might have done the same without alarming anybody much by the chinking of coin. (ch. 16)

Compared with this rich variety of gesture, it is something of an anticlimax when Job confirms the truth of what he has said by nodding significantly. Job's fondness for gesture is revealed again later when Mr Pickwick exposes Jingle at the house of Mr Nupkins. Mr Pickwick harangues the unrepentant Jingle, and Job 'with facetious gravity applied his hand to his ear, as if desirous not to lose a syllable he uttered' (ch. 25). Since Job uses tears for the purpose for which other men use language, these may perhaps be included as part of his gesture language:

> Job Trotter bowed low; and in spite of Mr Weller's previous remonstrance, the tears again rose to his eyes.
>
> 'I never see such a feller,' said Sam. 'Blessed if I don't think he's got a main in his head as is always turned on.' (ch. 16)

Gesture language is freely used by other characters in the same novel. Mr Jackson, after serving a subpoena on Mr

Pickwick on behalf of Dodson and Fogg, refuses to answer Mr Pickwick's questions and makes use of two gestures, one still familiar today, the other less so:

> Mr Jackson struck his forefinger several times against the left side of his nose, to intimate that he was not there to disclose the secrets of the prison-house . . .
>
> Here Mr Jackson smiled once more upon the company, and, applying his left thumb to the tip of his nose, worked a visionary coffee-mill with his right hand: thereby performing a very graceful piece of pantomime (then much in vogue, but now, unhappily, almost obsolete) which was familiarly denominated 'taking a grinder'. (ch. 30)

When Tony Weller greets his fellow-coachmen he uses a gesture which prompts the author to introduce an anecdote of two twin brothers who never exchanged any other greeting:

> The salutation between Mr Weller and his friends was strictly confined to the freemasonry of the craft; consisting of a jerking round of the right wrist and a tossing of the little finger into the air at the same time. (ch. 43)

Another gesture, showing that Dickens was a careful observer, is described when Mr Pickwick in prison reveals his ignorance of the customs of the place:

> At this inquiry Mr Martin looked, with a countenance of excessive surprise, at his two friends and then each gentleman pointed with his right thumb over his left shoulder. This action, imperfectly described in words by the very feeble term of 'over the left' when performed by any number of ladies or gentlemen who are accustomed to act in unison, has a very graceful and airy effect; its expression is one of light and playful sarcasm. (ch. 42)

Many of these gestures are of a kind whose meaning is clear only to the initiated. For a full understanding of gestures it is necessary to be on familiar terms with the person who uses them. Arthur Clennam shows some alertness in understanding Pancks:

> Mr Pancks in shaking hands merely scratched his eyebrow with his left forefinger and snorted once, but Clennam, who understood him better now than of old, comprehended that he had almost done for the evening and wished to say a word to him outside. (LD, Bk II, ch. 9)

Gesture language is most common among low-life characters, but it is not confined to them. Mr Pecksniff, in addressing the assembled members of the Chuzzlewit family, is described as 'crossing his two fore fingers in a manner which was at once conciliatory and argumentative' (*MC*, ch. 4). In *Little Dorrit* quite a lot of use is made of the gesture of simply closing the eyes. The bashful young Member of Parliament at Mr Merdle's party is so impressed by the greatness of Lord Decimus that he shuts his eyes tightly whenever that nobleman speaks (Bk II, ch. 12). Mrs General makes use of the same gesture in her conversation with Mr Dorrit (Bk II, ch. 5), and this action may be regarded as symbolical of Mrs General's habit of closing her eyes to all unpleasant or disturbing facts. Fanny Dorrit is more influenced by Mrs General than she likes to admit, and she may be assumed to have picked up the habit from her (Bk II, ch. 24).

Just as many Dickensian characters use habitual phrases, by which they can be recognized, some of them have habitual gestures. When Blandois is first introduced in *Little Dorrit* we are told that when he laughed, 'his moustache went up under his nose, and his nose came down over his moustache', and in the course of half-a-dozen pages this phrase occurs three times (Bk I, ch. 1). The result is that the reader learns to associate this phrase with Blandois, and when he re-appears later in the novel, this gesture serves to let the reader know who he is (Bk I, ch. 11). There are similarly repetitive gestures in *Great Expectations*. Pip in his prosperity suffers much from them: when he is with Pumblechook he is almost incessantly required to shake hands, and when he visits Wemmick he has to spend much of his time in nodding to the Aged Parent.[1]

One of the best-known linguistic characteristics of England and America in the nineteenth century was the reluctance to call a spade a spade. There are many examples of euphemism in Dickens, usually in the speech of characters in the novels but also in the passages where Dickens is writing as the narrator and in his letters. Miss Flite, wishing to say that Krook is mad, describes him as 'a little – M—' (*BH*, ch. 5). When Sir

[1] For further examples of habitual gestures in *Great Expectation* see Dorothy Van Ghent, *op. cit.* p. 130.

Leicester Dedlock complains that an election has cost the Party hundreds of thousands of pounds, his cousin Volumnia is so indiscreet as to ask 'What for?' and receives a stately rebuke:

> 'But as you, though inadvertently, and without intending so unreasonable a question, asked me "What for?" let me reply to you. For necessary expenses. And I trust to your good sense, Volumnia, not to pursue the subject, here or elsewhere.' (*BH*, ch. 40)

When Dickens himself indulges in euphemism, the reason as a rule does not seem to be a genuine desire to avoid unpleasant ideas; euphemisms are introduced as a joke between the author and his readers, as much as to say that the convention to avoid the use of certain words is a foolish one that both he and the reader would be willing to ignore, but he is observing the convention to avoid jarring on the sensibilities of other, more squeamish, readers. Thus he goes to the trouble to write *National participled* instead of *damned* (*CS, Somebody's Luggage*, ch. 2). When Mr Pickwick receives an unfriendly welcome from Simpson, with whom he has to share a room in prison, the author makes it clear what Simpson said, but he playfully avoids using the word *Hell*:

> The individual brought in his head and shoulders with great swiftness, and surveying Mr Pickwick from head to foot, demanded in a surly tone what the – something beginning with a capital H – he wanted. (*PP*, ch. 42)

The description of Mr Barley's curses in *Great Expectations* shows a similar coy reluctance to use the word *damn*:

> As we passed Mr Barley's door, he was heard hoarsely muttering within, in a strain that rose and fell like wind, the following Refrain; in which I substitute good wishes for something quite the reverse.
> 'Ahoy! Bless your eyes, here's old Bill Barley. Here's old Bill Barley, bless your eyes. Here's old Bill Barley on the flat of his back, like a drifting old dead flounder, here's your old Bill Barley, bless your eyes. Ahoy! Bless you.' (ch. 46)

Sometimes the playful use of euphemism involves the polysyllabic humour of which Victorian authors were fond. The introduction of Mr Pickwick as the fourth occupant of a room in the Fleet prison causes one of his room-mates to describe his arrival as 'very aggravating'. The other two share this view:

Mr Martin expressed the same opinion in rather stronger terms. Mr Simpson, after having let a variety of expletive adjectives loose upon society without any substantive to accompany them, tucked up his sleeves and began to wash the greens for dinner. (*PP*, ch. 42)

When Sir Barnet Skettles discovers that Mr Baps is a dancing-master, he is annoyed and we are told that 'he even went so far as to D Mr Baps to Lady Skettles, in telling her what had happened' (*DS*, ch. 14). Dickens thus avoids printing the word *damn*.

Oaths are often slightly corrupted by speakers who want to get the best of both worlds, and a particular corruption may become the favourite oath of one particular character. *Ecod* is the favourite oath of Jonas Chuzzlewit, and it is used too by Silas Wegg (*OMF*, Bk III, ch. 14). Major Bagstock says *By Gad, Sir!* (*DS*, ch. 14). Mrs Cluppins says *Lauk* for *Lord* (*PP*, ch. 26). Susan Nipper uses the same word, though the author spells it differently: *Lork* (*DS*, ch. 3). Rachael Wardle and her niece Emily both say *Lor* (*PP*, ch. 4), which is probably regarded as less vulgar than *Lauk*, while Mr Boffin says *Lard* (*OMF*, Bk I, ch. 5).

Euphemistic oaths come to be used by people who have little interest in etymology, and there is no reason to suppose, when Mrs Gamp uses the word *drat*, that she is conscious of its derivation from *God rot*. One can only speculate on whether Mrs Joe Gargery realizes that her *Lor-a-mussy-me!* is a slightly disguised variant of *Lord have mercy on me!* Miss Miggs is so astonished at seeing Simon Tappertit stealing out of the house that she rings the changes on one euphemistic oath:

At this spectacle Miggs cried 'Gracious!' again, and then 'Goodness gracious!' and then 'Goodness gracious me!' (*BR*, ch. 9)

Sometimes an oath is toned down to avoid offending the susceptibilities of another character in a novel rather than those of the reader. When Mr Venus is quarrelling with Silas Wegg, he says:

' . . . and as a point of fact I would have seen you – will you allow me to say, further?'

'I wouldn't say more than further, if I was you,' Mr Wegg suggests pacifically. (*OMF*, Bk II, ch. 7)

When Sam Weller is trying to persuade Arabella Allen to see
Mr Winkle, he resorts to circumlocution to avoid using the
word *damned*, perhaps because he is talking to a lady:

> 'he says if he can't see you afore to-morrow night's over, he vishes
> he may be somethin'-unpleasanted if he don't drownd hisself.' (*PP*,
> ch. 39)

It is not merely euphemism that leads to variety in oaths.
Bob Acres had oaths for all occasions and made free use of the
'oath referential' or 'sentimental swearing' (Sheridan, *The
Rivals*, II.i). There is something of this type of oath, combined
with euphemism, in the remark of Tom Smart in *The Bagman's
Story*, incorporated in *Pickwick Papers*:

> 'Damn my straps and whiskers. If this ain't pleasant, blow me.'
> (ch. 14)

Just as the word *damned* had to be avoided, so the word *Devil*
had to be paraphrased, although there was no objection to
easily identifiable references. Mrs Gamp reports Mrs Harris
as saying, 'Telling the truth then, ma'am, and shaming him as
shall be nameless betwixt you and me . . . ' (*MC*, ch. 25).
The taboos that are most productive of euphemisms in
English are death and sex, with money as a third taboo in
certain circles. Dickens, with his fondness for death-bed scenes,
is less influenced by the taboo on death than we are today, but
Joe Gargery is perhaps influenced by the taboo when he tries
to break gently to Pip the news of Miss Haversham's death:

> 'Is she dead, Joe?'
> 'Why, you see, old chap,' said Joe, in a tone of remonstrance,
> and by way of getting at it by degrees, 'I wouldn't go so far as to
> say that, for that's a deal to say; but she ain't—'
> 'Living, Joe?'
> 'That's nigher where it is,' said Joe; 'she ain't living.' (*GE*,
> ch. 57)

As an example of euphemism in relation to sex we may note
the coy reference in *Sketches by Boz* to the belief that a lion
would never harm a virgin:

> we have been deeply impressed with a becoming sense of the polite-
> ness they are said to display towards unmarried ladies of a certain
> state. (*SB, Some Particulars Concerning a Lion*)

Reluctance to mention money is shown by characters like Mrs General and Mrs Sparsit, who is anxious that her salary should be described as an 'annual compliment' (*HT*, Bk I, ch. 16).

Victorian prudery imposed taboos on the naming of certain articles of dress. Miss Mowcher is shy about mentioning garters: 'Oh my stars and what's-their-names!' (*DC*, ch. 29). Lavinia Wilfer and George Sampson get into trouble for mentioning underwear:

> 'But why one should go out to dine with one's own daughter or sister, as if one's under-petticoat was a backboard, I do not understand.'
>
> 'Neither do I understand,' retorted Mrs Wilfer, with deep scorn, 'how a young lady can mention the garment in the name of which you have indulged. I blush for you . . . '
>
> Here, Mr Sampson, with the view of establishing harmony, which he never under any circumstances succeeded in doing, said with an agreeable smile: 'After all, you know, ma'am, we know it's there.' And immediately felt that he had committed himself.
>
> 'We know it's there!' said Mrs Wilfer, glaring.
>
> 'Really, George,' remonstrated Miss Lavinia . . . (*OMF*, Bk IV, ch. 16)

Flora Finching pretends to be similarly shy about mentioning a skirt to Arthur Clennam, but her attitude is the not uncommon one of paying lip-service to the proprieties while claiming to be so emancipated as to set them aside:

> ' . . . who would have ever thought of seeing such a sight as this and pray excuse a wrapper for upon my word I really never and a faded check too which is worse but our little friend is making me a, not that I need mind mentioning it to you for you must know that there are such things a skirt, . . . ' (*LD*, Bk I, ch. 35)

One of the strongest taboos in Victorian times was that which forbade the use of the word *trousers*. In *Sketches by Boz* Dickens uses various polysyllabic euphemisms: *inexpressibles* (*The Out-and-Out Young Gentleman*), *indescribables* (*Scenes*, ch. 12), and *inexplicables* (*Tales*, ch. 2). In *Oliver Twist* the butler Giles is describing his actions on being disturbed by burglars:

> 'I tossed off the clothes,' said Giles, throwing away the table-cloth, and looking very hard at the cook and housemaid, 'got softly out of bed; drew on a pair of—'
>
> 'Ladies present, Mr Giles,' murmured the tinker.
>
> '—of *shoes*, sir,' said Giles, turning on him and laying great emphasis on the word. (ch. 28)

Victorian prudishness is turned to good account by the resource-ful Silas Wegg when asked by Mr Boffin to explain the difference between *Rooshan* and *Roman*:

> 'The difference, sir? – There you place me in a difficulty, Mr Boffin. Suffice it to observe, that the difference is best postponed to some other occasion when Mrs Boffin does not honour us with her company.' (*OMF*, Bk I, ch. 5)

Prudery imposed taboos on speech in North America as well as in England, and Dickens mentions an extreme example. Martin Chuzzlewit uses the expression 'with his naked eye' in conversation with Mrs Hominy:

> Mrs Hominy was a philosopher and an authoress, and con-sequently had a pretty strong digestion; but this coarse, this indecorous phrase, was almost too much for her. For a gentleman sitting alone with a lady – although the door was open – to talk about a naked eye!
> A long interval elapsed before even she, woman of masculine and towering intellect though she was, could call up fortitude enough to resume the conversation. (*MC*, ch. 22)

In general Dickens seems to have regarded euphemism as rather silly, and it is his foolish characters who are the most squeamish. The frame of mind that gives rise to euphemism is illustrated by the shocked rebuke of Cyrus Angelo Bantam, Master of Ceremonies at Bath, when Mr Pickwick refers to a 'fat old lady'. 'Hush, my dear sir – nobody's fat or old in Ba-ath' (*PP*, ch. 35). On the other hand, a sympathetic character, Miss La Creevy, makes use of euphemism in rather a tactful way when Ralph Nickleby calls on her:

> 'A miniature, I presume. A very strongly-marked countenance for the purpose, sir. Have you ever sat before?' (*NN*, ch. 3)

Quotations play a prominent part in the novels of Dickens; they are freely used both by the author in his narration and by the characters in the novels. The author's references to passages in books are generally concealed quotations incorporated into descriptive or narrative passages in such a way that a reader unfamiliar with their source might not realize that they are quotations. A curtain in Mrs Gamp's apartment is described as preventing the Zephyrs that were abroad in Kingsgate

Street from visiting Mrs Gamp's head too roughly (*MC*, ch. 49; cf. *Hamlet*, I, ii, 142); Miss Skiffins retained her green gloves during the evening as an outward and visible sign that there was company (*GE*, ch. 37; cf. *The Book of Common Prayer: A Catechism*), and Mr Pickwick and his friends are described as going in to dinner with good digestion waiting on appetite, and health on both, and a waiter on all three (*PP*, ch. 51; cf. *Macbeth*, III, iv, 38). Concealed quotations of this kind are often partial quotations in that one word of the original is deliberately altered to make the quotation fit its new context. The noise made by Sam Weller and his friends at the Angel at Bury was so great that it 'penetrated to Mr Pickwick's bedroom, and shortened the term of his natural rest by at least three hours' (*PP*, ch. 16). Again, in *Our Mutual Friend*,

> Mr Inspector having to Mr Riderhood announced his official intention of 'keeping his eye upon him', stood him in a corner of the fireplace, like a wet umbrella, and took no further outward and visible notice of that honest man . . . (Bk I, ch. 14)

There are, of course, other reasons for departing from the original or for ascribing a quotation to the wrong source. An author, like his characters, can make mistakes. When Dickens refers to 'rats and mice and such small gear' (*NN*, ch. 19), he may be relying on an editorial emendation of Edgar's 'such small deer', but when he says 'The only scriptural admonition that Ralph Nickleby heeded, in the letter, was "Know thyself"' (*NN*, ch. 44), he is giving a new meaning to the word 'scriptural'.

Misquotation, both deliberate and unintentional, and mistaken attribution are even more common among the characters in the novel than in the author's narrative. Mr Mould is perhaps too appreciative of his wife's deliberate misquotation:

> 'The woodpecker tapping the hollow elm tree,' observed Mrs Mould, adapting the words of the popular melody to the description of wood commonly used in the trade.
> 'Ha, ha!' laughed Mr Mould. 'Not at all bad, my dear. We shall be glad to hear from you again, Mrs M. Hollow elm tree, eh! Ha, ha! Very good indeed. I've seen worse than that in the Sunday papers, my love.' (*MC*, ch. 25)

Mr Micawber, like many other Dickensian characters, uses deliberate misquotation with comic effect:

'My dear,' said Mr Micawber, 'your papa was very well in his way, and Heaven forbid that I should disparage him. Take him for all in all, we ne'er shall – in short, make the acquaintance probably of anyone else possessing, at his time of life, the same legs for gaiters, and able to read the same description of print, without spectacles.' (*DC*, ch. 12)

Anticlimax is achieved by the unexpected conclusion, which is very much longer than the five words needed to complete the quotation correctly. The same sort of misquotation is used by Mr Mould: 'We do good by stealth, and blush to have it mentioned in our little bills' (*MC*, ch. 19).

The characters who are most fond of quotations are not as a rule those who are intellectually outstanding and it is therefore natural that there should be many unintentional misquotations. Quotations that get out of hand, often as a result of the mixture of two quotations, are a favourite form of Dickensian humour. When Mrs Gamp indulges in a quotation from the Bible, the surprising thing is not that she gets it wrong but that she should be in a position to attempt the quotation at all. The misquotations are of the kind that are inevitable when a speaker relies on verbal memory. The warehouseman who thanks the Cheeryble brothers at their party begins his speech:

'We're allowed to take a liberty once a year, gen'lemen, and if you please we'll take it now; there being no time like the present, and no two birds in the hand worth one in the bush, as is well known – leastways in a contrairy sense, which the meaning is the same.' (A pause – the butler unconvinced.) (*NN*, ch. 37)

The Dickensian character who is most fond of quotations is Captain Cuttle. Like Mrs Gamp, he produces startling and obscure aphorisms by combining two quotations:

'Turn again Whittington, Lord Mayor of London, and when you are old you will never depart from it.' (*DS*, ch. 4)

'Train up a fig-tree in the way it should go, and when you are old sit under the shade of it. Overhaul the – Well,' said the Captain, on second thoughts, 'I an't quite certain where that's to be found, but when found, make a note of.' (ch. 19)

It is natural that the quotations remembered by Captain Cuttle should include some that have become traditional among non-bookish people. Many children have indicated their

ownership of books by writing in them verses similar to the one
used by Captain Cuttle in introducing himself to Toots:

> 'Cap'en Cuttle is my name, and England is my nation, this here
> is my dwelling-place and blessed be creation – Job,' said the
> Captain as an index to his authority. (ch. 32)

Durdles produces another version:

> Mister Sapsea is his name,
> England is his nation,
> Cloisterham's his dwelling-place,
> Aukshneer's his occupation. (ED, ch. 18)

A similar verse occurs in the first few pages of James Joyce's
A Portrait of the Artist as a Young Man (1916), and another
version, having crossed the Atlantic, provided the title for
Thornton Wilder's *Heaven's My Destination*. Another often-
repeated quotation is that used by Captain Cuttle as a lament
for Sol Gills, which Bunsby was able to continue:

> 'Affliction sore, long time he bore, and let us overhaul the
> wollume and there find it.'
> 'Physicians,' observed Bunsby, 'was in vain.' (DS, ch. 39)

This is clearly a quotation from the traditional verse which
Matthew Arnold describes as one of the 'familiar memorial
inscriptions of an English churchyard':

> Afflictions sore long time I bore,
> Physicians were in vain,
> Till God did please Death should me seize
> And ease me of my pain.[1]

Like many people who are fond of quotations, Captain Cuttle
did not always achieve accuracy or appropriateness. His fondness
for combining two quotations produces startling results:

> 'He an't been heerd on, since he sheered off arter poor Wal'r. But,'
> said the Captain, as a quotation, 'Though lost to sight, to memory
> dear, and England, Home and Beauty.' (ch. 48)

> 'The wery planks she walked on,' murmured the Captain, looking
> at her drooping face, 'was as high esteemed by Wal'r, as the water
> brooks is by the hart which never rejices!' (ch. 49)

[1] Matthew Arnold, *On the Study of Celtic Literature and other Essays*,
Everyman's Library edition, p. 111. I am indebted to my colleague,
Mr Noel Lees, for this reference.

G

The author ironically calls attention to the inappropriateness of one of the Captain's quotations:

> 'If there is a man chock full of science in the world, it's old Sol Gills. If there is a lad of promise – one flowing,' added the Captain, in one of his happy quotations, 'with milk and honey – it's his nevy.' (ch. 10)

Inaccuracy of quotation is matched by inaccuracy of attribution. Captain Cuttle shows an almost medieval fondness for supporting his opinions by an appeal to authority, and he resembles a medieval author, too, in the frequent vagueness and inaccuracy of his attribution. His favourite authority is the Catechism:

> 'Love! Honour! And Obey! Overhaul your catechism till you find that passage, and when found turn the leaf down.' (ch. 4)

> 'Walk fast, . . . and walk the same all the days of your life. Overhaul the catechism for that advice and keep it!' (ch. 9)

> 'and with regard to old Sol Gills,' here the Captain became solemn, 'who I'll stand by, and not desert until death doe us part, and when the stormy winds do blow, do blow, do blow – overhaul the Catechism,' said the Captain parenthetically, 'and there you'll find them expressions . . . ' (ch. 23)

Captain Cuttle is fond of attributing quotations to the Catechism but sometimes he quotes it without thinking it necessary to identify so familiar a source:

> 'Wal'r,' said the Captain, his eyes glistening with the praise of his young friend, and his hook raised to announce a beautiful quotation, 'is what you may call a out'ard and visible sign of an in'ard and spirited grasp, and when found make a note of.' (ch. 23)

On occasion Captain Cuttle can appeal to other authorities:

> ' . . . I will think of them, when night comes on a hurricane and seas is mountains rowling, for which overhaul your Doctor Watts, brother, and when found make a note on.' (ch. 32)

> 'Hope is a buoy, for which you overhaul your Little Warbler, sentimental division.' (ch. 50)

and the authority is sometimes obscure:

> 'If you're in arnest, you see, my lad,' said the Captain, 'you're a object of clemency, and clemency is the brightest jewel in the crown of a Briton's head, for which you'll overhaul the constitution as laid

down in Rule Britannia, and, when found, *that* is the charter as
them garden angels was a singing of, so many times over. Stand
by!' (ch. 39)

Captain Cuttle is not the only character in *Dombey and Son*
to be vague or confused in his quotation. Mrs Skewton provides
one of the best-known examples:

'My dearest Edith, there is such an obvious destiny in it, that really
one might almost be induced to cross one's arms upon one's frock,
and say, like those wicked Turks, there is no What's-his-name but
Thingummy, and What-you-may-call-it is his prophet!' (ch. 27)

Montague Tigg is similarly vague:

'if I am gone to that what's-his-name from which no thingumbob
comes back.' (*MC*, ch. 4)

Captain Cuttle is not alone in the importance that he attaches
to the Catechism. There are allusions or quotations in several
of the novels. Durdles gives a new and more literal application
to one sentence from it when he says:

'You get among them Tombs afore it's well light on a winter morning,
and keep on, as the Catechism says, a-walking in the same all the days
of your life, and you'll know what Durdles means.' (*ED*, ch. 4)

References to the Catechism often allude to the part that it
played in our educational system. Ham Peggotty 'went to the
national school, and was a very dragon at his catechism' (*DC*,
ch. 1). Tinkler, Mr Dorrit's servant, was so solemn in his
behaviour that 'he left a vague impression on Mr Dorrit's mind
that he was a well-conducted young fellow, who had been
brought up in the study of his Catechism, by a widowed
mother' (*LD*, Bk II, ch. 5). Miss Peecher reminds both her
pupil and herself of the Catechism when she asks searching
questions about Lizzie Hexam:

'Is Lizzie a Christian name, Mary Anne?'
Mary Anne laid down her work, rose, hooked herself behind as
being under catechization, and replied: 'No, it is a corruption, Miss
Peecher.'
'Who gave her that name?' Miss Peecher was going on, from
the mere force of habit, when she checked herself, on Mary Anne's
evincing theological impatience to strike in with her godfathers and
her godmothers, and said: 'I mean of what name is it a corruption?'
'Elizabeth or Eliza, Miss Peecher.'
'Right, Mary Anne.' (*OMF*, Bk II, ch. 11)

The dangers of expecting children to memorize it when they are too young to understand it are illustrated in *Great Expectations*:

> I have a lively remembrance that I supposed my declaration that I was to 'walk in the same all the days of my life', laid me under an obligation always to go through the village from our house in one particular direction, and never to vary it by turning down by the wheelwright's or up by the mill. (ch. 7)

Another Dickensian character, though convinced of the importance of a knowledge of the Catechism, finds his recollection of it rather hazy:

> On young Woolwich's last birthday, Mr Bagnet certainly did, after observing on his growth and general advancement, proceed, in a moment of profound reflection on the changes wrought by time, to examine him in the catechism; accomplishing with extreme accuracy the questions number one and two, What is your name? and Who gave you that name? but there failing in the exact precision of his memory, and substituting for number three, the question And how do you like that name? which he propounded with a sense of its importance, in itself so edifying and improving, as to give it quite an orthodox air. (*BH*, ch. 49)

Passages from other parts of the Book of Common Prayer tend to be quoted by the most unexpected characters. Grandfather Smallweed is so annoyed at the thought of having no letters written by Captain Hawdon that he suddenly remembers a book that he has probably not read or heard read for some time:

> ' . . . I have nothing but his signature. Plague pestilence and famine, battle murder and sudden death upon him,' says the old man, making a curse out of one of his few remembrances of a prayer. (*BH*, ch. 26)

When Jobling quotes Shakespeare to Jonas Chuzzlewit, 'Your bosom's lord sits lightly on its throne', it is no doubt well-bred affectation that causes him to use the vague attribution 'as what's his name says in the play', though it is clear from the context that he is perfectly familiar with the play from which the quotation comes (*MC*, ch. 41).

Some quotations are clearly from popular songs or ballads for recitation. Miss Mowcher's 'Did he sip every flower, and change every hour, until Polly his passion requited?' (*DC*, ch. 22) is from *The Beggar's Opera* (Act I, Air XV). Sometimes rhyme and rhythm make it clear that a speaker is indulging in a quotation, often in a mangled form, as in the deathbed speech of Doctor Marigold's father:

'Now here my jolly companions every one – which the Nightingale club in a village was held, At the sign of the Cabbage and Shears, Where the singers no doubt would have greatly excelled, But for want of taste, voices and ears . . . ' (*CS, Doctor Marigold*, ch. 1)

The nineteenth century was a time when popular songs flourished. These songs were encouraged by performances like that at the Cider Cellar, to which Colonel Newcome took Clive, and they were the chief source of entertainment on convivial occasions when neither words nor music reached a high standard. Such an occasion was the party at Bob Sawyer's lodgings, where Jack Hopkins set the seal on a reconciliation after a tipsy quarrel:

'Now,' said Jack Hopkins, 'just to set us going again, Bob, I don't mind singing a song.' And Hopkins, incited thereto by tumultuous applause, plunged himself at once into 'The King, God bless him', which he sang as loud as he could, to a novel air, compounded of the 'Bay of Biscay', and 'A Frog he would'. The chorus was the essence of the song; and, as each gentleman sang it to the tune he knew best, the effect was very striking indeed. (*PP*, ch. 32)

It is at a similar party, after the cricket match between Dingley Dell and Muggleton, that Jingle sings a song 'in which the words "bowl" "sparkling" "ruby" "bright" and "wine" are frequently repeated at short intervals'. (*PP*, ch. 7).

Halfpenny ballads formed an important part of the stock-in-trade of Silas Wegg, and it was his ability to read them to his customers that brought him to the notice of the admiring Mr Boffin:

'Why, you know every one of these songs by name and by tune, and if you want to read or to sing any one on 'em off straight, you've only to whip on your spectacles and do it!' cried Mr Boffin. 'I see you at it.' (*OMF*, Bk I, ch. 5)

Silas Wegg had a habit, much appreciated by Mr Boffin, of giving popular ballads a personal application by interpolating the name of his listener along with other parenthetic remarks. Mrs Boffin, whose memory, like that of many unbookish

people, was excellent, was able to remember one such verse,
interpolations and all:

> I'll tell thee how the maiden wept, Mrs Boffin,
> When her true love was slain, ma'am,
> And how her broken spirit slept, Mrs Boffin,
> And never woke again, ma'am.
> I'll tell thee (if agreeable to Mr Boffin) how the steed drew nigh,
> And left his lord afar;
> And if my tale (which I hope Mr Boffin might excuse) should make
>   you sigh,
> I'll strike the light guitar. (Bk I, ch. 15)

If the parentheses are removed, this becomes a very smooth
and metrically regular verse of a ballad, but sometimes Wegg
produces a farrago which even the most tolerant listener could
not regard as an adequate quotation in spite of the preface
'For what says the Poet?':

> And you needn't, Mr Venus, be your black bottle,
> For surely I'll be mine,
> And we'll take a glass with a slice of lemon in it to which you're
>   partial,
> For auld lang syne. (Bk III, ch. 6)

Dickensian characters are always liable to burst into song,
although the bursts of song are not always appreciated by their
friends. Mr Chick greets his wife's moral reflections 'with the
singularly inappropriate air of "A cobbler there was"' and then
checks himself in some confusion, but gets into trouble again
by murmuring under his breath 'the equally unmeaning and
unfeeling remark of rump-te-iddity, bow-wow-wow' (*DS*,
ch. 2). Captain Cuttle has a more sympathetic audience when
he sings the ballad of 'Lovely Peg' to Sol Gills and Walter Gay
for the third time in one evening and is defeated by the rhyme
in his attempt to substitute the name 'Florence' for 'Peg' (*DS*,
ch. 10). Mrs Nickleby's neighbour, when found in the chimney,
is singing 'the once popular air of "Has she then failed in her
truth, the beautiful maid I adore!"' (*NN*, ch. 49), and Arthur
Gride, in preparing for his wedding, 'feebly chirruped forth the
fag end of some forgotten song, of which the burden ran:

> *Ta-ran-tan-too,*
> *Throw the old shoe,*
> *And may the wedding be lucky.'* (*NN*, ch. 51)

Mr Micawber sings about Jack's delight being his lovely Nan (*DC*, ch. 11). Jobling describes Krook on the night of his death humming 'the only song he knows – about Bibo and old Charon, and Bibo being drunk when he died, or something or other' (*BH*, ch. 32), and Inspector Bucket sings a song (*BH*, ch. 49). Joe Gargery teaches Pip the words and tune of another song which Pip afterwards teaches Miss Havisham and Estella:

> There was a song Joe used to hum fragments of at the forge, of which the burden was Old Clem. This was not a very ceremonious way of rendering homage to a patron saint; but I believe Old Clem stood in that relation towards smiths. It was a song that imitated the measure of beating upon iron, and was a mere lyrical excuse for the introduction of Old Clem's respected name. Thus, you were to hammer boys round – Old Clem! With a thump and a sound – Old Clem! Beat it out, beat it out – Old Clem! With a clink for the stout – Old Clem! Blow the fire, blow the fire – Old Clem! Roaring dryer, soaring higher – Old Clem! (*GE*, ch. 12)

Most of these songs are now almost completely forgotten and it is likely that not many of them had much literary merit. Their popularity in Victorian England belongs to the field of social history rather than literature.

One important function of language is to indicate the attitude of the speaker towards the hearer. In *Edwin Drood* Mr Crisparkle is anxious to impress on the Chief Verger that only the best English is good enough for use when addressing a dignitary of the Church:

> 'Mr Jasper was that, Tope?'
> 'Yes, Mr Dean.'
> 'He has stayed late.'
> 'Yes, Mr Dean. I have stayed for him, your Reverence. He has been took a little poorly.'
> 'Say "taken", Tope – to the Dean,' – the younger rook interposes in a low tone with this touch of correction, as who should say: 'You may offer bad grammar to the laity, or the humbler clergy, not to the Dean.'
> Mr Tope, chief Verger and Showman, and accustomed to be high with excursion parties, declines with a silent loftiness to perceive that any suggestion has been offered to him.
> 'And when and how was Mr Jasper been taken – for, as Mr Crisparkle has remarked, it is better to say taken – taken – ' repeats the Dean; 'when and how has Mr Jasper been Taken—'
> 'Taken, sir,' Tope deferentially murmurs.

'Poorly, Tope?'

'Why, sir, Mr Jasper was that breathed—'

'I wouldn't say "That breathed", Tope,' Mr Crisparkle interposes with the same touch as before. 'Not English – to the Dean.'

' "Breathed to that extent",' the Dean (not unflattered by this
indirect homage) condescendingly remarks, 'would be preferable.'
(ch. 2)

The choice of language appropriate to the person addressed
is not merely a question of choosing the right degree of
formality. There are many ways of indicating the degree of
respect which one entertains for one's hearers, and Dickens was
very successful in portraying the two extremes of sycophancy
and overbearing or patronizing behaviour.

The sycophancy of Dickensian characters is sometimes of a
quite disinterested kind. There seem to be no ulterior motives
in the behaviour of the 'loquacious young man called Mr
Quale', who delights in drawing out Mrs Jellyby about her
philanthropical work and in repeating her answers like an
interpreter (*BH*, ch. 4). The admiration of Mr Wititterly for
his wife's ill-health and delicate sensibility is simply a form of
pride in the glory reflected on himself, and so is the pride which
Mr Bayham Badger takes in his wife's two previous husbands,
Captain Swosser of the Royal Navy ('a very distinguished
officer indeed') and Professor Dingo ('of European reputation')
(*BH*, ch. 13). Bayham Badger's pride in his predecessors comes
very near to farce, and so does Sampson Brass's admiration for
Quilp:

'You're as slow as a tortoise and more thickheaded than a
rhinoceros,' returned his obliging client with an impatient gesture.

'He's extremely pleasant!' cried the obsequious Sampson. 'His
acquaintance with Natural History too is surprising. Quite a
Buffoon, quite.' (*OCS*, ch. 51)

Sampson Brass has his own variety of sycophancy by soliloquy.
Quilp's advances to Sally Brass arouse the admiration of her
brother:

'He's a very remarkable man indeed,' soliloquised Mr Brass.
'He's quite a Troubadour, you know; quite a Troubadour!' (ch. 51)

Stagg, in *Barnaby Rudge*, like Brass, finds that sycophancy
comes more easily in the third person, as though the object of
his admiration were too exalted to be addressed directly:

'My captain flies at higher game than Miggses. Ha, ha, ha! My captain is an eagle, both as respects his eye and soaring wings. My captain breaketh hearts as other bachelors break eggs at breakfast.' (ch. 18)

In *Great Expectations* Pumblechook, during his period of sycophancy, achieves a ludicrous effect by his desire to please:

Mr Pumblechook helped me to the liver wing, and to the best slice of tongue (none of those out-of-the-way No Thoroughfares of Pork now), and took, comparatively speaking, no care of himself at all. 'Ah! poultry, poultry! You little thought,' said Mr Pumblechook, apostrophising the fowl in the dish, 'when you was a young fledgling, what was in store for you. You little thought you was to be refreshment beneath this humble roof for one as – Call it a weakness, if you will,' said Mr Pumblechook, getting up again, 'but may I? *may* I—?' (ch. 19)

In *Nicholas Nickleby* we get the impression that sycophancy was expected from any employed woman as a normal part of her job. Fanny Squeers's maid is expected to flatter her employer; Miss Knag flatters Madame Mantalini and the girls in the workroom flatter Miss Knag. Miggs, in *Barnaby Rudge*, is a more malevolent type of sycophant. Her praise of Mrs Varden is reinforced by the two powerful motives of self-glorification and desire to wound Gabriel Varden, and the malevolence rises almost to frenzy in the last scene in which Miggs appears.

There are in Dickens many characters whose self-importance becomes apparent almost as soon as they open their mouths. They are, for the most part, minor officials like Bumble in *Oliver Twist*. In *Pickwick Papers* both Nupkins and Grummer, in their different ways, find balm for their vanity in the offices that they hold. Grummer equates himself with the king: 'No room's private to his Majesty when the street door's once passed' (ch. 24). The sergeant in *Great Expectations*, seeking Joe's help, makes a similar identification: 'Now, blacksmith! If you're ready, his Majesty the King is'(ch. 5).

One way of emphasizing the pomposity of the language is to show the official unable to keep it up. We then get examples of formal language mixed with substandard pronunciations and turns of phrase:

'Grummer,' said the magistrate.
'Your wash-up.'
'Is the town quiet now?'

'Pretty well, your wash-up,' replied Grummer, 'Pop'lar feeling has in a measure subsided, consekens o' the boys having dispersed to cricket.' (*PP*, ch. 24)

The kind of behaviour that Dickens is most fond of satirizing is neither the obsequious nor the overbearing, but the patronizing. Patronizing behaviour always has two causes: the speaker believes himself to be superior to his hearer or hearers, and he unsuccessfully tries or pretends to conceal this conviction beneath a veil of conventional courtesy. When Septimus Hicks says of Tibbs 'He's the best-natured little man in existence, if you manage him properly' (*SB*, *Tales*, ch. 1), the implicit disparagement is more obvious than the superficial praise. Mrs Gowan is one of the worst offenders; her son is a close runner-up. It is her practice to damn with faint praise but to make enormous tacit claims to consideration, claims which cannot be refuted because they are only hinted at. In her conversation with Arthur Clennam she expresses her contempt for artists:

> 'Perhaps you have heard that I have suffered the keenest distress of mind from Henry's having taken to a pursuit which – well!' shrugging her shoulders, 'a very respectable pursuit, I dare say, and some artists are, as artists, quite superior persons; still, we never yet in our family have gone beyond an Amateur, and it is a pardonable weakness to feel a little—' (*LD*, Bk I, ch. 26)

There is a similar offensive condescension in Mrs Gowan's practice of referring to her daughter-in-law as Pretty One and in addressing Mr and Mrs Meagles as Papa Meagles and Mama Meagles (Bk II, ch. 8), though on occasion she is willing to use the cruder insult of getting their names wrong as 'the Miggles people' (Bk I, ch. 26).

Mrs Merdle, in the same novel, has mastered the art of using insincere courtesy as an offensive weapon. In the scene where she and Fanny are describing to Little Dorrit the progress of Edmund Sparkler's infatuation, she is very free with her flattery of Fanny ('Quite accurate. A most admirable memory'), and very ingenious in her condescending way of reminding Fanny that she had been bought off:

> 'I also mentioned to your sister – I again address the non-professional Miss Dorrit – that my son would have nothing in the event of such a marriage, and would be an absolute beggar. (I mention that, merely as a fact which is part of the narrative, and

not as supposing it to have influenced your sister, except in the prudent and legitimate way in which, constituted as our artificial system is, we must all be influenced by such considerations.) Finally, after some high words and high spirit on the part of your sister, we came to the complete understanding that there was no danger; and your sister was so obliging as to allow me to present her with a mark or two of my appreciation at my dressmaker's.' (Bk I, ch. 20)

Mr Tulkinghorn is a master of that superficial courtesy that can be more offensive than direct rudeness. He replies to Guppy's stipulation that a friend should be present during their discussion:

> 'The matter is not of that consequence that I need put you to the trouble of making any conditions, Mr Guppy.' (*BH*, ch. 39)

The patronizing of one woman by another is especially common. The decencies are superficially preserved but the intention to express disparagement is obvious. One method is to slip in an adjective to indicate that the woman described is old. Mrs Wititterly, reproaching Kate Nickleby, refers to 'that respectable old female, your mother' (*NN*, ch. 28). It is in all innocence that Kate gets her own back by saying that she expected more sympathy 'from one so much her senior' as Mrs Wititterly, but the allusion offends her employer so much that she falls back upon the sofa, uttering dismal screams. Readers of Dickens generally think of Georgiana Podsnap as 'the young person', but Mrs Wititterly applies the term to Kate Nickleby long before the writing of *Our Mutual Friend*. Mrs Nickleby in her turn patronizes Miss La Creevy, and when the gentleman in the small-clothes transfers his affections to her, Mrs Nickleby describes her as 'that poor unfortunate little old maid' (ch. 49).

Patronizing speech is especially common in *Martin Chuzzlewit*. Before his reformation, young Martin is particularly liable to use it. He patronizes Tom Pinch and when he talks about him to Mary he makes frequent use of such phrases as 'a poor, strange, simple oddity, Mary; but thoroughly honest and sincere', 'There never was such a simple fellow! Quite an infant! But a very good sort of creature, I assure you' (ch. 14). He patronizes Mark Tapley, and addresses him as 'my good fellow' (ch. 21), just as he had earlier assured Tom Pinch that he was 'a good fellow' (ch. 6). The Pecksniff family are even worse offenders. Pecksniff's treatment of Tom Pinch is uniformly patronizing until he decides to dismiss him, and he extends the treatment to Tom's sister. The first meeting between Pecksniff and Ruth Pinch displays patronage in both speech and manner. Pecksniff introduces himself in a manner which shows how great is his consciousness of his own greatness: 'My name – compose yourself, Miss Pinch – is Pecksniff'. The author adds the comment:

> The good man emphasised these words as though he would have said, 'You see in me, young person, the benefactor of your race; the patron of your house; the preserver of your brother, who is fed with manna daily from my table; and in right of whom there is a considerable balance in my favour at present standing in the books beyond the sky. But I have no pride, for I can afford to do without it!' (ch. 9)

Pecksniff's reference to Tom has the combination of superficial courtesy with obvious contempt that is of the essence of patronizing behaviour:

> 'I cannot say, poor fellow, that he will ever be distinguished in our profession, but he has the will to do well which is the next thing to having the power and, therefore, we must bear with him. Eh?'

His reception of Ruth's expressions of gratitude is delightfully in character:

> 'Very grateful; very pleasant; very proper,' murmured Mr Pecksniff.

Certain adjectives, once wholly laudatory, have been so often used in patronizing contexts that they have become derogatory. *Honest* and *worthy* are such adjectives, and it is in keeping with this development that Pecksniff says that Mrs Lupin is, as far as he knows (the qualification of a man who is anxious to damn with faint praise), 'one of the worthiest creatures in this county' just when he is warning old Martin that her inn is not a suitable home for Mary Graham (ch. 30).

Charity Pecksniff is at her most patronizing when speaking to Augustus Moddle, and her habit of addressing him as 'my child' and 'my sweet child' is no doubt one of the chief causes of his flight to Van Dieman's Land with the resolve never to be taken alive (*MC*, ch. 54). Compared with this, the patronizing behaviour of Bailey to Poll Sweedlepipe (*MC*, ch. 26) is entertaining rather than offensive. It is noteworthy that the characters in Dickens who are treated in a patronizing manner are either figures of fun, like George Sampson or Augustus Moddle, or else rather attractive characters, like Tom Pinch or Poll Sweedlepipe, whose modesty makes them easy victims.

Patronizing behaviour needs constant feeding. When a character habitually acts in a patronizing way, there are generally other characters who encourage this conduct by their simple-minded hero-worship. Tom Pinch just makes Pecksniff worse; Pecksniff would have been a more admirable, though less amusing, character if all his pupils had been like John Westlock and young Martin. Similarly, the superior airs, as well as the selfishness, of old Mr Turveydrop are encouraged by the admiration of his son and daughter-in-law. Even when Miss Tox is anxious to be conciliatory, she patronizingly calls Polly Toodle 'a good-humoured creature'. The reaction of Polly Toodle and her husband to this form of address provides an interesting contrast:

> Polly was gratified, and showed it. Mr Toodle didn't know whether he was gratified or not and preserved a stolid calmness. (*DS*, ch. 38)

Offensiveness under a thin cloak of courtesy is not confined to the upper classes. When Kate Nickleby asks if Madame Mantalini is in, the footman who opens the door realizes that she can safely be treated disrespectfully:

> 'Not often out at this time, Miss,' replied the man in a tone which rendered 'Miss' something more offensive than 'My dear'. (*NN*, ch. 17)

Similarly, the expression 'my friend' is generally used offensively *de haut en bas*. Mr Jaggers uses it to Pip when questioning him about his debts (*GE*, ch. 36). Mr Tulkinghorn uses it to Krook in ordering him to hold a candle (*BH*, ch. 11) and when addressing the copying-clerk Nemo (*BH*, ch. 10), and Richard Carstone addresses Krook as 'my good friend' when sharply protesting at Krook's action in drawing one of Ada Clare's tresses through his hand (*BH*, ch. 5). Mrs Pardiggle addresses the brickmaker's family as 'My friends', but Esther adds the comment 'but her voice had not a friendly sound, I thought' (*BH*, ch. 8), and Sir John Chester addresses John Willet as 'my friend' when reproving him for familiarity (*BR*, ch. 10). Sir John Chester, in keeping with his attitude of patronizing superiority towards the world, uses the expression 'my good friend' frequently: to Hugh (ch. 23) and to Gabriel Varden (ch. 26). The habit of patronizing Varden is too common in *Barnaby Rudge*: Haredale calls him 'my good friend' (ch.26), and even the author calls him 'honest Gabriel' (ch. 26).

The phrase 'young person' seems to have more than one set of associations in the novels of Dickens. When the phrase is used of Georgiana Podsnap, it may be assumed to possess the highest respectability, but in the same novel it is used in a different sense. Reginald Wilfer is clearly unconscious of any derogatory implications when he speaks of two possible pupils of his wife's as 'young persons', but his wife has different views:

'Pardon me,' Mrs Wilfer again interposed; 'they were not young persons. Two young ladies of the highest respectability.' (*OMF*, Bk I, ch. 4)

Mrs Wilfer's interpretation of the phrase is shared by Mr Pecksniff, who corrects Mrs Lupin for referring to Mary Graham as a young lady. Since her relations with old Martin Chuzzlewit seem to lay her open to suspicion, Pecksniff suggests that 'young person' would be a better description (*MC*, ch. 3). The offensiveness of the phrase is emphasized by Pecksniff's unwillingness to use it in Mary's presence:

'What gentleman is this?' inquired the object of his virtuous doubts.
'Hush! don't trouble yourself, ma'am,' said Mr Pecksniff, as the landlady was about to answer. 'This young' – in spite of himself he hesitated when 'person' rose to his lips, and substituted another word: 'this young stranger, Mrs Lupin, will excuse me . . . ' (*MC*, ch. 3)

The superficial courtesy that characterizes all patronizing behaviour is sometimes exaggerated, and we then get 'the pride that apes humility'. Mr Dombey is a frequent offender. When Major Bagstock asks him if he is Mr Dombey, he replies 'I am the present unworthy representative of that name, Major' (ch. 10). This may simply be the courtesy of the time, but elsewhere the author underlines the insincerity of Mr Dombey's protestations:

' . . . I beg you to believe, Mrs Pipchin, that I am more than satisfied with your excellent system of management, and shall have the greatest pleasure in commending it whenever my poor commendation' – Mr Dombey's loftiness when he affected to disparage his own importance, passed all bounds – 'can be of any service.' (ch. 11)

The Bank Director who is one of Mr Dombey's guests is described as 'a wonderfully modest-spoken man, almost boastfully so':

[He] mentioned his 'little place' at Kingston-upon-Thames, and its just being barely equal to giving Dombey a bed and a chop, if he would come and visit it. Ladies, he said, it was not for a man who lived in his quiet way to take upon himself to invite – but if Mrs Skewton and her daughter, Mrs Dombey, should ever find themselves in that direction, and would do him the honour to look at a little bit of shrubbery they would find there, and a poor little flower-bed or so, and a humble apology for a pinery, and two or three attempts of that sort without any pretension, they would distinguish him very much. (*DS*, ch. 36)

7

PROPER NAMES

Goaded by the insistent questioning of Mr Boffin and anticipating the further questions which he has reason to fear will follow, Silas Wegg gives his name in a reply which has become famous: 'Silas Wegg. I don't know why Silas and I don't know why Wegg' (*OMF*, Bk I, ch. 5). Most readers of Dickens are content to follow his example, but the proper names of Dickens were not arrived at by accident. Inquiry into their origins may range from the certainty with which we recognize the appropriateness of the names of Mrs Leo Hunter or Eatanswill to speculation, incapable of proof or disproof, on the possibility that Silas Wegg got his name because it rhymes with, and is a telescoped form of, *wooden leg*. Somewhere between the two extremes we may put the suggestion that Estella Provis, Bella Wilfer and Helena Landless owe some part of their names to Ellen Lawless Ternan.[1]

The names of the major Dickensian characters are now so familiar that we tend to forget how unusual some of his best-known names are. Some names have plebeian or ludicrous associations which make them unsuitable for use in certain contexts. For example, it becomes clear to the discerning reader that Newman Noggs has made a mistake in his attempt to discover the object of Nicholas Nickleby's romantic attachment as soon as we are told that the girl he has followed is called Cecilia Bobster. Dickens was more willing than most novelists to give his heroes unusual or grotesque names, such as Chuzzlewit and Nickleby, but even in Dickens one cannot imagine a romantic hero with a name like Toodle. Mr Dombey has difficulty in imagining a wet-nurse with that name and insists on calling her Richards: 'an ordinary name and con-

---

[1] Edmund Wilson, 'Dickens: The Two Scrooges' in *The Wound and the Bow* (1941, revised ed. 1952), p. 62.

venient' (*DS*, ch. 2). In much the same way, there are offices where the office-boy is always called Fred. The indifference to the feelings of the person bearing the name which this practice implies is rightly resented, and even the patient Mrs Toodle hoped that 'perhaps if she was to be called out of her name, it would be considered in the wages'. There is mockery of the whole process of name-giving when Dick Swiveller has to choose a name for the Marchioness when she goes to school and decides on Sophronia Sphynx, 'as being euphonious and genteel, and furthermore indicative of mystery' (*OCS*, ch. 73).

Some names, of both places and persons, are based on rather elementary satire. Mudfog is clearly a descriptive place-name, and *Sketches by Boz* abounds in names like Mrs Queertable, the keeper of a boarding-house, and the Honourable Captain Fitz-Whisker Fiercy (*The Pantomime of Life*).

Dickens devoted a lot of care to the choice of suitable names for his characters. Some of the most familiar Dickensian names were arrived at only after many changes. Forster (IV, 1) records the variant forms that were considered before Chuzzlewit was finally adopted. Martin was constant throughout but the surname was in turn Sweezleden, Sweezleback, Sweezlewag, Chuzzletoe, Chuzzleboy, Chubblewig and Chuzzlewig.

Some Dickensian names are taken from life. There are, of course, familiar place-names and, with his customary careful observation, Dickens has sometimes preserved information about their pronunciation by spellings which he occasionally feels to need further identification, as when an omnibus conductor says ' . . . we will take him up to the Edge-er (Edgeware) Road for nothing, and set him down at Doory-lane when we comes back' (*SB*, *Tales*, ch. 11). Other names are thinly disguised. The second meeting of the Mudfog Association is held at Oldcastle, which is reached by sea from London (*SB*, *The Mudfog Papers*). The names of the public-houses in that town are parodies, such as the Black Boy and Stomach-ache or the Boot-jack and Countenance. The first meeting had been held in the town of Mudfog, and one can guess at the ancient rivalries underlying the names of the two inns where the meetings were held, the Pig and Tinder-Box and the Original Pig. Forster says (I, 5) that Dickens took the name of Mr Pickwick from that of a celebrated coach-proprietor of Bath, and he forestalls criticism by making Sam Weller accuse the coach-proprietor of stealing Mr Pickwick's name. Sam's own surname was no doubt suggested by that of Mary Weller, a servant who looked after Dickens when he was a child. It is reasonable to suppose that the name of Sir John Chester in *Barnaby Rudge* owes something to Lord Chesterfield, and the resemblance between the personalities of the two men is emphasized by a soliloquy in which Sir John sings the praises of his favourite author Lord Chesterfield (ch. 23). On the other hand, some names are obvious parodies, like that of the Honourable Augustus Fitz-Edward Fitz-John Fitz-Osborne (*SB, Tales*, ch. 5) or O'Bleary (*SB, Tales*, ch. 1) and the place-name Ballykillbabaloo (*SB, Sketches of Young Gentlemen*). If we did not know from other sources that Dickens regarded a professor as a figure of fun, his opinion would become clear from the names of the professors who attended the first meeting of the Mudfog Association for the Advancement of Everything: Snore, Doze, Wheezy, Nogo, Muff and Queerspeck.

In the autobiographical fragment which Dickens entrusted to Forster, he describes the help that he received, when working as a boy in the blacking warehouse, from an older boy who showed him how to tie knots and who once spent a half-day in filling empty blacking-bottles with hot water to apply to Dickens's side when he was in pain. The name of this benefactor was Bob Fagin (Forster, I, 2). Another name that goes back to the time when Dickens worked in the blacking warehouse is the Christian name of Poll Sweedlepipe in *Martin Chuzzlewit*. Dickens said that the name was derived from that of Paul Green, who worked with him and who was generally believed to have been christened Poll (Forster, I, 2).

Dickens's note-books include lists of Christian names with the sources from which they were taken: the Privy Council Education Lists. Forster's comment is that some of these names would have been reckoned too extravagant for anything but reality (IX, 7), and they show that one of the best ways of finding really fantastic names is to choose the names of living persons. The lists include the Christian names of Pleasant Riderhood and Bradley Headstone, together with that of Doctor Marigold (*CS*), whose name was chosen out of gratitude to the doctor who brought him into the world.

The Christian names are followed by a list of some 170 'available names' without any indication of their source. This list includes many surnames used in the later novels, such as Merdle, Casby, Plornish, Meagles, Pancks, from *Little Dorrit*, Higden, Twemlow, Rokesmith, Podsnap, Boffin, Wilfer, Riderhood, Wegg from *Our Mutual Friend*, Magwitch, Pumblechook, Gargery, Wopsle from *Great Expectations*, and Sapsea from *Edwin Drood*. Some of the names underwent minor changes: Lightword and Mulvey are no doubt the earlier forms of the names of Mortimer Lightwood and the Rev. Frank Milvey in *Our Mutual Friend*. Some names that are very familiar to readers of Dickens occur in more than one form: Dorrit occurs as a possible variant of Dorret, and Arthur Clennam's name seems at first to have been Blenham, followed by the letters *Cl* as a possible alternative to *Bl*. One can only regret that Dickens found no occasion to use some of the very Dickensian names in the list, such as Spessifer, Grimmer, Tuzzen, Bantinck and Chinkible.

One device which Dickens uses more than once is that of coining a series of names by the substitution of a different initial letter, thus producing a list of rhyming names. As if to call attention to the arbitrary nature of the device, the names are given in alphabetical order, and there are so many of them that the author seems to intend to run through the alphabet. In *Bleak House* one of the guests at Chesney Wold is Lord Boodle, who tells his host that, if the Government is overthrown, the choice of the Crown in the formation of a new Ministry would be between Lord Coodle and Sir Thomas Doodle, supposing it to be impossible for the Duke of Foodle to act with Goodle. The members of the Cabinet will include Joodle, Koodle, Loodle and Moodle, but the difficulty is how to provide for Noodle. Another view is that expressed by the Right Honourable William Buffy, who contends that the shipwreck of the country is attributable to Cuffy, who had been allowed to go over to Duffy, instead of forming an alliance with Fuffy, and so on, until we are left dependent on the mere caprice of Puffy (ch. 12).

At first, this may seem to be a rather mechanical device, to which an author is likely to resort when he is barren of new ideas for names, but lack of inventiveness in names is one of the last defects of which one could accuse Dickens. The similarity of names is better regarded as a deliberate satirical device, by means of which the author expresses his belief that politicians are all very much alike, and that it does not greatly matter which of them are in power. A similar device is used in *Our Mutual Friend* by young Blight, one of the many Dickensian characters of whom one would like to see more. Blight, Mortimer Lightwood's clerk, was 'apt to consider it personally disgraceful to himself that his master had no clients', and so, when giving Mr Boffin an appointment, he ran his finger down the day's appointments, murmuring, 'Mr Aggs, Mr Baggs, Mr Caggs, Mr Daggs, Mr Faggs, Mr Gaggs, Mr Boffin'. This done, he enters Mr Boffin's name in the Callers' Book after those of Mr Alley, Mr Balley, Mr Calley, Mr Dalley, Mr Falley, Mr Galley, Mr Halley, Mr Lalley and Mr Malley (Bk I, ch. 8).

An impersonal effect, similar to that achieved by this ringing of the changes on a single name, is achieved elsewhere by suppressing names altogether and replacing them by the names of professions. At the party given by Mr Merdle (*LD*, Bk II, ch. 25) we find Bar, Physician and Bishop (whose wife is Mrs Bishop and whose son is young Mr Bishop) engaged in conversation with one another and with 'the representatives of the Barnacle Chorus'. Similarly, in *Our Mutual Friend* the guests whom Twemlow meets when first invited to dine at the Veneerings are described partly by their professions and partly by their opinions or attributes as 'a Member, an Engineer, a Payer-off of the National Debt, a Poem on Shakespeare, a Grievance, and a Public Office' (Bk I, ch. 2).

Mrs Todgers's lodgers in *Martin Chuzzlewit* are for the most part unnamed, but their interests are mentioned:

Then the presentation took place. They included a gentleman of a sporting turn, who propounded questions on jockey subjects to the editors of Sunday papers, which were regarded by his friends as rather stiff things to answer; and they included a gentleman of a theatrical turn, who had once entertained serious thoughts of 'coming out', but had been kept in by the wickedness of human nature; and they included a gentleman of a debating turn, who was strong at speech-making; and a gentleman of a literary turn, who wrote squibs upon the rest, and knew the weak side of everybody's character but his own. There was a gentleman of a vocal turn, and a gentleman of a smoking turn, and a gentleman of a convivial turn;

some of the gentlemen had a turn for whist, and a large proportion
of the gentlemen had a strong turn for billiards and betting. They
had all, it may be presumed, a turn for business; being all com-
mercially employed in one way or other; and had, every one in his
own way, a decided turn for pleasure to boot. (*MC*, ch. 9)

The lack of names is a convenience to the reader, who is
relieved of the necessity of remembering the names of characters
who are not going to play a significant part in the action of the
novel.

Proper names and titles cause trouble to some of Dickens's
more simple-minded characters. Dick Swiveller is addressed by
a servant-girl as Mr Snivelling and by the Marchioness as Mr
Liverer (*OCS*, chs. 7, 64). Miss Flite has a vague idea that
Caddy Jellyby has some connexion with the wards in Jarndyce
and she therefore always calls her Fitz-Jarndyce (*BH*, ch. 14);
she acknowledges Mr George's military service by calling him
General George (ch. 47). Similarly in *Dombey and Son* Toots,
having become used to calling Captain Cuttle Captain Gills, is
for the moment uncertain how to address the real Solomon
Gills when he meets him but solves the problem by addressing
him as Mr Sols (ch. 56). Toots had arrived at Lieutenant
Walters as a suitable name for Walter Gay 'by a process
peculiar to himself' (ch. 50). Joe Gargery has difficulty with
the name Camilla:

> 'Mrs – what's the name of them wild beasts with humps, old
> chap?'
> 'Camels?' said I, wondering why he could possibly want to know.
> Joe nodded. 'Mrs Camels,' by which I presently understood he
> meant Camilla. (*GE*, ch. 57)

Persistently and deliberately to use the wrong name or title
of someone who is perfectly well known to the speaker is a
form of insult in which some of Dickens's unpleasant characters
indulge from time to time. Uriah Heep repeatedly addresses
David Copperfield as 'Master', each time correcting it to 'Mr'
with an apology whose only purpose is to call attention to the
slight. After Louisa Gradgrind's marriage to Mr Bounderby,
Mrs Sparsit continues to call her Miss Gradgrind, saying to
Harthouse 'I really cannot call her Mrs Bounderby' (*HT*,
Bk II, ch. 9). Both speakers have the same motive: to call
disparaging attention to the youth of someone they dislike.

Dickens made frequent use of names that, by obvious puns, reveal the character or occupation of their holders: Sir Mulberry Hawk, Mr Gallanbile, M.P. (*NN*, ch. 16), Bob Sawyer, Tite Barnacle. It is especially minor characters whose names are of this kind. In *Bleak House*, for example, we have Mr Gusher, 'a very fervid, impassioned speaker' (ch. 8) and the Honourable Bob Stables, who speaks of Lady Dedlock's 'points' (ch. 2). In *Great Expectations* we are told:

> Mr and Mrs Pocket had a toady neighbour; a widow lady of that highly sympathetic nature that she agreed with everybody, blessed everybody, and shed smiles and tears on everybody, according to circumstances.' (ch. 23)

It causes us no surprise when Dickens goes on: 'This lady's name was Mrs Coiler'. The proposed scene of the Great Winglebury Duel (*SB, Tales*, ch. 8) is Stiffun's Acre, and the challenger is called Hunter while his unwilling victim is called Trott. Different ways of ill-treating children are indicated by the name of the school Dotheboys Hall (*NN*) and that of the schoolmaster McChoakumchild (*HT*). Place-names like Eatanswill (*PP*), and Purechurch in the valley of Cashup (*NN*, ch. 57) are obvious puns. The names of Pyke and Pluck, Sir Mulberry Hawk's parasites, and of Wolf, who makes a brief appearance at Tigg Montague's party (*MC*, ch. 28) all reveal their predatory natures. Mrs Leo Hunter's name clearly describes her hobby and the joke is kept up in her address: The Den, Eatanswill (*PP*, ch. 15). Such names were frequent in Elizabethan and Restoration drama. The Reverend Melchisedech Howler (*DS*, ch. 15) is a name that might have come straight out of Ben Jonson, with its combination of a punning surname with a biblical Christian name. The appropriateness of the surname is made clear by the comment that he 'had consented, on very urgent solicitation, to give the world another two years of existence, but had informed his followers that, then, it must positively go' (ch. 60). The punning significance of a name is often thinly disguised by the spelling, like those of Count Smorltork (*PP*, ch. 15), Lord Frederick Verisopht, Sir Leicester Dedlock, and Colonel Fitz-Sordust (*SB, Sketches of Young Gentlemen*). The pun may be disguised for a modern reader by the disappearance of a variant form known to Dickens

and his contemporaries. Thus, the appropriateness of the surname of the very military Matthew Bagnet in *Bleak House*
becomes more clear when we find *bagginets* used as a variant of
bayonets in *Pickwick Papers* (ch. 19). A name may be the result
of an association of ideas, and the association is sometimes
ironical. Mr Dorrit's servant, Tinkler, clearly gets his name
because he answers the bell, and Edmund Sparkler equally
obviously gets his name because he doesn't sparkle.

Sometimes it is only part of a name that resembles a common
English word, but the resemblance is enough to make the name
significant; so we have Cheeryble and Gradgrind. Although we
sympathize with Mr Jellyby's sufferings, his spineless acquies-
cence makes his name appropriate.

Another group of names is made up of those which contain
groups of sounds which are likely to remind the reader of
common English words and which therefore indicate the
character of the bearer of the name. Thus we have Slurk, the
editor of the *Eatanswill Independent* (*PP*, ch. 51), whose name
reminds the reader of such words as *sly* and *lurk*. The un-
attractiveness of Chevy Slyme is only slightly disguised by the
spelling of his surname, and the significance of the name of
David Crimple in the same novel is underlined by the author's
statement that the name was originally Crimp but that the
owner of the name had altered it because 'the word was
susceptible of an awkward construction' (*MC*, ch. 27). Squeers
reminds us of *squint* and *queer*, and Peg Sliderskew reminds us
of *sly*, *slide* and *askew*. The associations are not always unpleasant: the name of Mr Crisparkle in *Edwin Drood* clearly
invites association of ideas with *crisp* and *sparkle*. Different
readers might select different words if asked about the associations of these names, but the author's general intention is clear.
The use of the initial group *Vh-*, which is contrary to English
habits of spelling, emphasizes the inhumanity of the least
attractive of the lawyers in *Bleak House*. Often there are no such
associations, but names of both persons and places seem to be
chosen because they sound pleasantly silly or grotesque,
especially in conjunction with other names. To this category
belong such names as Snittle Timberry (*NN*, ch. 48), Sir
Chipkins Glogwog (*SB*, *Sketches of Young Couples*), the
imaginary estate of Blinkiter Doddles in *Little Dorrit* (Bk II,

ch. 12), the firms Bilson and Slum and Tiggin and Welps mentioned by the bagman in *Pickwick Papers* (ch. 49), and Mrs Nickleby's former suitors: young Lukin, Mogley, Tipslark, Cabbery and Smifser (*NN*, ch. 41).

Christian names tell us more about the parents than about those who bear the names. What more natural than that the son of the successful ironmaster in *Bleak House* should be called Watt Roucewell (ch. 7) or that the son of Mr Turveydrop, who took the Prince Regent as his hero, should be called Prince? The children of Matthew Bagnet (*BH*, ch. 27) were not actually christened Quebec, Malta and Woolwich, but they were always called by these names in the family from the places of their birth in barracks. The names serve to remind the reader of their parents' military background.

A refusal to use Christian names can be very revealing. Mr Gradgrind shows his unsympathetic nature by addressing Sissy Jupe when a young child as 'Jupe' (*HT*, Bk I, ch. 6). It may be, of course, that his refusal to use Sissy's Christian name was due to his distaste for the abbreviated form, which he had made clear in the second chapter of the novel: 'Sissy is not a name. Don't call yourself Sissy. Call yourself Cecilia.' Bounderby goes to the other extreme and goes out of his way to refer to Gradgrind as Tom Gradgrind, and there is the comment that he does so 'for a bluff, independent manner of speaking; as if somebody were always endeavouring to bribe him with immense sums to say Thomas, and he wouldn't' (*HT*, Bk I, ch. 7).

One result of the wide appeal of the novels of Dickens is that the names of his characters have passed into our everyday language just as the names of Shakespearean characters have done. It is often a comparatively trivial incident or remark in a novel that gives the name its currency today, such as the willingness of Barkis, the use of a word in its Pickwickian sense or the friendliness of Codlin in comparison with Short. Many a university department with two professors is run on a Spenlow and Jorkins arrangement by which one professor blames his less active colleague for his own unpopular decisions.

One linguistic point which has a bearing on character-portrayal is the variety of ways in which husbands and wives address or refer to each other. The use of a surname without

any prefix by a wife in referring to her husband is now thought
of as characteristic of servants in large households where
husband and wife have the same employer, but it is not uncommon among Dickens's less affluent characters. Mrs Plornish
calls her husband Plornish (*LD*, Bk I, ch. 12), Mrs Quilp calls
hers Quilp (*OCS*, ch. 4), Mrs Varden addresses her husband
as Varden (*BR*, ch. 13) and Peggotty calls hers Barkis (*DC*,
ch. 27). Barkis himself has the idiosyncratic habit of referring
to his wife as C. P. Barkis. Flintwinch, in *Little Dorrit*,
generally calls his wife 'Affery woman'. It may seem characteristic of Mr Dombey's formality that, after ten years of married
life, he is still addressing his wife as 'Mrs Dombey' (*DS*, ch. 1)
and that he calls his brother-in-law 'Mr John' (ch. 5). Such
formal address, however, was not uncommon in Victorian times.
Gradgrind and his wife address each other as 'Mrs Gradgrind'
and 'Mr Gradgrind', though Mrs Gradgrind draws the line at
addressing her son-in-law as 'Mr Bounderby' (*HT*, Bk I,
ch. 15).

An eccentricity of nomenclature is shared by two very
dissimilar characters: Major Bagstock (*DS*) and Durdles (*ED*)
habitually refer to themselves by name in the third person.

Nicknames play a large part in the novels of Dickens, and
they become firmly fixed in the reader's memory as a result of
the author's willingness to go on repeating them; the nickname
is often better remembered than the real name, which may
never be mentioned at all. Deputy in *Edwin Drood* is always
called by that name. Short, of the Codlin and Short partnership,
is best known by his nickname, and there is a circumstantial
account of how he acquired it:

> The real name of the little man was Harris, but it had gradually
> merged into the less euphonious one of Trotters, which, with the
> prefatory adjective, Short, had been conferred upon him by reason
> of the small size of his legs. Short Trotters, however, being a
> compound name, inconvenient of use in friendly dialogue, the
> gentleman on whom it had been bestowed was known among his
> intimates either as 'Short', or 'Trotters', and was seldom accosted
> at full length as Short Trotters, except in formal conversations and
> on occasions of ceremony. (*OCS*, ch. 17)

The nicknames are of two kinds: those which the characters in
the novels give to one another and those which are given by

the author. Examples of the first kind of nickname are Mealy Potatoes (*DC*, ch. 11), the Marchioness (*OCS*), Daisy (Steerforth's name for David Copperfield) and old bricks and mortar (Mr Lenville's name for Vincent Crummles because his style of acting is heavy, *NN*, ch. 23). Examples of the second type, all from *Dombey and Son*, are 'the black-eyed' (Susan Nipper), the Dowager (Mrs Pipchin) and Cleopatra (Mrs Skewton). The nicknames which Dickens gives to his characters would form a good basis for an examination paper to be answered by Dickens enthusiasts. Questions in this paper would be of the type 'Who are the following and why are they so called?' A few of the easier questions would refer to the Golden Dustman (*OMF*), the Old Soldier (*DC*) and the Patriarch (*LD*).

When Mr Snagsby is looking for Jo, he learns something of the wealth of nicknames in use in London's underworld:

> As few people are known in Tom-all-Alone's by any Christian sign, there is much reference to Mr Snagsby whether he means Carrots, or the Colonel, or Gallows, or Young Chisel, or Terrier Tip, or Lanky, or the Brick . . . At last there is a lair found out where Toughy, or the Tough Subject, lays him down at night; and it is thought that the Tough Subject may be Jo. (*BH*, ch. 22)

Similar exuberance is illustrated elsewhere. The boots at Mrs Todgers's boarding-house is generally called Bailey, but this is only one of many names:

> Benjamin was supposed to be the real name of this young retainer, but he was known by a great variety of names. Benjamin, for instance, had been converted into Uncle Ben, and that again had been corrupted into Uncle; which, by an easy transition, had again passed into Barnwell, in memory of the celebrated relative in that degree who was shot by his nephew George, while meditating in his garden at Camberwell. The gentlemen at Todgers's had a merry habit, too, of bestowing upon him, for the time being, the name of any notorious malefactor or minister; and sometimes when current events were flat, they even sought the pages of history for these distinctions; as Mr Pitt, Young Brownrigg, and the like. At the period of which we write, he was generally known among the gentlemen as Bailey junior; a name bestowed upon him in contra-distinction, perhaps, to Old Bailey; and possibly as involving the recollection of an unfortunate lady of the same name, who perished by her own hand early in life, and has been immortalised in a ballad. (*MC*, ch. 9)

Bella Wilfer's father acquires a variety of nicknames as a result of his secretiveness about his real name. These are quoted at length, along with the origin of his usual nickname Rumty (*OMF*, Bk I, ch. 4).

Such names often throw light on the characters of those who bear them and even more of those who bestow them. For example, the strain of insensitiveness that underlies the cheerful good nature of Mr Meagles is illustrated by his choice of the name Tattycoram for the foundling Harriet Beadle. It is left for the hypersensitive Miss Wade to point out (*LD*, Bk I, ch. 2) how offensive the daily use of the name Tattycoram might be as a reminder that its holder was taken from the Foundling Hospital founded by Thomas Coram. A similar callousness towards illegitimacy is shown by a character whom the author clearly regards sympathetically. When Betty Higden is asked whether Sloppy is called by his right name, she replies:

'Why, you see, speaking quite correctly, he has no right name. I always understood he took his name from being found on a Sloppy night.' (*OMF*, Bk I, ch. 16)

Some nicknames were in the nineteenth century, and still are, traditionally assigned to a particular surname or to a particular distinctive feature or trait of character. In *Oliver Twist* (ch. 31) Conkey Chickweed is mentioned, and the explanation that Conkey means Nosey is brushed aside as superfluous.

Nicknames are sometimes used because of a desire to avoid using the real name of a character. Mr Dick never uses his surname, because it reminds him of his family, who have not treated him well. Affery Flintwinch is reluctant to mention the name of Mrs Clennam. Her awe is too great to allow her to use a nickname, and she therefore either uses a personal pronoun or refers to her husband and Mrs Clennam collectively as 'them two clever ones' (*LD*, Bk I, ch. 3). Another attitude towards nicknames is satirized in Edward Dorrit's allusion to Arthur Clennam: 'your Clennam, as he thinks proper to call himself' (*LD*, Bk II, ch. 3). A simple-minded person, having taken a dislike to someone, is liable to regard it as a grievance that the object of his animosity has a name at all.

Nicknames flourish in prisons, where the prisoners often prefer not to be reminded of their identity, and where slang, which has a good deal in common with the use of nicknames, also flourishes. It is in the Marshalsea that Edward Dorrit becomes Tip, through the intermediate stage Ted (*LD*, Bk I, ch. 7), and the prisoners who left gifts for the Father of the Marshalsea often assumed facetious names, such as the Brick, Bellows, Old Gooseberry, Wideawake, Snooks, Mops, Cutaway, and the Dogs-meat Man, but the recipient of the gifts thought these names in bad taste and was always a little hurt by their use (*LD*, Bk I, ch. 6).

Sam Weller uses nicknames freely as a sign of his refusal to tolerate any self-importance in his fellow men. Such nicknames are quite compatible with respect, as well as affection, for the person to whom they are applied. In the course of the novel Sam's attitude to Mr Pickwick changes from patronizing tolerance to devotion, but it is nearly at the end of the novel that, on hearing of his stepmother's death, he says cheerfully 'I must apply to the hemperor for leave of absence' (*PP*, ch. 52). Here, as elsewhere, the use of a nickname is a sign of affection. Esther Summerson is regarded with deep affection by her friends, and she is therefore frequently addressed by such names as Dame Durden and Mother Hubbard (*BH*, ch. 9). The affectionate Mr Meagles has nicknames for his entire household: Mother, Pet and Tattycoram (*LD*), but, when nicknames are applied to strangers or mere acquaintances, they are generally disrespectful. When Jingle sends 'love to Tuppy' Mr Pickwick is indignant: 'The villainy... which could first borrow money of his faithful follower, and then abbreviate his name to "Tuppy" was more than he could patiently bear' (*PP*, ch. 9).

A particular nickname will sometimes be used by only one character in a novel. The author calls Mr Boffin the Golden Dustman (*OMF*, Bk I, ch. 16); Mrs Boffin calls him Noddy (Bk IV, ch. 13); Silas Wegg calls him variously Dusty Boffin (Bk III, ch. 14) and, in that strain of rather obscure poetry which Dickensian characters sometimes adopt, 'that minion of fortune and worm of the hour' (Bk III, ch. 14). Similarly, only Jenny Wren calls Fledgeby Little Eyes (*OMF*, Bk IV, ch. 8), only Eugene Wrayburn calls Jenny's father Mr Dolls (*OMF*, Bk III, ch. 10), and only Captain Cuttle calls Florence Dombey Heart's Delight (*DS*, ch. 48). Jenny's real name is Fanny Cleaver, but throughout the book she is called by the name

Jenny Wren, which 'she had long ago chosen to bestow upon herself' (*OMF*, Bk II, ch. 2).

In reading a novel we do not as a rule learn the names of the characters as soon as they are introduced. The usual method is to introduce characters by brief descriptive phrases and to add the name only when the character in question has made one or two remarks which give him individuality in the reader's mind. In *Dombey and Son* Toodle is introduced as 'the apple-faced man' (ch. 2), but we are soon told his name. Susan Nipper is introduced as 'a short, brown, womanly girl of fourteen'. After a few speeches she is described as Spitfire and finally we are told her name (*DS*, ch. 3).

Dickens sometimes devotes a good deal of detail to the description of a character who turns out to be so unimportant that we are never told his name. There is, for example, the 'youngish sallowish gentleman in spectacles, with a lumpy forehead' who causes a profound sensation at Podsnap's party by saying '*esker*' to the foreign gentleman, another character whose name is never given (*OMF*, Bk I, ch. 11). Dickens often crystallizes the brief descriptive phrase into a nickname, which may be all that we are given, or it may prolong the period of anonymity before the actual name is mentioned. We thus become familiar with the Mature Young Lady and the Mature Young Gentleman at Veneering's party before learning that their names are Alfred Lammle and Sophronia Akersham (*OMF*, Bk I, ch. 10). Veneering's butler is at first called a 'retainer'; the nickname Analytical, by which he is known throughout the book, is a reminder of a joke made by the author soon after his first appearance (Bk I, ch. 2) that when he handed food to a guest, he was like a gloomy Analytical Chemist, always seeming to say 'You wouldn't if you knew what it's made of'. Another butler described by a nickname is Mr Merdle's Chief Butler, the Avenging Spirit, who is also called 'that respectable Nemesis' (*LD*, Bk II, ch. 12). Both these butlers occur in the later novels. No doubt, as Dickens prospered, he saw more of butlers, and he seems to have found them rather overwhelming.

Dickens sometimes applies to his characters epithets which remind the reader of one of their characteristics. Silas Wegg is described as 'that ligneous sharper' because of his wooden leg

(*OMF*, Bk I, ch. 5), and Mrs General is 'that eminent varnisher' and 'the fair varnisher' (*LD*, Bk II, ch. 5). It is Sir Leicester Dedlock who first calls Mr Rouncewell, the ironmaster, 'the iron gentleman', but the author takes up the term and repeats it several times, varying it once with 'that ferruginous person' (*BH*, ch. 48). Sometimes the epithet is a pun on the character's name. When Dick Swiveller is employed by Sampson Brass he is said to be 'passing through the street in the execution of some Brazen errand' (*OCS*, ch. 38), and Brass is elsewhere described as Quilp's 'brazen friend' (ch. 33).

The best-known Dickensian nickname is that of Dickens himself, Boz. The origin of this name in a family joke is described by Forster:

> This was the nickname of a pet child, his youngest brother Augustus, whom in honour of the *Vicar of Wakefield* he had dubbed Moses which being facetiously pronounced through the nose became Boses, and being shortened became Boz. (I, 4)

This etymology suggests that the usual pronunciation of *Boz* with a short *o* is not the one originally intended. There is some evidence that Dickens, at least for a time, thought of the vowel as long, since in a letter to Forster he speaks of himself as 'Monsieur de Boze' (Forster, V, 7). Dickens was fond of giving nicknames to his children. The girls were Mild Glo'ster and Lucifer Box; the boys were Flaster Floby, Ocean Sceptre and Plornishmaroontigoonter.

A nickname which Dickens often applied to himself was 'the Inimitable'. This name was given to him by the Baptist minister William Giles, whose school Dickens attended as a boy (Forster, I, 1).

Appendix

SUBSTANDARD GRAMMAR

Phonology
Consonants

1. Confusion between [w] and [v] is often thought of as one of the most important characteristics of the London dialect, but it may be that this view is due in large measure to the popularity of the novels of Dickens, who makes very free use of words illustrating the confusion. (cf. Wyld, *HMCE* pp. 143, 292, *SHE* § 282 (5)). A. J. Ellis[1] pointed out that the confusion is common in various regional dialects, notably in Norfolk, Essex and Kent. When the waiter at Yarmouth speaks of broken *wittles* (*DC*, ch. 5), he may therefore be illustrating a feature of regional dialect, but the confusion is so common in Dickens that it is better to regard the use of [w] for [v] as a feature that is liable to occur in the speech of any of his low-life characters. It is especially common in the speech of the two Wellers. Gerson (§ 44.3) counted 330 examples from Sam and 154 from his father. The following examples all occur in the first chapter of *Doctor Marigold* (*CS*): *aggrawation, awaricious, conwulsion, indiwidual, rewerse, uniwersal, wenturesomeness, wermilion, wiolence, wiolin, woters*. Examples of the use of [w] for [v] by Sam Weller include *inwenter* and *wixin* (*PP*, ch. 31). Other examples are *wacant* (Billickin, *ED*, ch. 22) and *wisibly* (Tony Weller, *PP*, ch. 33).

The use of [v] for [w] is less common in London speech than the use of [w] for [v], but there are several examples in Dickens, such as *vich* and *elsevere* (Mrs Gamp, *MC*, ch. 29) (cf. Gerson § 45.1.1). The most famous example of all, which suggests that the distinction between the two sounds was not always clear, is that provided by the Weller family at the trial of Bardell against Pickwick. Sam's preference for 'V' is confirmed by his father: 'Quite right, too, Samuel, quite right. Put it down a we, my Lord' (*PP*, ch. 34). Other examples used by

---

[1] *Early English Pronunciation*, iv, p. 1330.

Sam include *vy, vorth, archvay* and *veskit* (all in ch. 10). Sam's *vun* for *one* (ch. 31) suggests that the change of [w] to [v] is later than the introduction of the regional pronunciation with initial [w] which is the basis of the present-day pronunciation of the word.

2. [g] was often unvoiced to [k] when it occurs finally after [ŋ] (cf. Wyld *HMCE*, p. 290, Gerson § 34.3). Examples are: *everythink* and *nothink* (Riderhood, *OMF*, Bk IV, ch. 15), *think* (Mrs Gamp, *MC*, ch. 40).

3. The loss of *g* in spelling in the group *-ng* in lightly-stressed final positions, usually indicates the replacement of the velar nasal [ŋ] by the alveolar nasal [n]. The change is well-evidenced at least as far back as the late fourteenth century (cf. Wyld, *HMCE*, pp. 69, 289, *SHE*, § 282 (2), Gerson § 34.2). Examples from Dickens are: *screamin', kickin', mornin', missin', nothin', affectin', feelin's* (all by Sam Weller in *PP*, ch. 31), *knowin'* (Jackson, *PP*, ch. 31), *considerin'* (Mrs Gamp, *MC*, ch. 26), *earnins* (Mrs Gamp, *MC*, ch. 40). Wardle's use of *ev'nins* (*PP*, ch. 4) serves as a reminder that this pronunciation is not confined to the London poor.

4. The change of [ŋ] to [n] led to confusion between the two sounds, and we consequently sometimes find *-ng* for *-n* in lightly-stressed syllables (cf. Gerson § 33). Examples are: *parding* (Mrs Raddle, *PP*, ch. 32), *Chicking* (Maggy, *LD*, Bk I, ch. 9), *wepping* 'weapon' (*BH*, ch. 11), *sov'ring* (Jo, *BH*, ch. 31). The change of the lightly-stressed vowel to [i] may be due to confusion with the common inflexional ending *-ing*. The form *thousing* 'thousand' (Guster, *BH*, ch. 19) suggests that final [ŋg] and [nd] had both been reduced to [n] in lightly-stressed syllables.

5. *Chim(b)ley* is a widespread dialectal variant of *chimney* (cf. Gerson § 33.2). Dickensian examples are: *chimbley* (Sam Weller, *PP*, ch. 30), *chimbley-corner* (Wegg, *OMF*, Bk II, ch. 7), *chimbley-piece* (Mrs Gamp, *MC*, ch. 19). The [b] is the result of faulty timing in the movement of the organs of speech from [m] to [l], and has a parallel in standard English *thimble*.

6. The use of [ʃ], spelt *sh*, for medial or final *s* is recorded from the fourteenth century (cf. Wyld, *HMCE*, p. 291, *SHE*, § 282(4)). Mrs Gamp speaks of a *gash balloon* (*MC*, ch. 29.)

7. The change of initial [ʃ] to [s] before [r] is found in some regional dialects, but in Dickens it is regarded as a vulgarism (cf. p. **100** and Gerson § 38.2). Examples are *rum-srub* (*SB, Scenes,* ch. 22), *srimps* (*SB, Tales,* ch. 4).

8. The consonant [t] was sometimes voiced before a nasal consonant, as in *pardner* (Mrs Gamp, *MC,* ch. 49; Hexam and Riderhood, *OMF,* Bk I, ch. 1) (cf. Gerson § 40.1). *Bardlemy's* is mentioned as a variant of *Bartlemy's* frequently used by nurses (*MC,* ch. 49). Voicing of [t] when not followed by a nasal is found in *alphabeds* (Mr Boffin, *OMF,* Bk I, ch. 5).

9. The group *-ture* is often spelt *ter* or *tur,* suggesting that the pronunciation may have been [tə]: *feater* (Betsey Prig, *MC,* ch. 29), *picter* (Mrs Boffin, *OMF,* Bk IV, ch. 13), *wentur* (Tony Weller, *PP,* ch. 20), *creetur* (Tony Weller, *PP,* ch. 9), *torters* (Mrs Gamp, *MC,* ch. 49), *departer* (Riderhood, *OMF,* Bk II, ch. 12), *furniter* (Sam Weller, *PP,* ch. 10), *lecters* (Riderhood, *OMF,* Bk IV, ch. 15), *manafacter* (Sam Weller, *PP,* ch. 31), *naterally* (Kenwigs, *NN,* ch. 36) (cf. Gerson § 43.1). Similarly, the affricate [tʃ] has been replaced by the plosive consonant *t* in *fort'ns* (*PP,* ch. 10), *unfort'nate* (Cuttle, *DS,* ch. 49).

10. The sound-change of medial [di] to [dʒ] has affected a few standard English words, such as *grandeur* and *soldier,* but its use in words like *hideous* and *odious* is now confined to a few old-fashioned speakers (Wyld, *SHE* § 283(3)). Guppy's *tremendjous* (*BH,* ch. 64) may show this change combined with confusion between the suffixes *-ous* and *-ious* (cf. § 59).

11. Between vowels [d] is sometimes weakened to [r] as in *imperent* 'impudent' (Mrs Gamp, *MC,* ch. 29; Sam Weller, *PP,* ch. 35). Cf. RP *porridge,* earlier *pottage.*

12. Between [r] and a vowel the voiced pre-dental [ð] sometimes becomes the alveolar [d], as in *farden* (Mrs Gamp, *MC,* ch. 29), *furder* (Tony Weller, *PP,* ch. 52).

13. The voiceless plosives [p], [t], [k] were liable to be confused with one another, as in *Barklemy's* (*MC,* ch. 49), *Ankworks* for *Antwerp* (Mrs Gamp, *MC,* ch. 40), *mankleshelf* (Betsey Prig, *MC,* ch. 25), *ast* for *ask* (Mrs Gamp, *MC,* ch. 25).

14. From the fifteenth century there are examples of the substitution of [f] for [θ] and of [v] for [ð]. Today these substitutions seem to be a personal idiosyncrasy, though they

H

are especially common in what H. C. Wyld describes as 'a very low type of Cockney English' (*SHE*, § 282(3)). There are occasional examples in Dickens, such as *nuffin* 'nothing' (*SB, Scenes*, ch. 20, *Characters*, ch. 12).

15. Metathesis of two consonants or of a vowel and a consonant is a change that takes place from time to time in both standard and substandard speech. Jo, in *Bleak House*, habitually calls Mr Snagsby *Mr Sangsby* (as in ch. 46).

16. Complete or partial assimilation of two consecutive consonants is another consonant change that is liable to take place at any time, though it is not always recorded in spelling. Mrs Gamp's *Gammy* 'Grandma' (attributed to a baby, *MC*, ch. 49) provides an example of this change and of the loss of [r] after an initial consonant, which may be assumed to be due to a child's difficulty in pronouncing the consonant-group [gr]. The Marchioness's *sangwitches* (*OCS*, ch. 64) shows partial assimilation of the group ([dw] to [gw].

17. Loss of initial [h] in French loan-words, such as *hour* and *honour*, and in lightly-stressed words, such as *him*, is normal in standard English, but the loss of initial [h] in strongly-stressed words of native or Scandinavian origin is one of the best known characteristics of substandard speech (cf. Dobson § 426, Gerson § 28.5.1). Examples are: *a 'arty old cock* (Wegg, *OMF*, Bk I, ch. 5), *'ouse* (Mrs Raddle, *PP*, ch. 32), *'ed* (Deputy, *ED*, ch. 18), *'appiness* (Mrs Gamp, *MC*, ch. 26), *art* for *heart* (Mrs Gamp, *MC*, ch. 26), *usband* (Mrs Mac-Stinger, *DS*, ch. 60), *appy* (Mrs MacStinger, *DS*, ch. 60). Uriah Heep's dropping of the *h* is very consistent (*I'm a very umble person*, *DC*, ch. 16) and is clearly intended to be a feature of class dialect.

18. In the effort to avoid dropping the [h], some speakers insert it without etymological justification. The insertion of [h] takes place only in stressed syllables and the habit has probably always been regarded as a vulgarism (Wyld *SHE* § 285 (4), Gerson § 28.4). Examples are: *hordit* (Tony Weller, *PP*, ch. 55), *hexpedite* (Tony Weller, *PP*, ch. 55), *hout* (Joe Gargery, *GE*, ch. 13), *herth* 'earth' (Mrs MacStinger, *DS*, ch. 39), *hinfant* (*PP*, ch. 5), *hi* 'eye' (*OMF*, Bk I, ch. 5), and *I listened with hadmiration amounting to haw* (Mr Boffin, *OMF*, Bk I, ch. 5). This practice is especially common in Sam Weller's speech, as in *hinfants* (ch. 31), *horgan* (ch. 10) and *hobvious* (ch. 16). Sam Weller's fondness for inorganic [h] shows that one reason for its use is not the only one: it is especially used by those who feel socially insecure. No one could accuse Sam of this failing, but Fanny Squeers is just the sort of person who might be expected to make use of a feature which had its origin in an unwillingness to 'talk common'. She speaks of her father's *henemies* (*NN*, ch. 64), and when she says 'This is the hend, is it?' (*NN*, ch. 42), the author adds the comment: 'Miss Squeers, . . . being excited, aspirated her h's strongly'. He achieves the same result by italicizing an *h* which is normally silent to show that the speaker pronounces it as in '*h*onours' (Kenwigs, *NN*, ch. 15), '*h*onour' (Kenwigs, *NN*, ch. 52). In describing the speech of the disreputable Smangle in addressing Mr Pickwick, the author makes doubly sure:

> Allow me the *h*onour,' said the gentleman with the whiskers, presenting his dexter hand, and aspirating the h. (*PP*, ch. 41)

19. Several words which in normal spelling contain the group *-rs-* are spelt with *ss* or *s*. In such words it is probable that the [r] had disappeared in pronunciation well before the time of Dickens (Wyld, *HMCE*, p. 299), and the omission of the *r* in spelling is therefore probably to be regarded as a method of indicating shortening or change of quality of the preceding vowel. Examples are *fust* 'first' (*PP*, ch. 2), *busted* (Squeers, *NN*, ch. 57), *wost* 'worst' (Sam Weller, *PP*, ch. 10), *mossel* (Mrs Gamp, *MC*, ch. 25), *nussed* (Mrs Gamp, *MC*, ch. 25), *I des-say* 'I dare say' (Sam Weller, *PP*, ch. 10). *Missus* (Sam Weller, *PP*, ch. 10) represents a pronunciation that is too widespread to be regarded as substandard; the *-ss-* is the result of assimilation of the group *str* in *mistress*. The loss of [r] after a consonant, as in *Febooary* (*PP*, ch. 31), is commonly found today.

20. The insertion of *r* in spelling in such words as *arter* 'after' (Mrs Gamp, *MC*, ch. 40), *arternoon* (Mrs Gamp, *MC*, ch. 46) is probably a device to indicate vowel-length (cf. Gerson § 26.4). Some such device became necessary after the disappearance of the *f*, because of the ambiguity of the letter *a*, which can represent a wide variety of different vowel-sounds in English. It may be that some such pronunciation of *after*

is to be assumed in the nursery rhyme *Jack and Jill*, to improve
the rhyme of *after* with *water*.

21. In lightly-stressed syllables [w] often disappears before
vowels, as in *orkard* (Sam Weller, *PP*, ch. 30), *unekal* (Sam
Weller, *PP*, ch. 41), *twopennorth* (*NN*, ch. 5), *summat* (*SB*,
Tales, ch. 10), *ekally* (Plornish, *LD*, Bk I, ch. 12), *back'ards*
(Mrs Gamp, *MC*, ch. 25), *ekalled* (Cuttle, *DS*, ch. 48), *for'ard*
(Mrs Gamp, *MC*, ch. 40), *allus* (Jo, *BH*, ch. 46), *summun*
'someone' (Magwitch, *GE*, ch. 42), *consekens* (Grummer, *PP*,
ch. 24), *up'ard* (Toodle, *DS*, ch. 20), (cf. Gerson § 45.2). A
similar disappearance of [w] takes place in monosyllabic words
with light sentence-stress, as in *'ud* (*PP*, ch. 2) and *'un*
(Sloppy, *OMF*, Bk II, ch. 10). The disappearance of initial
[w] in *woman* is probably due to the close phonetic resemblance
between the [w] and the following vowel (cf. Gerson § 45.2).
The form without initial consonant, spelt *'ooman*, is used by a
wide variety of Dickensian characters, including Sam Weller
(*PP*, ch. 10), Tony Weller (*PP*, ch. 33), Wardle's mother
(*PP*, ch. 6), Mrs Gamp (*MC*, ch. 46), and the turnkey of the
Marshalsea (*LD*, Bk I, ch. 6).

22. [l] often disappears medially, especially next to another
consonant: *a'most* (Cuttle, *DS*, ch. 32), *particklery* 'particularly' (Sam Weller, *PP*, ch. 37), *orvis* 'always' (*SB*, *Tales*,
ch. 4) (cf. Gerson § 31.2).

23. [t] often disappears medially before or after [l], [n] or
[r]. Examples are *gen'lm'n* (Sam Weller, *PP*, ch. 10), *Cap'en*
(Mrs MacStinger, *DS*, ch. 60), *chris'n* 'Christian' (Mrs Gamp,
MC, ch. 26). Captain Cuttle habitually calls Walter Gay
Wal'r, but this may be regarded as an individual eccentricity,
since it is not understood by Perch, who assumes that the
reference is to the poet Waller (*DS*, ch. 17).

24. Final consonants sometimes disappear in polysyllabic
words. The loss of the final consonant is especially common in
kerchief and compounds of which it is the final element. Examples
are *ketcher* (Riderhood, *OMF*, Bk IV, ch. 15), *neckhankercher*
(Riderhood, *OMF*, Bk IV, ch. 15), *ankercher* (Sam Weller, *PP*, ch.
27). Final [t] is lost after a voiceless plosive in *kep* (Sam Weller,
PP, ch. 31; Mrs Gamp, *MC*, ch. 49), and *werdick* (Tony Weller,
PP, ch. 43). In *fypunnote* (*CS*, *Doctor Marigold*, ch. 1) the
final consonant of the first element of a compound has disappeared.

25. The present-day standard English distinction between the forms of the indefinite article, which keeps *a* before a consonant and *an* before a vowel, is not preserved; there are many examples of the use of *a* before a vowel (cf. Horn-Lehnert § 422). Thus we have: *a angel* (Tony Weller, *PP*, ch. 33), *a errand connexion* (Wegg, *OMF*, Bk IV, ch. 14), *a old bird* (Mr Boffin, *OMF*, Bk I, ch. 5), *a ingein* (Boffin, *OMF*, Bk II, ch. 10), *a air* (Lillyvick, *NN*, ch. 30), *a unsatisfying sort of food* (Riderhood, *OMF*, Bk III, ch. 11), *a idle willin* (Sam Weller, *PP*, ch. 31), *a ackney coach* (*LD*, Bk I, ch. 6). In a few words in standard English, such as *newt*, an *n* has been transferred from the indefinite article to the following noun, and other words, such as *apron* and *umpire*, have lost an initial *n* by a similar transfer. Such a transfer, known as metanalysis, accounts for Uriah Heep's *a numble abode* (*DC*, ch. 16).

26. In the course of the history of English there has been variation between [n] and [nd] arising from imperfect timing of the movements of the organs of speech. We thus have *thunder* (OE *ðunor*) and *sound* (OF *son*), beside *lawn* (OF *launde*) (cf. Gerson § 24.7). In substandard speech the confusion extends to words which do not show it in standard English, as in *gownd* (Jo, *BH*, ch. 22). The verb *drown* is particularly liable to take on an extra *d*, as in *drownd* (Tony Weller, *PP*, ch. 52), *drownded* (Miggs, *BR*, ch. 19), *a drowndin' herself* (Tony Weller, *PP*, ch. 33). False etymology may have combined with the sound-change of [n] to [nd] in Mr Peggotty's reply when David Copperfield asks him if his brother is dead: 'Drowndead'. (*DC*, ch. 3). The converse change of [nd] to [n] is seen in *unnerstand* (Magwitch, *GE*, ch. 42) and *Are you in the Funns?* (Wegg, *OMF*, Bk I, ch. 5), *the funs* (Tony Weller, *PP*, ch. 52), *twenty-poun' note* (Bailey, *MC*, ch. 26), *fi'typunnote* (Game Chicken, *DS*, ch. 56).

27. A few words in standard English show the insertion of a nasal consonant before [g] or [dʒ] in lightly-stressed syllables of polysyllabic words, as in *passenger* (OF *passager*) and *nightingale* (OE *nihtegale*). In substandard speech this development is found also before [t] and [d]. Examples are: *skellinton* (Sam Weller, *PP*, ch. 15), *crorkindills* 'crocodiles' (Peggotty, *DC*, ch. 2), *milintary* (Perch, *DS*, ch. 53; John Willet, *BR*, ch. 13).

28. The addition of final [t] after [n] is found in a number of standard English words, such as *ancient* (Fr *ancien*), *pheasant* (Fr *faisan*), *parchment* (Fr *parchemin*). In other words it is substandard (cf. Wyld, *HMCE*, p. 309, *SHE*, § 285 (2)). Magwitch uses the form *warmint* (*GE*, ch. 3) in the etymological sense 'vermin'.

29. The addition of [t] after [s] in *whilst* is a perfectly well recognized standard English sound-change, but the parallel addition of [t] to *once* and *twice* has remained substandard. Other examples of the same sound-change are: *wunst* (Scaley, *NN*, ch. 21; Jo, *BH*, ch. 47), *once't or twice't* (Game Chicken, *DS*, ch. 56) (cf. Gerson § 40.7).

Strongly-Stressed Vowels

30. There is a tendency for vowels of several different origins to be raised to [i] by a process similar to that which has caused *James* to become *Jim*. The vowel most often affected is [e] as in *ingine* (Sam Weller, *PP*, ch. 31) with *ingein* (Boffin, *OMF*, Bk II, ch. 10) as a spelling variant, *ingein-driver* (Toodle, *DS*, ch. 59), *twenty-sivin* (Miggs, *BR*, ch. 41), *kittle* (*PP*, ch. 32), *niver* (*OMF*, Bk I, ch. 5), *forgit* (Mrs Raddle, *PP*, ch. 46), and *Jinkins*, the name of Tom Smart's rival in *The Bagman's Story* (*PP*, ch. 14). Montague Tigg calls Chevy Slyme *Chiv* (*MC*, ch. 4). In *Sketches by Boz* we are told that Jemima Evans was called *Ivins* by most of her friends (*Characters*, ch. 4). It is sometimes possible to discover a variant which may have given rise to the form with *i*. Thus, *kivering* (Venus, *OMF*, Bk IV, ch. 14) has its parallel in *kiver*, beside *kever*, still extensively used in dialects as a variant of *cover*. The forms with *e* and *i* are from the OF stressed form *cuevre*, *queuvre* of the present singular, whereas *cover* is from OF *cuvrir* or *covrir* (see *OED* sv. Cover, v. 1). Similarly, *sich* (Tony Weller, *PP*, ch. 33) may not be derived from *such*, but both *sich* and *such* are to be traced back to Middle English dialectal variants developed from OE *swylc*. Examples of the raising of vowels other than [e] are: *jist kitch* (*PP*, ch. 5), *agin* (Sam Weller, *PP*, ch. 19), *mim* 'madam' (Miggs, *BR*, ch. 7 and frequently elsewhere) *cabmin* (*PP*, ch. 46). The raising of vowels to [i] is a feature of the pronunciation of Jo in *Bleak House*: *stritched* (ch. 11), *unkiver* (ch. 16), *yinder* 'yonder' (ch. 16). Gerson derives *yinder* from ME *yender*, a variant of *yonder* (Gerson § 4.3, Dobson p. 566).

31. There is a rather less strong tendency for vowels of various origins to become [e]. Mrs Gamp's *shetters* (*MC*, ch. 29) may be a South-Eastern dialectal form (cf. OE *scyttan*), but [e] is found also in *jest* (Sam Weller, *PP*, ch. 26) (cf. Dobson p. 111, Gerson § 5.3).

32. ME [a:], lengthened in open syllables of disyllabic words, has had two developments. Sam Weller's *rayther* (*PP*, ch. 34) shows the regular development, as found in RP *name*, whereas RP *rather* is from a variant with a short stem-vowel in ME (cf. Wright *EHNEG*, § 94). There is evidence also of a more close vowel: *reether* (Bailey, *MC*, ch. 26), *neem* (footman, *MC*, ch. 36).

33. French loan-words containing [i:] have had two different developments in English according to the date of introduction. Those borrowed early enough to undergo the change of [i:] to [ai], which began in the fifteenth century, have [ai], as in *arrive* and *crime*; those borrowed later have [i:], as in *machine* and *unique*. In the seventeenth and eighteenth centuries *oblige* was treated as a late loan-word and was consequently pronounced with [i:], as it still is in many regional dialects (Wright *EHNEG* § 73.8, *EDG* § 223, Horn-Lehnert § 119, Dobson p. 664f, Gerson § 13.3.1). In the nineteenth century both pronunciations were current, but the use of the spelling *obleege* shows that the pronunciation with [i:] was the less common of the two in that it needed a special spelling to represent it, and it is clear from the speakers who use [i:] in Dickens that he thought of this pronunciation as substandard. Examples are: *obleeging* (Wegg, *OMF*, Bk III, ch. 7), *obleege* (Old Smallweed, *BH*, ch. 33; Riderhood, *OMF*, Bk IV, ch. 15), *obleeged* (Billickin, *ED*, ch. 22; Tony Weller, *PP*, ch. 45).

34. The normal development of ME [o:] in RP is [u:], as in *do* and *soon*, but there are spellings in Dickens with *oe*, probably derived from ME lightly-stressed forms with a short vowel, later lengthened to [o:] and still later diphthongized to [ou]. (cf. Dobson § 4, Gerson § 11.9). Examples are *untoe* (Pumblechook, *GE*, ch. 58; Chadband, *BH*, ch. 19), *doe* (Cuttle, *DS*,

ch. 23), and *fur toe* (Plornish, *LD*, Bk II, ch. 13). ME [oː]
has probably become a diphthong [iu] or [ju] in *tew* (Little
Swills, *BH*, ch. 32).

35. The shortening of ME [oː] appears in present-day
English as both [u] and [ʌ], the difference between the two
probably depending on the date of shortening. The spelling *sut*
(Joe, *GE*, ch. 13), probably represents [ʌ], compared with the
standard English [u]. A similar pronunciation of the stem-
vowel is no doubt indicated by Captain Cuttle's *buzzums* (*DS*,
ch. 23; cf. Gerson § 6.2). In *boozums* (Kenwigs, *NN*, ch. 52)
shortening has apparently not taken place at all.

36. [ɔː] is sometimes unrounded to [aː], as in *sarser*
'saucer' (Boffin, *OMF*, Bk I, ch. 8), *da'ater* and *grand-da'aters*
(Wardle's mother, *PP*, ch. 8), *the nail and sarspan business*
(*PP*, ch. 13), *darters* (Mrs Gamp, *MC*, ch. 46), *sarse* (Cuttle,
DS, ch. 49; Sam Weller, *PP*, ch. 43). In *sassage* (Sam Weller,
PP, ch. 31) the unrounded vowel resulting from this change
has been shortened (cf. Dobson § 238, Gerson § 4.1.1).

37. [æ] is sometimes rounded and retracted to [ɔ], as in
sot 'sat' (Joe, *GE*, ch. 2), *wropped* (Sam Weller, *PP*, ch. 3),
cotcht (*SB*, *Scenes*, ch. 20).

38. The pronunciation of *girl* as [gæl] is not exclusively
substandard, but the characters who use it in Dickens include
some speakers of substandard English, such as Tom the clerk
(*NN*, ch. 16), Quilp's boy (*OCS*, ch. 11), Mrs Brown (*DS*,
ch. 34), beside Wardle (*PP*, ch. 4) and Fledgeby (*OMF*, Bk
III, ch. 1) (cf. Gerson § 12.1).

39. Spellings with *oo* suggest that the *u* in *Russia* and *Prussia*
was a back close rounded vowel [u] or [uː] rather than the
vowel [ʌ] which is used in these names in standard English
today (cf. Gerson § 5.7). Examples are *Roosher* (*NN*, ch. 43),
Rooshan and *Prooshan* (Mrs Gamp, *MC*, ch. 19), *Rooshan*
(Boffin, *OMF*, Bk I, ch. 5).

40. A Middle English sound-change that had varied results
in a number of English words was that of [e] to [a] before [r]
when not followed by a vowel. The change is seen in its simplest
form in words such as *far* and *parson*; in *person* and *servant* the
change has not taken place or the older form has been restored
by the influence of the spelling; in *clerk* and *Derby* the change
has affected the pronunciation but not the spelling, and in

American English it has not even affected the pronunciation of these words. In substandard speech the change is found in words that do not show it in standard English, such as *warmin* 'vermin' (*DC*, ch. 12), *arning* (Betty Higden, *OMF*, Bk II, ch. 14), *arnest* (Cuttle, *DS*, ch. 39), *consarn* sb. (Scaley, *NN*, ch. 21) (cf. Gerson § 12.6). The spelling *fur* for *far* (Joe, *GE*, ch. 7; Riderhood, *OMF*, Bk III, ch. 8) may be due to the influence of the OE comparative adverb *fyrr* or of *further* (Dobson pp. 410f, Gerson §8.10).

41. The first element of the diphthong found in standard English *chair* is sometimes raised, as in *cheer* 'chair' (Tony Weller, *PP*, ch. 33; Cuttle, *DS*, ch. 17), *aweer* (Mrs Raddle, *PP*, ch. 32), *a harm-cheer* (Tony Weller, *PP*, ch. 45), *cheerman* (*SB*, *Scenes*, ch. 20) (cf. Gerson § 16.3.1).

42. ME [ui], which was generally written *oi*, became [ai] in the late sixteenth or early seventeenth century and fell together with the [ai] from ME [i:], although the spelling *oi* (or its variant *oy*) generally remained. The pronunciation with [ai] was common in the eighteenth century, but from the middle of the century words which had *oi* in spelling generally came to be pronounced [ɔi] by the influence of the spelling (Wright *EHNEG* § 88.2, Wyld *HMCE* p. 249, Gerson § 18.1). Forms with *i* or *y* are common in Dickens, but they are clearly regarded as vulgarisms. Examples are: *pint* (Sam Weller, *PP*, ch. 12; Boffin, *OMF*, Bk I, ch. 5), *bilin'* (Sam Weller, *PP*, ch. 30), *jintly* (Wegg, *OMF*, Bk III, ch. 14), *appinted* (Riderhood, *OMF*, Bk III, ch. 11), *pison* (Tony Weller, *PP*, ch. 27), *jines* (Mrs Gamp, *MC*, ch. 29), *nisy* (Mrs Gamp, *MC*, ch. 40), *disapinting* (Cuttle, *DS*, ch. 50).

43. The monophthongization of [ju:] to [u:] is today thought of as an Americanism, but it is found also in a number of English dialects (cf. Wright *EDG* § 226, Gerson § 29). Dickensian examples are *dooty* (Tony Weller, *PP*, ch. 52; Sloppy, *OMF*, Bk II, ch. 10), *constitootion* (Scaley, *NN*, ch. 21), *constitooshun* (Bailey, *MC*, ch. 9), *stoopid* (Bailey, *MC*, ch. 26). The same change takes place in lightly-stressed syllables in *toomultuous* (Lillyvick, *NN*, ch. 25) and *fluctooatin'* (Tony Weller, *PP*, ch. 52).

44. There have been variations in the length of vowels between standard and substandard English. The variation

generally goes back to a period earlier than the Great Vowel
Shift, and the variation today is therefore often one between a
short vowel and a diphthong. Short vowels occur in *babby* (Sam
Weller, *PP*, ch. 10; Kenwigs, *NN*, ch. 52), *swips* 'sweeps'
(*SB*, *Scenes*, ch. 20), *ten pund ten* (Mould, *MC*, ch. 19),
Simmun (Miggs, *BR*, ch. 22). Long vowels or their development occur in *leetle* (Boffin, *OMF*, Bk IV, ch. 14) and *paira-
mount* (Sam Weller, *PP*, ch. 44). *Leetle* has had an independent
sense-development which has given it the meaning 'very little';
it is used when the speaker is afraid of seeming greedy or
causing offence, as in *When we're a leetle more perfect, I think it
will go admirably* (*SB*, *Tales*, ch. 9) (cf. Horn-Lehnert § 341,
Gerson § 3.8). OE [æ:] has sometimes been shortened to [æ],
sometimes to [e], the quality of the vowel depending on the
date and dialect of the shortening. Consequently OE *ǣrende* has
given both standard English *errand* and the Dickensian *arrand*
(Sam Weller, *PP*, ch. 10; Mrs Gamp, *MC*, ch. 46).

45. Substandard speech sometimes preserves an historically
correct form that has been replaced in standard English by a
spelling pronunciation. Such a pronunciation is that of *cucumber*
(OF *co(u)combre*), which was pronounced [kaukʌmbə] until
the beginning of the nineteenth century (Wright, *EHNEG*,
§ 77, note 1). Dickensian spellings with *ow* show that [au]
was no longer the normal pronunciation but was an unusual
pronunciation to which Dickens wished to call special attention.
The form *cowcumber* is used by Mrs Gamp (*MC*, ch. 25) and
Inspector Bucket (*BH*, ch. 54).

46. It is not certain what pronunciation is indicated by Captain
Cuttle's *ould* 'old' (*DS*, ch. 62). The *ou* may represent [au],
as it does in such words as *house*. If so, it points to a fronting
and lowering of the first element of the diphthong [ou].
Another possibility is that the first element of the diphthong is
the central vowel [ə].

Lightly-Stressed Vowels

47. When the first syllable of a polysyllabic word is lightly
stressed, it is liable to disappear (cf. Gerson § 7.17.1). This
change is especially common in the speech of Sam Weller.

Examples from his speech are *'spectable* (*PP*, ch. 31), *'Merriker* (ch. 31), *'casion*, v. (ch. 26), *'lection* (ch. 13), *'cordin* (ch. 19), *'cos* (ch. 20). Other examples are: *'prenticeship* (Cuttle, *DS*, ch. 23), *backer* 'tobacco' (Toodle, *DS*, ch. 38), *'sheenery* 'machinery' (*SB*, *Scenes*, ch. 20), *'dustrious* (*SB*, *Scenes*, ch. 23), *'mancipation* (*SB*, *Characters*, ch. 5), *'Merrikin* (Tony Weller, *PP*, ch. 45), *'Delphi* (*SB*, *The Pantomime of Life*). Sometimes the syllables that disappear follow the chief stress of the word, as in *gents* (Mrs Gamp, *MC*, ch. 19), *rheumatiz* (Tony Weller, *PP*, ch. 20). Sam Weller's *compo* (*PP*, ch. 12), in the sense 'combination', may be a curtailment of *composition*.

48. In pretonic syllables *u* of the prefix *un-* sometimes becomes *o*: *You are oncommon in some things. You're oncommon small. Likewise you're a oncommon scholar* (Joe, *GE*, ch. 9). This is a feature of many regional dialects (cf. Gerson § 5.5).

49. It may be that *formilior* (Cuttle, *DS*, ch. 56), *formiliar* (Tony Weller, *PP*, ch. 20; Sam Weller, *PP*, ch. 25) is to be regarded as a blend-word of *form* and *familiar*, but the possibility of a sound-change of [ə] to [ɔ:] cannot be completely ruled out.

50. There are many examples, especially in *Pickwick Papers*, of the occurrence of [i], especially before [n], in lightly-stressed syllables where standard English has [ə]: *wagginload* (*PP*, ch. 5), *ribbins* (*PP*, ch. 5), *willin* 'villain' (*PP*, ch. 9), *wagginer* (Sam Weller, *PP*, ch. 16), *melincholly* (Sam Weller, *PP*, ch. 44), *drunkin* (Mrs Gamp, *MC*, ch. 29), *fortin* 'fortune' (*SB*, *Scenes*, ch. 12) (cf. Dobson p. 904, Gerson § 7.3).

51. The diphthong [ju:] is often monophthongized to [i], less often [ə], in lightly-stressed syllables (cf. Gerson § 48.18). Examples of [i] are: *walley* 'value' (Sam Weller, *PP*, ch. 19), *eddication* (Tony Weller, *PP*, ch. 20), *argueyment* (Wegg, *OMF*, Bk I, ch. 15), *ockypied* (Wegg, *OMF*, Bk III, ch. 14), *monneyment* (Squeers, *NN*, ch. 57), *stattit* 'statute' (Grummer, *PP*, ch. 24), *corpilence* (Sam Weller, *PP*, ch. 33), *ockipy* (Tony Weller, *PP*, ch. 33), *innokilated* (Sam Weller, *PP*, ch. 47), *depitty* (Sam Weller, *PP*, ch. 48), *nevy* (Cuttle, *DS*, ch. 17). Examples of [ə] are: *penderlum* (Sam Weller, *PP*, ch. 28), *ackerate* (Tony Weller, *PP*, ch. 55), *agers* (Squeers, *NN*, ch. 57), *obderrate* (Stiggins, *PP*, ch. 27). The change is most frequent in polysyllabic words, but it also affects the pronoun *you* when it occurs in a lightly-stressed position: *How de do?*

(*PP*, ch. 31), *Thankee* (Sam Weller, *PP*, ch. 10). *Lookee* (Magwitch, *GE*, ch. 1). The triphthong [juə] is reduced to [i] in *mantie-making* (Scaley, *NN*, ch. 21), and to [ə] in *inwallable* (Mrs Gamp, *MC*, ch. 19). The reduction to [ə] leads to the introduction of an intrusive *r* in *acterally* (*PP*, ch. 46).

52. When the diphthong [ju:] is followed by a vowel, it sometimes undergoes a shift of stress and is spelt *iw*. The change in pronunciation is not so great as the difference in spelling between *u* and *iw* might suggest. The diphthong [ju:] is a rising diphthong, of which the first element has been slightly raised so as to become a semi-vowel; the diphthong represented by the spelling *iw* is a falling diphthong, of which the second element has become a semi-vowel which, when followed by a vowel, becomes consonantal [w]. Examples are: *sitiwation* (*OT*, ch. 28; Wegg, *OMF*, Bk IV, ch. 3), *actiwally* (Tony Weller, *PP*, ch. 33), *punctiwal* (Tony Weller, *PP*, ch. 33). The [w] that arises from the shift of stress sometimes undergoes the further change to [v] (cf. § 1), as in *Samivel* (Tony Weller, *PP*, ch. 23), *gradivally* (Sam Weller, *PP*, ch. 43). Unless the replacement of *w* by *v* is a mechanical spelling variation, such forms suggest that the shift of stress in the diphthong is earlier than the change of [w] to [v].

53. A glide-vowel, usually spelt *e* and probably pronounced [ə], often develops between a consonant and [r], as in *aggerawated* (Tony Weller, *PP*, ch. 33), *aggerawatin'* (*PP*, ch. 2), *properiator* (Sam Weller, *PP*, ch. 27), *Henery* and *Henerietty* (Boffin, *OMF*, Bk I, ch. 5), *kerhewelty* (*SB*, *Scenes*, ch. 20), *sapparised* 'surprized' (*PP*, ch. 37), *umberella* (Sam Weller, *PP*, ch. 52) (cf. Gerson § 7.16.1). A similar glide develops before [v] (from [w]) in *ekervally* (Joe, *GE*, ch. 18). The glide is no doubt to be regarded as a mark of sanctimonious speech when Chadband speaks of *Terewth* (*BH*, ch. 25).

54. Shortening of long vowels is frequent in the lightly-stressed second element of a compound: *shipmet* (Bunsby, *DS*, ch. 23), *veskits* (Sam Weller, *PP*, ch. 27), *workus* (*MC*, ch. 13), *custom'us* (Mrs Gamp, *MC*, ch. 46), *fourpunten* (*CS*, Doctor Marigold, ch. 2), *fypunnote* (*CS*, Doctor Marigold, ch. 1).

55. The following spellings probably indicate a shift of stress: *proprieator* (Sam Weller, *PP*, ch. 35), *irrepairabel* (*PP*, ch.

37), *con-spiraytors* (Sam Weller, *PP*, ch. 47), *contrairy* (Susan Nipper, *DS*, ch. 5), *theayter* (Mrs Bagnet, *BH*, ch. 27; Bucket, *BH*, ch. 54).

56. Words of two or more syllables are often printed with a hyphen after the first syllable. The hyphen may indicate a pause and it may also indicate that the word is pronounced with something approaching level stress. Examples are: *Ram-paged* (Joe, *GE*, ch. 2), *Ram-page* (Joe, *GE*, ch. 7), *Mo-gul* (Joe, *GE*, ch. 7), *gen-teel* (Dennis, *BR*, ch. 39), *dex-terity* (Dennis, *BR*, ch. 39), *sure-ly* (Wardle's Mother, *PP*, ch. 6).

57. Medial vowels often disappear in lightly-stressed syllables, as in *indiwiddle* (Rob, *DS*, ch. 59), *cord'l* (Toodle, *DS*, ch. 59), *nat'ral* (Sam Weller, *PP*, ch. 3; Boffin, *OMF*, Bk I, ch. 8), *nat'rally* (Riderhood, *OMF*, Bk III, ch. 11), *d'rectly* (*PP*, ch. 35), *b'sides* (Sam Weller, *PP*, ch. 10), *b'longs* (Sam Weller, *PP*, ch. 10), *sing'ler* (Tony Weller, *PP*, ch. 22), *fort'nate* (Rob, *DS*, ch. 39), *partickler* (Tapley, *MC*, ch. 48). A more drastic curtailment is Jo's *cumfbler* 'comfortabler' (*BH*, ch. 47), and Magwitch reduces the lightly-stressed preposition *with* to *er* in *alonger* (*GE*, ch. 39). This change has taken place in many words in standard English, and the replacement of a letter by an apostrophe in *ev'ry* (*PP*, ch. 2) and *bis'ness* (Sam Weller, *PP*, ch. 31) simply records the normal standard pronunciation of these words, as does the spelling *'nd* for *and* (Tony Weller, *PP*, ch. 34).

58. Final [ou], spelt *o*, *ow*, is often weakened to [ə], spelt *er*, less often *ar*: *elbers* (Squeers, *NN*, ch. 34), *lumbagers* (Squeers, *NN*, ch. 57), *tobacker* (*DC*, ch. 19), *piller* (Betsey Prig, *MC*, ch. 25), *feller* (Sam Weller, *PP*, ch. 19), *widder* (Tony Weller, *PP*, ch. 20), *mellers* (Wegg, *OMF*, Bk I, ch. 5), *swaller* (Riderhood, *OMF*, Bk IV, ch. 7), *follerin'* (Sam Weller, *PP*, ch. 31), *pianner forty* (Tony Weller, *PP*, ch. 45), *taters* 'potatoes' (*DC*, ch. 19) (cf. Gerson § 9.6.1).

59. After consonants [i] often disappears, as in *Willum*, the name of Doctor Marigold's father (*CS, Doctor Marigold*, ch. 1) and *amable* (Tony Weller, *PP*, ch. 23), *odous* (*PP*, ch. 50), *garden angels* (Cuttle, *DS*, ch. 39), *curous* (*BH*, ch. 57), *serous* (Joe, *GE*, ch. 7) (cf. Horn-Lehnert § 324, Gerson § 3.12.1).

60. Perhaps as a consequence of the loss of [i] in suffixes, some speakers, anxious to avoid this defect, insert an [i] (sometimes spelt *e*) without etymological justification: *mis-cheevious* (*BH*, ch. 34), *felion* (*DS*, ch. 39), *favior* (*NN*, ch. 18), *per-annium* (Joe, *GE*, ch. 57), *barbareous* (*SB*, *Scenes*, ch. 20) (cf. Gerson § 3.11.2). Mrs Gamp is especially fond of this extra *i*, as in *goldian* for *golden* (*MC*, ch. 25), *guardian* for *garden* (ch. 46), *mortial* for *mortal* (ch. 49), *serpiant* for *serpent* (ch. 49), *bragian* for *brazen* (ch. 49). When Mrs Gamp (ch. 49), says *aperiently* for *apparently*, she is illustrating this change, but the word is also, no doubt, to be regarded as a malapropism with a special appropriateness to Mrs Gamp's profession. On one occasion the author calls attention to the pronunciation and suggests a reason for it:

> 'My informiation,' retorted the Billickin, throwing in an extra syllable for the sake of emphasis at once polite and powerful . . . (*ED*, ch. 22)

61. Final [ə] (spelt *a*) is often weakened to [i], as in *Jamaikey* (Wegg, *OMF*, Bk II, ch. 7), *Chaney* (Susan, *DS*, ch. 3), *Indy* (Tapley, *MC*, ch. 23), *Sairey* (Mrs Gamp, *MC*, ch. 25), *sofy* (Bucket, *BH*, ch. 54) (cf. Gerson § 7.3).

62. Final [iə] (spelt *-ia*, or *-ea*) is sometimes weakened to [i] or [ə]: *airy* 'area' (Mrs Gamp, *MC*, ch. 49), *Australey* (Mrs Bagnet, *BH*, ch. 27), *Inder* (Bucket, *BH*, ch. 53).

Accidence

63. After numerals, nouns without inflexional ending are often used. These are no doubt developed from OE partitive genitives in *-a*, though French loan-words are also affected in this way, as in *eleven pair o' boots* (Sam Weller, *PP*, ch. 10). Examples are: *better nor six mile* (*PP*, ch. 9), *four hundred pound* (Sam Weller, *PP*, ch. 10), *going on four year* (Heep, *DC*, ch. 16), *I'm going to earn from five to ten thousand pound* (Riderhood, *OMF*, Bk I, ch. 12), *eight and thirty year* (Mrs Gamp, *MC*, ch. 40), *twenty year* (Mrs Gamp, *MC*, ch. 25), *five mile* (*BH*, ch. 19).

64. The irregular plurals of nouns of foreign origin are sometimes replaced by analogical forms in *-s*. Mr Lillyvick, for example, says *phenomenons* (*NN*, ch. 25).

65. Double genitives are occasionally found, as in *the lambses' time* (Riderhood, *OMF*, Bk IV, ch. 15). Deputy, in *Edwin Drood*, when asked the way to Mr Tope's, replies "Ow can I stay here and show you which is Topeseses?' (ch. 18). Names ending in *-s* sometimes have *-es* added, as in *Coavinses* (*BH*, ch. 6), and *them old Skettleses* (Susan Nipper, *DS*, ch. 23), *your Toxes and your Chickses* (Susan Nipper, *DS*, ch. 3).

66. In standard English comparison of adjectives by the addition of the suffixes *-er* and *-est* is normally restricted to short adjectives, but in substandard speech these suffixes are used more freely: *seasonablest* (Tony Weller, *PP*, ch. 56), *blesseder*, *blessedest* (Susan Nipper, *DS*, ch. 44), *uprighter* (Wegg, *OMF*, Bk IV, ch. 3), *smilinest* (Mrs Gamp, *MC*, ch. 46), *charmingest* (Tigg, *MC*, ch. 7), *soberest* (Mrs Gamp, *MC*, ch. 25), *favouritest* (Mrs Gamp, *MC*, ch. 40), *awfullest* (Mrs Gamp, *MC*, ch. 46), *certainest* (Mrs Gamp, *MC*, ch. 46), *devotedest* (Susan Nipper, *DS*, ch. 56), *longest-sufferingest* (Miggs, *BR*, ch. 22), *innocentest* (Susan Nipper, *DS*, ch. 56). The suffix *-est* is sometimes added to a noun, a pronoun, or an adverb: Fledgeby calls Riah *the dodgerest of all the dodgers* (*OMF*, Bk III, ch. 13); Riderhood calls Bradley Headstone *T'otherest* (*OMF*, Bk IV, ch. 7), and Mrs Gamp says *oftener than you would suppose* (*MC*, ch. 40). Substandard speech often has analogical forms where standard English has irregular comparisons: *Oh! a deal badder* (*MC*, ch. 25).

67. Double comparatives and superlatives of adjectives are formed by adding the *-er* or *-est* suffix to a form that is already comparative or superlative and by using the word *more* with the comparative form of the adjective. Examples are: *worser* (Sam Weller, *PP*, ch. 22), *more tenderer* (Tony Weller, *PP*, ch. 33), *the juniorest Palmer* (Fanny Squeers, *NN*, ch. 57), *a nicerer* (Fat Boy, *PP*, ch. 54), *more comfortabler* (Tony Weller, *PP*, ch. 52), *more flatterer* (*OCS*, ch. 26).

68. A new pronoun *tother* comes into existence as a result of misdivision of *that other*. When the origin of the initial *t* is forgotten, the new pronoun is preceded by the definite article: *the t'other one* (Sam Weller, *PP*, ch. 30), *the T'other Governor* (Riderhood, *OMF*, Bk I, ch. 12).

69. In substandard speech, as in many dialects of the Midlands and South, variant forms of the possessive pronouns with a final -*n* are often found when the pronouns are not used attributively: *that friend of yourn* (Mrs Gamp, *MC*, ch. 49), *this here proposal o' yourn* (Cuttle, *DS*, ch. 39), *His'n, miss* (Charley, *BH*, ch. 37), *that there chest o'yourn* (Sam Weller, *PP*, ch. 52).

70. *hisself, theirselves* (on the analogy of such forms as *myself*) are common in Dickens, as in dialects: *he may make his-self easy, Sammy* (Tony Weller, *PP*, ch. 33), *he rashly converted his-self into sassages* (Sam Weller, *PP*, ch. 31), *gettin' theirselves inwolved* (Tony Weller, *PP*, ch. 52).

71. The verb *to do* often has forms of the third sing. pres. ind. without -*s* in both the positive and the negative: *he do* (Sloppy, *OMF*, Bk I, ch. 16), *she don't* (Tony Weller, *PP*, ch. 20), *How lovely your hair do curl to-night* (*NN*, ch. 12). These forms are not exclusively substandard. Pecksniff says *He don't deserve it* (*MC*, ch. 30) and Charity Pecksniff says *Why don't he then?* (*MC*, ch. 32). The form without -*s* occurs in narrative, not assigned to any character: *The morning luminary is built out, and don't shine there* (*DS*, ch. 57).

72. Past participles of strong verbs sometimes end in -*en* in standard English. In substandard speech the final -*n* often disappears, as in *spoke* (Sam Weller, *PP*, ch. 56), *broke* (Sam Weller, *PP*, ch. 35), *forgot* (Sam Weller, *PP*, ch. 33), *froze* (Jo, *BH*, ch. 31), *eat* (Barnaby, *BR*, ch. 10).

73. Preterite forms of strong verbs are often used as past participles. By the time of Dickens this construction was a vulgarism but a century earlier it was used by many writers who cannot be regarded as substandard. Parson Woodforde, in 1794, has the severe comment on a social note that he received: 'Note shockingly bad wrote'.[1] Dickensian examples are: *took* (Riderhood, *OMF*, Bk III, ch. 8), *wrote* (Sam Weller, *PP*, ch. 10), *fell* (Riderhood, *OMF*, Bk III, ch. 8), *drank* (Kenwigs, *NN*, ch. 36), *drove* (Tony Weller, *PP*, ch. 52), *ate* (Mrs MacStinger, *DS*, ch. 39), *undertook* (Mrs Gamp, *MC*, ch. 19), *mistook* (Mrs Gamp, *MC*, ch. 40).

74. Substandard speech sometimes preserves preterite forms that have been replaced by analogical forms in standard English.

---

[1] *Woodforde: Passages from the Five Volumes of the Diary of a Country Parson 1758–1802*, ed. by John Beresford, O.U.P., 1935, p. 369.

OE *drīfan* 'to drive' had a preterite singular *drāf* and a plural *drifon*. From the first of these, ME *drove* is derived; from the second we have *driv*, extended by analogy to the first person singular (*SB, Tales*, ch. 8).

75. Jo, in *Bleak House*, uses distinctive forms of the preterite of both strong and weak verbs by adding *-n* to the present stem: *Jo . . . excitedly declares . . . that he never known about the young lady, that he never heern about it* (ch. 46), *. . . Jo, wot he known once, is a-moving on* (ch. 47). Such forms are probably to be regarded as past participles which have come to be used as preterites as a result of the disappearance of a lightly-stressed auxiliary *have* or *had*.

76. Apparent examples of the use of the present tense of strong verbs with a preterite sense are often to be explained as survivals of Old English preterites, singular or plural, which have been replaced by analogical forms in standard English. Examples are: *come* (*PP*, ch. 44), from OE pret. sg. *cōm* or pl. *cōmon*, beside *came* by analogy with such forms as OE *geaf* pret. sg. of *giefan* 'to give'; *run* (*PP*, ch. 9) from OE pret. pl. *urnon*, beside *ran* from OE pret. sg. *ærn*. The preterite *driv* (cf. § 74) may have provided the basis for the analogical preterites *give* (Mrs Gamp, *MC*, ch. 40), *giv* (Magwitch, *GE*, ch. 39).

77. A number of strong verbs have weak forms of the preterite and past participle. Examples of preterites are: *know'd* (Sam Weller, *PP*, ch. 30), *seed* (*SB, Tales*, ch. 10). Examples of past participles are: *drawd* (Sam Weller, *PP*, ch. 56), *throw'd* (Rob, *DS*, ch. 39), *flowed* (Rob, *DS*, ch. 25). *Heerd*, used both as a preterite (Mrs Gamp, *MC*, ch. 46) and as a past participle (Sam Weller, *PP*, ch. 26), is a new formation with a long vowel on the analogy of the infinitive; standard English *heard* shows the development of a vowel that has been shortened. *Afeared* (Affery, *LD*, Bk I, ch. 3) and *afeerd* (Joe, *GE*, ch. 7) are regularly developed from OE *āfǣred* pp; standard English *afraid* has been influenced by OF *esfreer*. In the past participle of the verb *hang* a distinction is often made according to meaning: when the verb refers to a sentence of death, the past participle is usually *hanged;* otherwise *hung* is used. This distinction is not generally made in substandard speech, and Mrs Blockson says: *and that's the truth if I was to be hung this minute* (*NN*, ch. 18). The past participle

I

busted (Squeers, *NN*, ch. 57) is a new formation of a verb originally strong.

78. Strong verbs are often confused with their weak causative cognates: *little do we know wot lays afore us* (Mrs Gamp, *MC*, ch. 40), *But I see how the land laid* (Riderhood, *OMF*, Bk IV, ch. 15), *I laid all of a heap* (Squeers, *NN*, ch. 34), *he'll stand and see me a settin' here* (Tony Weller, *PP*, ch. 56), *set down agin* (Sam Weller, *PP*, ch. 37).

79. In substandard speech, *durst*, the old preterite of *dare*, is commonly used. Like *must* (from OE *mōste*, pret. of *mōt*), it has come to be used with present meaning as well as in the preterite. The examples in Dickens are usually in the negative. Tony Weller uses *dustn't* in the preterite (*PP*, ch. 52), and Jo uses the same form in the present (*BH*, ch. 46). Plornish uses *dursn't* in the present (*LD*, Bk I, ch. 12).

80. Forms of the verb *to be* are often lightly-stressed, and variants are liable to occur as the result of variations of stress. Standard English *are* [ɑ:] and *were* [wə:] are from lightly-stressed forms; the strongly-stressed variants are spelt *air* and *ware* in Dickens: *you air* (Sam Weller, *PP*, ch. 37), *his observation generally air* (Perch, *DS*, ch. 22), *which he wish to know what the shilling ware for* (Guster, *BH*, ch. 19) (cf. Gerson §§ 8.13.1 and 12.9).

81. Special negative forms of the verb *to be* come into use. *Am not* becomes *an't*, *ain't*, and is extended to other persons of the singular and the plural: *ain't us* (Joe, *GE*, ch. 7), *an't this capital?* (Wardle, *PP*, ch. 4), *I ain't mistaken* (*PP*, ch. 31). *Warn't* is used by Betsey Prig (*MC*, ch. 25), Sam Weller (*PP*, ch. 31) and Tony Weller (*PP*, ch. 22) and *worn't* by Sam Weller (*PP*, ch. 16).

Syntax

82. There are many examples of lack of concord between the subject of a sentence and its verb. The verb 'to be' is particularly subject to variation. Examples are: *fourteen unpolled electors as was a stoppin' in the house* (Sam Weller, *PP*, ch. 13); *Rum creeturs is women* (*PP*, ch. 14); *don't you wish you was me?* (*NN*, ch. 16); *Yes, it were, sir* (*PP*, ch. 34); *apologies* *was due* (John Chivery, *LD*, Bk II, ch. 27); *my nerves is so unstrung* (Perch, *DS*, ch. 22); *You was, was you?* (Betsey Prig, *MC*, ch. 49); *It were understood, and it are understood, and it ever will be similar according* (Joe, *GE*, ch. 18). In other verbs apparent examples of false concord are the result of the extension of the third person singular ending to other persons of the singular and to the plural. Examples are: 1 *sg. I knows, I has, I wants* (Fat Boy, *PP*, ch. 8), *I find I gets on better at supper when I does* (Sam Weller, *PP*, ch. 35), *I spells it with a 'V'* (Sam Weller, *PP*, ch. 34); 2 *sg. you takes* (Sam Weller, *PP*, ch. 44), *You knows me of old, sir* (Mrs Gamp, *MC*, ch. 19), *you wants* (Betsey Prig, *MC*, ch. 49); 1 *pl. we sends* (Sam Weller, *PP*, ch. 26), *we bears* (*PP*, ch. 2); 3 *pl. he and the gen'l'm'n looks werry hard at each other* (Sam Weller, *PP*, ch. 13), *her friends comes in* (*PP*, ch. 26), *They puts things into old gen'lm'n's heads* (Sam Weller, *PP*, ch. 10). The verbal form *summons* in *I'll summons you* (Squeers, *NN*, ch. 38) is a new formation from the plural of the substantive.

83. Double negatives are very common, as they are in early English and in many regional dialects. The purpose of the double negative is to give added emphasis, and substandard English knows nothing of the dictum of the school-room that two negatives make an affirmative. Examples are: *I never said nothing to her* (Sam Weller, *PP*, ch. 10); *Don't let's have no words* (*PP*, ch. 31); *don't ask me whether I won't take none* (Mrs Gamp, *MC*, ch. 19), *he couldn't stand it no longer* (Sam Weller, *PP*, ch. 31), *I don't believe there's no sich a person:* (Betsey Prig, *MC*, ch. 49). John Chivery achieves the emphasis that is the aim of those who make use of double negatives, but he does it by parenthesis:

'I hadn't,' John declared, 'no, I hadn't, and I never had, the audaciousness to think, I am sure, that all was anything but lost. I hadn't, no, why should I say I hadn't if I ever had, any hope that it was possible to be so blest.' (*LD*, Bk II, ch. 27)

84. Substandard syntax rejects the view that the superlative of an adjective should not be used when two things are compared. Thus, Sam Weller, asking Arabella Allen to identify her brother, asks: *Is it the dirtiest vun of the two?* (*PP*, ch. 39).

85. Adjectives are used adverbially because loss of final *-e* in pronunciation had blurred the distinction between many adjectives and the corresponding adverbs. Examples are: *I didn't want it particular before today* (*PP*, ch. 32), *uncommon fat* (Sam Weller, *PP*, ch. 10), *uncommon well* (Wardle, *PP*, ch. 4), *we can act according* (Sam Weller, *PP*, ch. 16), *It's positive indelicate* (*NN*, ch. 12), *an immense rich heiress* (Job Trotter, *PP*, ch. 16), *if he wasn't too far gone to do it creditable* (*NN*, ch. 12). This syntactic feature is found especially in the speech of low-life characters, but not exclusively so. Sir Mulberry Hawk, for example, says *I'm infernal selfish* (*NN*, ch. 29).

86. *Them* is used as a demonstrative adjective in both subjective and objective cases. Examples are: *Are them brutes going?* (*PP*, ch. 32), *to them old Skettleses* (Susan Nipper, *DS*, ch. 18), *one o' them fits* (Sam Weller, *PP*, ch. 31), *What do you think them women does t'other day?* (Tony Weller, *PP*, ch. 22), *open them ears o' yourn* (Sam Weller, *PP*, ch. 43), *if them shepherds had let her alone* (Sam Weller, *PP*, ch. 52).

87. *This here*, *these here*, and *that 'ere* are often used as emphatic forms of the demonstrative adjectives. The form *'ere* is probably from *there*, with the initial *th* first assimilated to the final *t* of the preceding word and with the resulting *tt* then simplified. These forms are particularly common in the speech of Sam Weller. Examples, all used by him, are: *this here shop* (*PP*, ch. 31), *this here young lady* (ch. 16), *these here boots* (ch. 10), *these here ones* (ch. 30), *that 'ere shop* (ch. 31), *that 'ere statement* (ch. 33). Other examples are: *that there blessed Bull* (Mrs Gamp, *MC*, ch. 29), *that there kitchin winder* (Jo, *BH*, ch. 16).

88. In standard English *many* is never directly preceded by the indefinite article, though we have phrases like *a great many*. In substandard speech it is often preceded by *a* both when adjective and when pronoun: *a many sizes too large* (Sam Weller, *PP*, ch. 10), *a many visitors* (Susan, *DS*, ch. 18), *a many hours* (Tony Weller, *PP*, ch. 52), *sich a many things* (Tony Weller, *PP*, ch. 52), *a many words* (Cuttle, *DS*, ch. 32), *a many places* (Mrs Gamp, *MC*, ch. 19), *there an't a many like him* (Mrs Gamp, *MC*, ch. 25), *a many Bolters* (Joe, *GE*, ch. 2).

89. The objective case of personal pronouns is sometimes used for the subjective, especially when coupled with a noun. Examples are: *me and my family ain't a goin' to be choked* (Sam

Weller, *PP*, ch. 31); *Can't us?* (Mrs Boffin, *OMF*, Bk I, ch. 15); *Mrs Boffin and me grow older* (Boffin, *OMF*, Bk I, ch. 8); *Us London lawyers don't often get an out* (Guppy, *BH*, ch. 7); *ain't us* (Joe, *GE*, ch. 7); *Me and Plornish says* (Mrs Plornish, *LD*, Bk I, ch. 12); *This young man and me will go on in the chaise* (Squeers, *NN*, ch. 7); *which me and another friend of mine took notice of* (Mrs Gamp, *MC*, ch. 46). The use of the subjective pronoun where we should expect the objective is less common. It is used by characters whose speech is not habitually substandard and is probably often an attempt to avoid the more common vulgarism of using *me* for *I*: *between you and I* (Perker, *PP*, ch. 10), *let he and I say good night together* (Nicholas, *NN*, ch. 30); *Leave Nell and I to toil and work* (Nell's grandfather, *OCS*, ch. 2).

90. Masculine and feminine pronouns sometimes refer to inanimate objects: *Why, pudding, he was four!* (Sloppy, *OMF*, Bk II, ch. 10), *Bought him at a sale* (of a book) (Mr Boffin, *OMF*, Bk I, ch. 5), *She'll bile in a couple of minutes* (of a kettle) (Mr Venus, *OMF*, Bk III, ch. 7).

91. The preposition *of* is often replaced by *on*, especially before pronouns or at the end of a sentence. Confusion between the two prepositions is old and there are many examples in Shakespeare (cf. Abbott, *A Shakespearian Grammar*, § 175). Examples in Dickens are: *I'll take care on him* (Sam Weller, *PP*, ch. 39), *he'll be the death on her* (Sam Weller, *PP*, ch. 31), *one on you* (Riderhood, *OMF*, Bk I, ch. 12), *I don't exactly want him, if it's made a favour on* (Scaley, *NN*, ch. 21), *one or another on 'em* (*LD*, Bk I, ch. 6), *one of the jolliest look-outs for domestic architecture that ever I heerd tell on* (Tapley, *MC*, ch. 13), *a person as I took care on* (Gamp, *MC*, ch. 49), *Now I've got rid on it* (Tapley, *MC*, ch. 52).

92. *Off of* is used as a strengthened form of *of*: *she couldn't very well be off o' that* (Sam Weller, *PP*, ch. 37), *I was never to go away without having had a good 'un off of meat and beer and pudding* (*OMF*, Bk II, ch. 10).

93. *For to* (or *fur to*) is sometimes used instead of *to* with the infinitive: *He was allus willin fur to give me somethink* (*BH*, ch. 46), *How unfortnet do you want me fur to be?* (*BH*, ch. 46), *I wouldn't attempt for to go and do it* (Rob, *DS*, ch. 42), *Don't I never mean for to go to church?* (*BH*, ch. 8), *Mr Merdle was*

*the one . . . to bring us all safe home as much we needed, mind you,
fur toe be brought* (Plornish, *LD*, Bk II, ch. 13). The use of *for
to* was a mannerism that could be ridiculed by exaggeration. A
clown at Astley's caused great amusement by saying: *Now,
Miss Woolford, what can I come for to go, for to fetch, for to bring,
for to carry, for to do, for you, ma'am?* (*SB, Scenes*, ch. 11).

94. *Which* is used as a conjunction with the meaning 'and' or
'although'. Examples are: *at the very last case as ever I acted,
which it was but a young person* (Mrs Gamp, *MC*, ch. 19), *And
wishing that your elth may be better than your looks, which your
inside must be bad indeed if it's on the footing of your out* (Riderhood, *OMF*, Bk III, ch. 11), *I knows a lady, which her name,
I'll not deceive you, Mrs Chuzzlewit, is Harris* (Mrs Gamp, *MC*,
ch. 46).

95. The use of *and* together with *which* produces a clause
which is neither co-ordinate nor subordinate: *I maintains my
indepency with your kind leave, and which I will till death* (Gamp,
MC, ch. 40).

96. *As* is used as a relative with the meaning 'who', 'whom'
or 'which': *Vun o' the truest things as you've said for many a long
year* (Sam Weller, *PP*, ch. 31), *and I am a man as gets my
living* (Riderhood, *OMF*, Bk I, ch. 12), *him as had his arm hurt*
(Fat Boy, *PP*, ch. 8), *it's him as wants* (*PP*, ch. 10), *them as
has treated us so handsome* (*NN*, ch. 37), *all as knows you* (Mrs
Gamp, *MC*, ch. 46), *a patient much about the same age, as I once
nussed* (Mrs Gamp, *MC*, ch. 46).

97. *As* is often used after verbs of saying or thinking with
the meaning 'that' (cf. *OED* sv. *As*, sense B28). Examples are:
I thought everybody know'd as a Sawbones was a Surgeon (Sam
Weller, *PP*, ch. 30), *you must inform your angel wife and lovely
family as you won't sleep at home for three nights to come* (Scaley,
NN, ch. 21).

98. *Nor* (sometimes reduced to *er*) is used in the sense
'than': *No more nor you do* (Sam Weller, *PP*, ch. 10), *better er
seven mile* (*PP*, ch. 5), *Where can I possible move to, sir, more nor
I do move?* (Jo, *BH*, ch. 19), *I have been moved on, and moved
on, more nor ever I was afore* (Jo, *BH*, ch. 31), *Your poor dear
wife as you uses worser nor a dog* (*SB, Scenes*, ch. 23), *I perceive
a worthier visitor nor myself is just entered* (*SB, Mr Robert
Bolton*).

99. *That* is used in the sense 'so, to such an extent'; *Mr Jasper was that breathed* (Tope, *ED*, ch. 2), *I had felt that unreasonable towards Pickleson* (*CS, Doctor Marigold*, ch. 3).

100. *What* is used as a relative pronoun for *who* and *which*: *Have I read the little book wot you left?* (*BH*, ch. 8).

101. As in Elizabethan English, speakers and writers of the present day often claim the right to use one part of speech for another. This claim is often challenged by those who condemn expressions like *to contact* on the grounds that *contact* is a noun. Substandard English is more tolerant: *one as monthlied* 'one who was employed by the month' (Mrs Gamp, *MC*, ch. 29), *It ain't wery likely I should want him to be Inkwhich'd* (Jo, *BH*, ch. 46). On the analogy of pairs like *do* and *don't* Joe Gargery produces: *be it so or be it son't* (*GE*, ch. 9).

102. The subjunctive is even less frequent in substandard speech than in standard English, and we find the indicative used after *if*: *If it wasn't for the nerve a little sip of liquor gives me* (Mrs Gamp, *MC*, ch. 19), *If they wos made accordin' to our wishes* (Mrs Gamp, *MC*, ch. 25). Mrs Wilfer, on the other hand, uses a special kind of substandard speech, which apes gentility, and in such speech subjunctives flourish: *it were the insanity of humility, to deem him worthy of a better assistant* (*OMF*, Bk I, ch. 16).

103. There was much confusion in Middle English between the verbal noun in *-ing* and the present participle (cf. T. F. Mustanoja, *A Middle English Syntax Part I* (Helsinki, 1960), pp. 566ff.). There are survivals of this confusion in substandard speech in the use of the prefix *a-* (a weakened form of the preposition *on*) with present participles of verbs used transitively. When the form in *-ing* is both preceded by *a-* and followed by the preposition *of*, it can best be regarded as a verbal noun. Examples of the construction with *of* are: *I see her a kissin' of him agin* (Fat Boy, *PP*, ch. 8), *I think it was the attic which had been a cleaning of himself* (*NN*, ch. 3), *masterses and missesses a teaching of you everything continual* (Susan Nipper, *DS*, ch. 12), *Missis's compliments to Miss Pinch, and begs to know wot my young lady is a-learning of just now* (*MC*, ch. 9), *that's the way he's been a-conductin of himself* (Betsey Prig, *MC*, ch. 29), *without wanting to go a-boarding of it* (Mrs Gamp, *MC*, ch. 40), *never mind a-contradicting of me* (Mrs Gamp, *MC*, ch. 40), *Now he's a-taking of her down* (Mrs Gamp, *MC*, ch. 40), *Did you see him a-jerking of her wrist, then?* (Mrs Gamp, *MC*, ch. 40), *you're a settlin' of it* (Mrs Gamp, *MC*, ch. 46). Examples without *of* are: *a fretting herself* (Scaley, *NN*, ch. 21), *no use a-lookin'* (*OMF*, Bk II, ch. 11), *Blowed if the gen'lm'n worn't a gettin' up* (*PP*, ch. 5), *all a-blowin and a-growin* (Bailey, *MC*, ch. 29), *Person's a waitin'* (Sam Weller, *PP*, ch. 15). Mark Tapley and Mrs Gamp are especially fond of this construction. The former says *a-coming* (*MC*, ch. 7), *a-going* (ch. 7), *a-rambling* (ch. 13), *a-toddling* (ch. 13), *a-getting up* (ch. 13), *a-mixing* (ch. 13), *a-thinking* (ch. 7), *a-going on* (ch. 7); the latter says: *a-looking* (ch. 46), *a-whisperin'* (ch. 46), *a-ringing* (ch. 49), *a-comin' in* (ch. 49), *a-goin' out* (ch. 49).

104. Some verbs are constructed with *of* although in standard English they are used without a preposition: *she keeps on abusing of him* (Sam Weller, *PP*, ch. 31), *a-worming and plodding and tracing and turning and twining of hisself about* (Squeers, *NN*, ch. 57), *here's thanking of 'em for all their goodness* (*NN*, ch. 37), *Except of me Mary my dear as your walentine* (Sam Weller, *PP*, ch. 33), *a Busted B'low-Bridge steamer which drownded of me* (Riderhood, *OMF*, Bk III, ch. 11), *I shall have the honour of stokin' of you down* (Toodle, *DS*, ch. 20), *will you be so good as consider of it* (Tapley, *MC*, ch. 13), *Who deniges of it?* (Mrs Gamp, *MC*, ch. 49), *he remembered of 'em in his hour of need* (Cuttle, *DS*, ch. 49).

105. Verbs usually intransitive are sometimes used transitively in substandard speech: A police constable replies to Jo's gestures of distress by saying: *Don't you come none of that* (*BH*, ch. 19).

106. A substandard way of achieving emphasis is to repeat a statement with inversion of the subject and the verb and with some re-wording of the subject. Squeers is addicted to this construction, as in *She's a rum 'un, is Natur* (*NN*, ch. 45); *this is a pretty go, is this here* (*NN*, ch. 57).

107. The auxiliary verb *have* is often reduced to *ha* or *a*, as in *you'd ha' made* (Tony Weller, *PP*, ch. 23) or the admirably concise *do adun* (Mary, *PP*, ch. 39). This reduced form is sometimes used redundantly in addition to *had*: *Why, I've been drunk for three days: and I'd a been drunk four, if I'd a had the money* (*BH*, ch. 8).

SUBSTANDARD VOCABULARY

The following list includes words, like *afore* and *cove*, which might be used by any Dickensian characters who speak substandard English, together with various semi-technical vocabularies, such as the cant used by the Artful Dodger, the pugilistic slang of the Game Chicken and the circus slang of Kidderminster. Only a single reference is normally given for each word quoted, though some words occur several times. The meanings of many of the words are supplied by the author as narrator or by other characters in the novels, and the disapproving comments of other characters often provide useful indications about which words were regarded as substandard.

ABEAR, *v.* to bear, endure (Mrs Gamp, *MC*, ch. 49).

AFORE, *prep. and cj.* before (Cuttle, *DS*, ch. 49; Tapley, *MC*, ch. 13).

AGAINST, *cj.* until (Rob, *DS*, ch. 38).

AGEN, AGIN, *prep.* against (Mrs Gamp, *MC*, ch. 25; Tapley, *MC*, ch. 23).

AGGRAVATED, *ppl. adj.* annoyed (Susan Nipper, *DS*, ch. 5).

AGGRAVATING, *adj* annoying (Lavinia Wilfer, *OMF*, Bk II, ch. 8; Fanny Dorrit, *LD*, Bk II, ch. 7).

AGGRAVATION, *sb.* desire to be troublesome (Squeers, *NN*, ch. 57).

ALONG OF, on account of (Scaley, *NN*, ch. 21).

ASKINGS, *sb. pl.* publication of the banns of marriage (Cuttle, *DS*, ch. 56).

BALMY, *sb.* sleep (Swiveller, *OCS*, ch. 8).

BANG-UP, *adj.* excellent, first-rate (*OMF*, Bk II, ch. 8).

BANNER, *sb.* a leap (Kidderminster, *HT*, Bk I, ch. 6).

BARKER, *sb.* a pistol (Toby Crackit, *OT*, ch. 22).

BEAK, *sb.* a magistrate (Artful Dodger, *OT*, ch. 8).

BENDER, *sb.* a sixpence (*SB, Scenes*, ch. 12).

BLABBING, *sb.* indiscreet talk (Rob, *DS*, ch. 46).

BLADE, *sb.* term of praise applied to a man (Westlock, *MC*, ch. 36).

BLOW, *v. blow upon*, to betray (Bill Sikes, *OT*, ch. 13); *blow on*, to reveal (Game Chicken, *DS*, ch. 56); *blow up*, to scold (Sam Weller, *PP*, ch. 16).

BLUNT, *sb.* money (Blathers, *OT*, ch. 31).

BOB, *sb.* a shilling (Artful Dodger, *OT*, ch. 8).

BOBBISH, *adj.* well (Squeers, *NN*, ch. 57).

BONE, *v.* to take away unjustly (Egbert Pardiggle, *BH*, ch. 8).

BOOTY, *sb. to play booty*, to act unfairly or treacherously (Fagin, *OT*, ch. 9).

BOUT, *sb.* illness, indisposition. Mrs Edmund Sparkler is scornful about her husband's use of the word (*LD*, Bk II, ch. 24).

BRAT, *sb.* a child (Nancy, *OT*, ch. 15).

BROWN GEORGE, *sb.* theatrical wig (worn by Vincent Crummles) (*NN*, ch. 25).

BULL, *sb.* a five-shilling piece (Jo, *BH*, ch. 46).

BUNG, *v.* to close up the eyes of an opponent with a blow (Game Chicken, *DS*, ch. 44).

CACKLER, *sb.* speaker (Childers, *HT*, Bk I, ch. 6).

CAD, *sb.* a bus conductor (*SB, Scenes*, ch. 17).

CASTOR, *sb.* a beaver hat (Toby Crackit, *OT*, ch. 25).

CATCH-'EM-ALIVE O, *sb.* a fly-paper (*LD*, Bk I, ch. 16).

CHAFF, *sb.* banter, ridicule (*BR*, ch. 8).

CHANCERY, *sb. to get into Chancery* (of a boxer) to get the head under one's opponent's arm to be punched with his other arm (Game Chicken, *DS*, ch. 44).

CHAUNTER, *sb.* a fraudulent horse-dealer (Plornish, *LD*, Bk I, ch. 12).

CHIVY, *v.* to chase (Rob, *DS*, ch. 22).

CHUCK, *v.* to throw (Cuttle, *DS*, ch. 49).

CHUMMAGE TICKET, *sb.* ticket assigning a prisoner to a particular room (*PP*, ch. 42).

CHUMMY, *sb.* a chimney sweep (*SB, Scenes*, ch. 20).

CLAP ON, *v.* to hurry (Cuttle, *DS*, ch. 48).

CLEAN OUT, *v.* to deprive someone of all his money (*OT*, ch. 39).

CLINCHER, *sb.* convincing argument (Swiveller, *OCS*, ch. 2).

CODGER, *sb.* old man or woman (Tapley, *MC*, ch. 34).

COMBUSTION, *sb.* fuss, uproar (*SB, Tales*, ch. 10).

COMFOOZLED, *ppl. adj.* overwhelmed (Sam Weller, *PP*, ch. 39).

CONKEY, *adj.* nosey (Blathers, *OT*, ch. 31).

CONSTABLE, *sb. outrunning the constable*, living beyond one's means (Jaggers, *GE*, ch. 20).

COVE, *sb.* man, person (Sam Weller, *PP*, ch. 10).

COVEY, *sb.* boy, young fellow (Artful Dodger, *OT*, ch. 10).

CRACK, *v.* to break open (Bill Sikes, *OT*, ch. 19); *sb.* a burglary (Toby Crackit, *OT*, ch. 22).

CRACKSMAN, *sb.* a housebreaker (Toby Crackit, *OT*, ch. 25).

CRANKY, *adj.* ill-tempered (Swiveller, *OCS*, ch. 7).

CRIB, *sb.* a house (Nancy, *OT*, ch. 15).

CRUEL JACK, *sb.* poor law official (Betty Higden, *OMF*, Bk I, ch. 16).

CUT, *v.* to run away (Toby Crackit, *OT*, ch. 25). Also *cut away*, *cut off*.

DAB, *sb.* expert (Mr Boffin, *OMF*, Bk I, ch. 5).

DAMP, *sb.* a drink (Tony Weller, *PP*, ch. 27).

DARKY, *sb.* a dark lantern used by housebreakers (Toby Crackit, *OT*, ch. 22).

DO, *sb.* a swindle (*PP*, ch. 48); *v. do over*, to swindle (*SB*, *Scenes*, ch. 17).

DODGE, *sb.* variety of stage performance (Sleary, *HT*, Bk IV, ch. 7).

DOLLY, *adj.* foolish (Bella Wilfer, *OMF*, Bk I, ch. 4).

DOWN, *adj. down in the mouth*, in low spirits (Artful Dodger, *OT*, ch. 16).

DOWNY, *adj.* shrewd, alert (Artful Dodger, *OT*, ch. 18).

DRAIN, *sb.* a drink (Toby Crackit, *OT*, ch. 22).

DRAT, *v.* to curse (Mrs Gamp, *MC*, ch. 29).

EARWIG, *v.* to cajole (Fagin, *OT*, ch. 47).

FAMILY, *sb.* the thieving fraternity (Blathers, *OT*, ch. 31).

FANCY, *adj.* worthy of the boxing world (Game Chicken, *DS*, ch. 56).

FANTEEG, *sb.* an unpleasant experience (Sam Weller, *PP*, ch. 38).

FEN, *v.* (I) forbid (Jo, *BH*, ch. 16).

FENCE, *sb.* a receiver of stolen goods (Bill Sikes, *OT*, ch. 13).

FETCH, *v. fetch a crack*, to strike a blow (*BH*, ch. 11).

FIB, *v.* to strike, thrash (Game Chicken, *DS*, ch. 44).

FILE, *sb.* man, fellow (Artful Dodger, *OT*, ch. 43); pickpocket (Toby Crackit, *OT*, ch. 25).

FLASH, *adj.* connected with the underworld (Artful Dodger, *OT*, ch. 8).

FLAT, *sb.* a simpleton (Artful Dodger, *OT*, ch. 18).

FLOORED, *ppl. adj.* exhausted (Bob Sawyer, *PP*, ch. 51).

FLY, *adj.* knowing; *I'm fly*, I understand (Jo, *BH*, ch. 16).

FOGLE, *sb.* a silk handkerchief; *fogle-hunter*, a pickpocket specialising in handkerchieves (*OT*, ch. 11).

FORK OUT, *v.* to pay (Swiveller, *OCS*, ch. 2).

GAB, *sb. gift of the gab*, eloquence (*SB, Scenes*, ch. 23).

GALLOWS, *sb.* one deserving to be hanged (*OT*, ch. 11).

GAME, *adj.* plucky, wide-awake (Game Chicken, *DS*, ch. 56).

GAMEY, *adj.* sporting, dashing (Bailey, *MC*, ch. 11).

GAMMON, *sb.* nonsense (Game Chicken, *DS*, ch. 56).

GENT, *sb.* gentleman (Mrs Gamp, *MC*, ch. 25).

GILLS, *sb.* chin (Bailey, *MC*, ch. 29).

GLIM, *sb.* a light (Bill Sikes, *OT*, ch. 16).

GO, *sb.* a portion (*SB, Characters*, ch. 11); state of affairs (Sam Weller, *PP*, ch. 35).

GOER, *sb.* active man (*PP*, ch. 42).

GONOPH, *sb.* thief (*BH*, ch. 19).

GOOSE, *v.* to hiss (Childers, *HT*, Bk I, ch. 6).

GOOSEBERRY, *sb. to play old Gooseberry*, to make mischief (Jonas Chuzzlewit, *MC*, ch. 38).

GRAB, *v.* to arrest (Bill Sikes, *OT*, ch. 16).

GRASS, *v.* to bring to the ground (Game Chicken, *DS*, ch. 44).

GRAVELLED, *adj.* at a loss: 'I was gravelled – an expression which your Ladyship, moving in the higher circles, will be so good as to consider tantamount to knocked over' (Guppy to Lady Dedlock, *BH*, ch. 55).

GREEN, *sb.* green tea (Charley Bates, *OT*, ch. 39).

GREEN, *adj.* ignorant, inexperienced (Artful Dodger, *OT*, ch. 8).

GREENLAND, *sb.* the country of greenhorns (Artful Dodger, *OT*, ch. 8).

GROGGY, *adj.* weak, unsteady (Game Chicken, *DS*, ch. 44).

GRUB, *sb.* food (Artful Dodger, *OT*, ch. 8).

GUM-TICKLER, *sb.* rum drunk neat (Wegg, *OMF*, Bk IV, ch. 3).

HEAVY-SWELL, *adj.* fashionable (Charley Bates, *OT*, ch. 16).

HIGH FLYER, *sb.* one who is enthusiastic or proficient (Mrs Boffin, *OMF*, Bk I, ch. 5).

HOOKING IT, running away (Jo, *BH*, ch. 16).

HORSE CHAUNTER, a dishonest horse-dealer (*PP*, ch. 42).

HUMBUG, *sb.* a bounder (*SB, Characters*, ch. 4).

HUSSY, *sb.* term of abuse applied to a woman (Mrs Gamp, *MC*, ch. 40).

JAPAN, *v.* to black (boots) (Artful Dodger, *OT*, ch. 18).

JEMMY, *sb.* (1) a sheep's head; (2) a housebreaking implement (Bill Sikes, *OT*, ch. 20).

JIFFY, *sb.* a moment (Mrs Pipchin, *DS*, ch. 59).

JIGGERED, *pp.* damned. A favourite word of Orlick's: 'He attached no definite meaning to the word that I am aware of, but used it, like his own pretended Christian name, to affront mankind, and convey an idea of something savagely damaging' (*GE*, ch. 17).

JOCKEY, *sb.* clerk, office-boy (*DS*, ch. 6).

Joskin, *sb.* a carter (Sleary, *HT*, Bk IV, ch. 7).

KEN, *sb.* a house, especially one occupied by thieves (Artful Dodger, *OT*, ch. 13).

KENNEL, *sb.* gutter (Fagin, *OT*, ch. 42).

KIDDY, *sb.* a stage-coach (*SB, Characters*, ch. 11).

KINCHIN, *sb.* young child; *kinchin lay*, robbing children sent on errands (Fagin, *OT*, ch. 42).

KIT, *sb.* lot, set (Magwitch, *GE*, ch. 40); *all the kit of 'em*, the whole lot of them (Game Chicken, *DS*, ch. 56).

KNOCKED OVER, at a loss (Guppy, *BH*, ch. 55).

KYE-BOSK, *sb.* one shilling and sixpence; *put the kye-bosk on her*, don't stand any nonsense from her (*SB, Scenes*, ch. 5).

LAG, *v.* to transport, send to penal servitude (Bill Sikes, *OT*, ch. 16).

LARK, *sb.* trick (Jo, *BH*, ch. 16).

LARRUP, *v.* to beat, thrash (Bounderby, *HT*, Bk I, ch. 5).

LAUNDRESS, *sb.* office cleaner (*PP*, ch. 20).

LAY, *sb.* a scheme, illicit occupation; *on the lay*, at work (Fagin, *OT*, ch. 39).

LEG, *sb.* a turf swindler (*PP*, ch. 42); a person (Toby Crackit, *OT*, ch. 39).

LEG-BAIL, *sb. to give leg-bail*, to escape (Fagin, *OT*, ch. 19).

LIE, *sb.* liar (*BH*, ch. 8).

LIFER, *sb.* one sentenced to transportation for life (Fagin, *OT*, ch. 43).

LIMB, *sb.* term of abuse applied to a boy (*MC*, ch. 29).

LINE, *sb. get into a line*, to persuade to become an accomplice (Bill Sikes, *OT*, ch. 19).

LONDON PARTICULAR, *sb.* thick fog (Guppy, *BH*, ch. 3).

LUCKY, *sb. make one's lucky*, to make one's escape (Sam Weller, *PP*, ch. 10).

LUKE, *adj.* lukewarm (Sam Weller, *PP*, ch. 33).

LUMMY, *adj.* first-rate (Charley Bates, *OT*, ch. 43).

LUSH, *v.* to drink (Charley Bates, *OT*, ch. 39).

MAGPIE, *sb.* a halfpenny (Artful Dodger, *OT*, ch. 8).

MAN AND A BROTHER, *sb.* a slave (Caddy Jellyby, *BH*, ch. 14).

MILL, *sb.* a fight (*DS*, ch. 41).

MILL, *sb.* a treadmill (Artful Dodger, *OT*, ch. 8); *v.* to send to the treadmill (*OT*, ch. 25).

MINDER, *sb.* child left to be looked after (Betty Higden, *OMF*, Bk I, ch. 16).

MIZZLE, *v.* to disappear, go away (Miss Mowcher, *DC*, ch. 22).

MORRIS, MORRICE, *v.* to run away (Sleary, *HT*, Bk I, ch. 6; Artful Dodger, *OT*, ch. 8).

MOVE, *sb.* motive (Artful Dodger, *OT*, ch. 18).

MUG, *sb.* a face (Toby Crackit, *OT*, ch. 22); *v.* to grimace, (*LD*, Bk I, ch. 20).

NAB, *v.* to arrest (Fagin, *OT*, ch. 44).

NATURAL, *sb.* an imbecile (Betty Higden, *OMF*, Bk I, ch. 16).

NIGHTCAP, *sb.* the cap placed over the head of a condemned man by the hangman (Bill Sikes, *OT*, ch. 15).

NOB, *sb.* aristocrat (Tigg, *MC*, ch. 7).

OCHRE, *sb.* money (Kidderminster, *HT*, Bk I, ch. 6).

OFFICE, *sb.* information (Magwitch, *GE*, ch. 3); *What's the office?* What's the matter? (*PP*, ch. 42).

OUT-AND-OUTER, *sb.* excellent thing of its kind (*PP*, ch. 40).

PAD, *v. to pad the hoof*, to go out on foot (Charley Bates, *OT*, ch. 9).

PAL, *sb.* friend, companion (Artful Dodger, *OT*, ch. 8).

PARTY, *sb.* person (Guppy, *BH*, ch. 55).

PEACH, *v.* to turn informer (Fagin, *OT*, ch. 9).

PECK, *sb.* a meal (Riderhood, *OMF*, Bk IV, ch. 7).

PEG AWAY, *v.* to continue (Ben Allen, *PP*, ch. 30).

PEPPER, *sb. to receive pepper*, to be punched (of a boxer) (Game Chicken, *DS*, ch. 44).

PERSUADER, *sb.* a weapon (Toby Crackit, *OT*, ch. 22).

PIERCER, *sb.* a bitterly cold day (Bill Sikes, *OT*, ch. 19).

PIPE, *v.* to pant, breathe hard (Game Chicken, *DS*, ch. 44).

PLANT, *sb.* a scheme, plot (Bill Sikes, *OT*, ch. 19); a prospective victim (Charley Bates, *OT*, ch. 10).

PLUCK, *sb.* courage (Game Chicken, *DS*, ch. 56).

PLUMMY, *adj.* satisfactory; *plummy and slam*, (used as a password) all right (Artful Dodger, *OT*, ch. 8).

PIN, *sb.* a leg (Artful Dodger, *OT*, ch. 8).

POLL PARROTING, *sb.* talking (Riderhood, *OMF*, Bk II, ch. 12).

POLL-PRY, *v.* to interfere inquisitively (*BH*, ch. 8).

PONGING, *sb.* somersaulting (Kidderminster, *HT*, Bk I, ch. 6).

POUND, *v.* to beat, punish (Rob, *DS*, ch. 22).

POUND, *v.* to wager (Sleary, *HT*, Bk I, ch. 6).

PRAD, *sb.* a horse (Blathers, *OT*, ch. 31).

PRECIOUS, *adv.* very (Chuckster, *OCS*, ch. 20).

PRIG, *sb.* a thief (*DC*, ch. 13).

PROFEEL MACHEEN, *sb.* a kind of camera (Sam Weller, *PP*, ch. 33).

PUT-UP, *adj. put-up job*, a burglary arranged beforehand by conspiracy with the servants (Bill Sikes, *OT*, ch. 19).

QUENCHER, *sb.* drink (Swiveller, *OCS*, ch. 36).

QUOD, *sb.* prison (Riderhood, *OMF*, Bk I, ch. 6).

RASPER, *sb.* term of praise applied to a man (Mould, *MC*, ch. 38).

RECEPTION, *sb.* applause from the audience when an actor first comes on the stage (Folair, *NN*, ch. 29).

RHEUMATICKS, *sb.* rheumatism (Toodle, *DS*, ch. 38).

RIG, *sb.* awkward situation (*PP*, ch. 42).

ROW, *sb.* disturbance; *What's the row?* What's the matter? (Artful Dodger, *OT*, ch. 8).

RUM, *adj.* strange (Charley Bates, *OT*, ch. 39).

RUMMY, *adj.* strange (*SB, Scenes*, ch. 12).

SACK, *sb. get the sack*, lose one's job (Jobling, *BH*, ch. 20).

SAWBONES, *sb.* a surgeon (Sam Weller, *PP*, ch. 30).

SCOUT, *v.* to dislike, deride (*SB, Our Parish*, ch. 5).

SCRAG, *v.* to hang (Charley Bates, *OT*, ch. 18).

SCREWED, *adj.* tipsy (*MC*, ch. 25).

SCROUDING, *pres. part.* crowding (Mrs Gamp, *MC*, ch. 40).

SELL, *sb.* betrayal (*OT*, ch. 26).

SHAVER, *sb.* a boy (Tapley, *MC*, ch. 33).

SHINER, *sb.* a guinea, sovereign (Bill Sikes, *OT*, ch. 19).

SHOP, *v.* to send to prison (Bill Sikes, *OT*, ch. 16).

SLACK-JEFF, *sb.* slack-rope walking (Kidderminster, *HT*, Bk I, ch. 6).

SLAM, *sb.* a trick; used in the password *plummy and slam* (Artful Dodger, *OT*, ch. 8).

SLAP-BANG, *sb.* a small cook-shop where no credit is given (*SB, Characters*, ch. 11); *adj.* excellent (*BH*, ch. 20).

SLAP-UP, *adj.* excellent (*OMF*, Bk II, ch. 8).

SLAVEY, *sb.* servant (Swiveller, *OCS*, ch. 13).

SLUED, *adj.* tipsy (*MC*, ch. 28).

SMASH, *v.* to attack, set upon (Pyke, *NN*, ch. 27).

SMIFLIGATE, *v.* to attack, set upon (Pyke, *NN*, ch. 27).

SNEAKING, *adj.* pilfering (Noah Claypole, *OT*, ch. 42).

SNEEZE-BOX, *sb.* a snuff-box (Charley Bates, *OT*, ch. 43).

SNOB, *sb.* low-class person (Bailey, *MC*, ch. 26).

SOAP, *v.* to flatter (*CS, Doctor Marigold*, ch. 1).

SPANKER, *sb.* very beautiful woman (*DS*, ch. 31).

SPANKING, *adj.* excellent (Chuckster, *OCS*, ch. 40).

SPLIT UPON, *v.* to inform against (*OT*, ch. 25).

SPOONEY, *adj.* foolish (*GE*, ch. 20).

SPOUT, *sb. up the spout*, ready to pawn something (*SB, Scenes*, ch. 23).

START, *sb.* strange state of affairs (Bob Sawyer, *PP*, ch. 38); man, person (Sam Weller, *PP*, ch. 12).

STIFF, *adj.* dignified; *the stiff 'un*, Mr Dombey (Game Chicken, *DS*, ch. 56).

STONE JUG, *sb.* prison (Artful Dodger, *OT*, ch. 8).

STOW, *v.* to cease, leave off (Bill Sikes, *OT*, ch. 15); abstain from (Jo, *BH*, ch. 16).

STRETCHER, *sb.* an implement used by boatmen (Hexam, *OMF*, Bk I, ch. 1).

STUMP, *v.* to pay (Artful Dodger, *OT*, ch. 8).

STUMPY, *sb.* money (*SB, Scenes*, ch. 17).

SWAG, *sb.* booty (Fagin, *OT*, ch. 19).

SWELL, *sb. heavy swell*, a man worthy of admiration (*OT*, ch. 39). See HEAVY-SWELL, *adj.*

SWIPES, *sb.* small beer (Toby Crackit, *OT*, ch. 39).

SWIPEY, *adj.* drunk (Bailey, *MC*, ch. 28).

TANNER, *sb.* sixpence (*MC*, ch. 37).

TAP, *v.* to strike (Game Chicken, *DS*, ch. 44).

TICKER, *sb.* a watch (Artful Dodger, *OT*, ch. 18).

TIGER, *sb.* a smart-liveried boy-groom (*SB*, *Scenes*, ch. 6).

TIGHT-JEFF, *sb.* tight-rope walking (Kidderminster, *HT*, Bk I, ch. 6).

TILE, *sb.* hat (Sam Weller, *PP*, ch. 10).

TIME, *sb. that's the time of day*, described as 'a very strong expression of approbation: an uncommonly hearty welcome' (Bill Sikes, *OT*, ch. 20).

TIN, *sb.* money (*SB*, *Scenes*, ch. 20).

TINKLER, *sb.* a bell (Bill Sikes, *OT*, ch. 15).

TIP, *sb.* a job, duty; *to miss one's tip* (of a circus performer), to fail at a jump (Childers, *HT*, Bk I, ch. 6).

TITTIVATED, *ppl. adj.* carefully tended (Betsey Prig, *MC*, ch. 29).

TOGS, *sb.* clothes (Charley Bates, *OT*, ch. 16).

TOUCHER, *sb. as near as a toucher*, as near as can be (Guppy, *BH*, ch. 4).

TRAP, *sb.* a policeman (Artful Dodger, *OT*, ch. 13).

TROTTER-CASE, *sb.* a boot (Artful Dodger, *OT*, ch. 18).

TRUMP, *sb.* good fellow (Jobling, *BH*, ch. 20).

TWIG, *sb.* style, fashion; *in twig*, on form (*BR*, ch. 11).

UNBEKNOWN, *adj.* unknown (Mrs Gamp, *MC*, ch. 46).

UP, *adv. You're up to that?* Do you understand that? (*PP*, ch. 42).

WAG, *v.* to play truant (Rob, *DS*, ch. 22).

WALKER, *sb.* rubbish (*PP*, ch. 27).

WEAL AND HAMMER, *sb.* a veal and ham pie (Wegg, *OMF*, Bk I, ch. 5).

WHISTLING-SHOP, *sb.* room in prison where spirits are sold (Job Trotter, *PP*, ch. 45).

WHITE-LIVERED, *adj.* cowardly (Fagin, *OT*, ch. 9).

WHOP, *v.* to strike violently (*PP*, ch. 42).

WILKS, *sb.* a species of snail (*SB*, *Scenes*, ch. 12).

WIND, *sb. when the wind's low*, when money is short (Artful Dodger, *OT*, ch. 8).

WINDER, *sb.* an effort that leaves one out of breath (Joe, *GE*, ch. 5).

WIPE, *sb.* a pocket handkerchief (Charles Bates, *OT*, ch. 9).

WORK OFF, *v.* to hang (Dennis, *BR*, ch. 37).

WORRIT, *sb.* worry, cause of worry (Susan Nipper, *DS*, ch. 23).

YELLOW-BOY, *sb.* sovereign (*OCS*, ch. 42).

YOKEL, *sb.* a countryman (Blathers, *OT*, ch. 31).

YOUNKER, *sb.* boy (Bill Sikes, *OT*, ch. 22).

SELECT BIBLIOGRAPHY

The number of books and articles on Dickens is enormous. Not many of them deal exclusively with his language, but many critical works contain some material of linguistic interest. The following list includes a few studies of this kind, as well as monographs on the language of Dickens and linguistic works to which reference is made by abbreviated titles.

A. Studies of the Language of Dickens

Brook, G. L., 'Dickens as a Literary Craftsman', *Bulletin of the John Rylands Library*, xlix (1966) 47–68.

Brook, G. L., 'The Language of Dickens', *Bulletin of the John Rylands Library*, xlvii (1964) 32–48.

Franz, W. 'Die Dialektsprache bei Ch. Dickens', *Englische Studien*, xii (1889) 197–244.

Gerson, Stanley, *Sound and Symbol in the Dialogue of the Works of Charles Dickens*, Stockholm, Almqvist & Wiksell, 1967; Stockholm Studies in English, xix (Gerson).

Pound, Louise, 'The American Dialect of Charles Dickens', *American Speech*, xxii (1927) 124–130.

Quirk, Randolph, *Charles Dickens and Appropriate Language*, University of Durham, 1959. An inaugural lecture.

Quirk, Randolph, 'Some Observations on the Language of Dickens', *A Review of English Literature*, ii (1961) 19–28.

Weekley, Ernest, 'Mrs Gamp and the King's English' in *Adjectives and Other Words*, John Murray, 1930, pp. 138–161.

B. Books on the English Language

Dobson, E. J., *English Pronunciation* 1500–1700, 2 vols, Oxford, 1957 (Dobson).

Horn, W. *Laut und Leben: Englische Lautgeschichte der neueren Zeit* (1400–1950). Bearbeitet und herausgegeben von Martin Lehnert, 2 vols. Berlin, 1954 (Horn-Lehnert).

Matthews, William, *Cockney Past and Present*, Routledge, 1938.
The Oxford English Dictionary, ed. J. A. H. Murray, H. Bradley, W. A. Craigie and C. T. Onions, 13 vols, including Supplement, Oxford, 1888–1933 (*OED*).
Partridge, Eric, *A Dictionary of Slang and Unconventional English*, Routledge and Kegan Paul, fifth edition, 1961.
Wright, Joseph, *An English Dialect Grammar*, Oxford, 1905 (*EDG*).
Wright, Joseph and Elizabeth Mary, *An Elementary Historical New English Grammar*, Oxford, 1924 (Wright *EHNEG*).
Wyld, Henry Cecil, *A History of Modern Colloquial English*, Third edition, Blackwell, 1936 (Wyld *HMCE*).
Wyld, Henry Cecil, *A Short History of English*, Third edition, John Murray, 1927 (Wyld *SHE*).

C. Biographical and Critical Works

Butt, John and Tillotson, Kathleen, *Dickens at Work*, Methuen, 1957.
Forster, John, *The Life of Charles Dickens* (Library edition, 2 vols., revised, 1876; originally published in 3 vols., 1872–4). Reference is by book and section (Forster).
Johnson, Edgar, *Charles Dickens, His Tragedy and Triumph*, 2 vols., Victor Gollancz, 1953.
Leavis, F. R., *The Great Tradition*, Chatto and Windus, 1948. Chapter V is 'An Analytic Note' on *Hard Times*.
Miller, J. Hillis, *Charles Dickens: The World of his Novels*, Cambridge, Mass., Harvard University Press, 1965.
Van Ghent, Dorothy, *The English Novel: Form and Function*, 1953; Harper Torchbooks edition, New York, Harper and Row, 1961. Includes, on pp. 125–138, a study of *Great Expectations*.

INDEX

In this index completeness is not aimed at. References to particular novels and characters are given if the passages referred to throw light on those novels or characters but not if the chief interest of the quotation is linguistic. For this reason the Index does not as a rule include references to quotations in the Appendix.